T0366734

THE I TATTI
RENAISSANCE LIBRARY

James Hankins, General Editor

BEMBO

LYRIC POETRY

ETNA

ITRL 18

PIETRO BEMBO
✦ ✦ ✦
LYRIC POETRY
ETNA

LYRIC POETRY
EDITED AND TRANSLATED BY

MARY P. CHATFIELD

ETNA TRANSLATED BY

BETTY RADICE

THE I TATTI RENAISSANCE LIBRARY
HARVARD UNIVERSITY PRESS
CAMBRIDGE, MASSACHUSETTS
LONDON, ENGLAND
2005

English translation of *Etna* by Betty Radice, reprinted by permission of
William Radice, from the edition published by Giovanni Mardersteig
and the Officina Bodoni, 1969

Series design by Dean Bornstein

Library of Congress Cataloging-in-Publication Data

Bembo, Pietro, 1470–1547.
[Poems. English & Latin]
Lyric poetry ; Etna / Pietro Bembo ;
edited and translated by Mary P. Chatfield.
p. cm. — (The I Tatti Renaissance library ; 18)
Includes bibliographical references and index.
ISBN 0-674-01712-9 (cloth : alk. paper)
1. Bembo, Pietro, 1470–1547 — Translations into English.
2. Latin poetry, Medieval and modern — Translations into English.
3. Etna, Mount (Italy).   I. Chatfield, Mary P.
II. Bembo, Pietro, 1470–1547. Aetna. English and Latin.
III. Title: Etna.   IV. Title.   V. Series.
PA8475.B5 [A235 2005] 851′.3 — dc22   2004060580

Contents

༄༅༄

Introduction

༄༅༄

Pietro Bembo, humanist, lover, and churchman, was born on May 20, 1470, the eldest son of Bernardo Bembo, a distinguished Venetian public servant and man of letters. Surrounded as a boy by his father's extraordinary library and educated by humanist tutors until he was eighteen, Bembo was destined for a high place in public life. As a young man he accompanied his father on various of his embassies, and in 1487–88 visited Rome, seeing for the first time the ancient sites about which he had already read with consuming interest.

Although he was officially initiated into Venetian political life in 1490, his studies, and the writing in which he was already engaged, were moving him towards a career in literature. This direction was further confirmed when in 1491 the famed poet and humanist Angelo Poliziano visited the Bembo house in Venice. The young Pietro seems to have made an impression on Poliziano, who referred to him as "a knight's son, a young man devoted to literature" (*equitis filius, studiosus litterarum adulescens*).

Between 1491 and 1493 Bembo was in Messina, studying Greek with Constantine Lascaris, in the company of his friend Angelo Gabriel. Halfway through his sojourn in Sicily he made a trip to Naples to visit Giovanni Pontano, founder of the famous Accademia Pontaniana. The visit was obviously appreciated by the older man, as Pontano dedicated the seventh volume of his last work, *De rebus caelestibus*, to Bembo. Soon after he returned to Venice Bembo wrote *De Aetna*, a lively dialogue in Latin between his father and himself about his climb up the volcano. This he dedicated to his friend and fellow-student, Gabriel. *De Aetna* was printed in 1495 by Aldus Manutius, in Francesco Griffo's first roman font, the modern version of which is now commonly known as Bembo roman. This edition is famous in the history of typography as the first example of Bembine.

The year 1494 found Bembo in Padua studying philosophy at the university, where he remained until 1497, when he accompanied his father, the newly appointed *visidomino*, or co-ruler, to Ferrara. While there he continued his philosophical studies under Niccolò Leonico Tomeo (see Poem XXXVI), and he did not return to Venice when his father's appointment in Ferrara was concluded. His life as a student and lover of letters, outside the orbit of his father's influence and ambitions, was beginning.

The intellectual pleasures of the Ferrarese court and the leisure to write and study given him by the generosity of Ercole d'Este bore fruit in *Gli Asolani*, Bembo's first long work in Italian. A dialogue about the joys and pains of love, held among three young gentlemen and three beautiful ladies temporarily without their husbands, this work illustrates both Bembo's concern to preserve the language and style of the best Italian writers of the recent past and his fascination with the possibility of Platonic love. In 1488, while accompanying his father on a mission to Florence, he had come to know and love the Tuscan dialect, and it was in an archaic version of this dialect, the language of Petrarch and Boccaccio, that he wrote. Though he was chided by friends (see Poem XVII) for writing a literary work in his mother tongue, he continued to write voluminously in Italian all his life.

For Bembo the delights of the literary life went hand in hand with other, more earthly pleasures. Though we know nothing of his first love beyond her initials, "M.G.," Bembo preserved and edited for publication almost all the letters which he wrote to Maria Savorgnan, his second *inamorata*. These carefully modulated expressions of an ardor at once both controlled and richly elaborated played an important part in the refining and revising of *Gli Asolani*, which was published by Manutius in 1505. The dedication, however, was to Lucrezia Borgia, with whom by then he had fallen deeply in love or, as he put it, "consigned himself to the flames for the third time."[1]

Even before the publication of *Gli Asolani* Bembo, as a rising young humanist, had been in collaboration with Manutius in a project to bring to print the great writers of the classical past. In 1501, with Bembo as editor, Manutius brought out the works of Virgil and Horace, as well as the *Rime* of Petrarch. In 1502, also under Bembo's editorship, he published the *Divine Comedy* under the title *The Terze Rime of Dante*. Yet as if to emphasize what he considered Pietro's real profession, Bernardo Bembo had between 1503 and 1504 proposed his son for several embassies; each time Pietro had been turned down. Seeing that there was no future for him in Venice and at heart not wanting there to be one, Bembo went to live in Urbino in 1506, a move which marked his final break with the city of his birth and with his father's political ambitions for him there. Whatever difficulties arose from insisting on his choice of profession, his style does not seem to have been affected by them. The urbanity, the polish, the carefully modulated expressions of love, and the high tone of encomium show how much his spirit was at home in the world of Castiglione's ideal courtier. In the court of Urbino, as we see it come to refined life in *The Book of the Courtier*, Bembo was not yet the master of Latin prose that would emerge in a few years, but a writer in the vulgar tongue, the author of *Gli Asolani*, the explicator and defender of Platonic love.

Meantime, how was he to make his way, if not up the political ladder in Venice? The answer seemed to him to lie in taking up the clerical life, which he did in 1508 during the pontificate of Julius II, the formidable Giuliano della Rovere, a proud and implacable man, determined to defend and enlarge the papal domain, but also a genuine lover of the arts (see Poem XXVIII). Bembo hoped to use his own and his father's contacts to find himself a position at the Vatican in which his talents as a humanist and *litterateur* might shine. In this he was disappointed. Since no post proved available, he committed himself wholeheartedly to the intellectual and amatory pleasures of the court of Urbino.

Bembo was popular both for his charming manners and his intellectual brilliance, and it was with good reason that Castiglione provided him with two special moments in *The Courtier*. The first, in Book I, has Bembo insisting on the superiority of letters over arms. The second forms the lengthy climax to the fourth book in which he describes the noble love which befits a courtier who is no longer young — a love which "remember(s) always that the body is something very different from beauty, and not only does not increase beauty but lessens its perfection."[2] It was a worthy lesson, but one which Bembo, even late in life, chose not to follow.

At last, in 1513, with the accession to the papacy of Giovanni de' Medici as Leo X, Bembo found favor in Rome. Through the good offices of his friend Bernardo Dovizi da Bibbiena, himself also a character in *The Courtier*, he became apostolic secretary to the pope, charged with composing the papacy's official correspondence with foreign powers. He shared this office with Jacopo Sadoleto, another celebrated Latinist, and their nominations "marked the victory of Ciceronian humanism in prose (and) Virgilian humanism in poetry."[3] Gradually, however, his subordination of the life of letters to the politics that were of necessity the lot of a papal servant soured his ambition. Already in June 1513 he was complaining in a letter to Lucrezia Borgia of "the cares of my office,"[4] and by 1518 he was exhausted and ill.

In March of that year he asked for leave to go to Venice to restore his health and to see his dying father. As heir he had to deal with the affairs of a much-depleted estate, so it was not until 1520 that he returned to Rome. Meanwhile his friend Bibbiena had died, and with his passing Bembo's hopes to be named to the cardinalate sank. In 1521 he left papal service entirely and went to Padua to convalesce and begin a new life. In order to keep his ecclesiastical benefice, on the income of which he depended, he made his full profession in the Order of St. John of Jerusalem. In spite of his vow of chastity he chose a former courtesan, Faustina Morosina, to share his life and together they had three children, Lucilius, Torquato, and Elena, all of whom he not only acknowledged but loved dearly (see Poem XL).

The relationship seemed to offer him new confidence and strength, and he gave himself to work with an intensity which he had not shown since his youth. In 1524 he finished *Prose della volgar lingua*, a treatise on the proper language for Italian literature, a work begun in 1514, but interrupted by his duties for Leo X. He dedicated it to the new pope, Clement VII, and went to Rome to present it in person. While there he hoped to ingratiate himself with Giovan Matteo Giberti, the bursar to the Vatican, with nomination as cardinal never far from his thoughts. To that end he also wrote and had printed a eulogy to Giberti titled "Benacus," the longest of the Latin poems which he included in the *Carminum libellus* (Poem XVIII).

The eulogy did not have its desired effect, but the *Prose della volgar lingua* was a huge success. Between 1525 and 1530 he worked intensely to promote his ideas about the proper language and style for those who would write in Italian, and he attracted many young writers to his coterie. He published his collected Italian poems, the *Rime*, which went into forty editions before 1595, as well as a second edition of *Gli Asolani*. His eldest son, Lucilius, died in 1532 and Morosina in 1535, but he kept to his work, and in 1537 he was in love again, this time with a young Venetian gentlewoman, Elisabetta Massolo, née Querini, who inspired his final sonnets.

Appointed by the Signoria official historiographer of Venice, he wrote an *Historia Veneta* in both Latin and Italian and in 1536 brought out an edition of the Latin *breve* he had written as secretary to Leo X.[5] He dedicated the book to the new pope, Paul III, hoping that it would be a reminder of his service to the Curia and of his humanist endeavors. This time he did not fail. In 1539 Pope Paul created as cardinals three men of high culture, Reginald Pole, Gasparo Contarini, and Pietro Bembo, calling Bembo "easily the leading man of our time in learning and eloquence" (*doctrina et eloquentia nostrae aetatis facile princeps*). Sometime in 1542 Titian painted a three-quarter-length portrait of Bembo in his cardinal's robes, a painting which is now in the National Gallery in Washington. It shows a tall, bearded man, surprisingly fit-looking for his age, with a sensitive face and keen dark eyes.

In the years leading up to the Council of Trent, when reformist passions were high, Bembo, by virtue of his many friendships with churchmen young and old, was able to play a part in moderating some of the extreme positions of the reform party. Though he rose in the church, becoming bishop of Gubbio in 1541 and in 1544 bishop of Bergamo and Cardinal of San Clemente, he was revered in his time not so much as a churchman but as one of the foremost humanists of his day. He died on January 18, 1547, and was buried behind the main altar of the church of Santa Maria sopra Minerva between the tombs of Leo X and Clement VII.

Bembo's literary executors were two good friends, Girolamo Querini, brother of Elisabetta Massolo, and Carlo Gualteruzzi. As a Roman, the latter wished to publish Bembo's works in Rome and Florence. But the Signoria of Venice intervened in favor of the Venetian, Querini, and the *Lettere*, the *Historia Veneta* (in both Latin and Italian), *Gli Asolani*, the *Epistolae Familiares*, and the *Carminum libellus* were all published in Venice between 1550 and 1553. The latter, under the editorship of Gualtero Scotto, was the last to be brought out. Though Bembo, as a Latinist, is most noted for the exquisitely modelled Ciceronian *brevia* composed while he was Papal Secretary, the *Carminum libellus*, as revised and carefully prepared for posthumous publication by his own hand, gives us a glimpse of the Bembo who loved and imitated Virgil, Catullus, Ovid, Horace, and the Greek pastoral poets. His intimate knowledge of Virgil shows in many small allusions throughout the *Carminum*, but most noticeably in Poem XIII, "Amica ad Gallum." "Sarca," a poem excluded from the *Carminum libellus*, describes Virgil as the "wellspring of Latin poesy" (608–10) and warmly praises the hexameter works of Pontano and Sannazaro, two great Renaissance Virgilians, both of whom were old friends and models.

The *Carminum libellus* is an eclectic collection, which seems to have been put together by Bembo to demonstrate his skill at composing in various meters and for various occasions. The text as Bembo arranged it, exclusive of the juvenilia he omitted and the poems later MSS attributed to him without certainty, is organized to mirror the passage of his emotional life. Faunus, in all his aspects, appears as an important character in the first seven poems: Faunus, guardian of shepherds-poets and their sheep, Faunus, the lascivious and unsatisfied voyeur, and "Faunus, the lover of the fleeing nymphs" (Horace, *Odes* 3.18.1). The careful devotee of the poet's craft, the ardent correspondent of "M.G." and Maria Savorgnan, the seeker after the delight of beautiful women's company, the witty, self-mocking, but also earnest, lover are all subsumed in the persona of Faunus. These poems, and the "Priapus" which follows them, are the works of someone whose heart is young and whose mind delights in showing off what it knows. They also, however, portray a sensitivity to the power a beautiful woman can have over a man and an understanding of the tender art of lovemaking; they support all that we otherwise know of Bembo as a life-long Romeo.

With Poem IX we begin to hear the voice of someone more mature, someone who has lost good friends to death, who is troubled by others' sorrows as well as his own, and who knows the frustrations of being in the service of another when he would like to be free. The placing of the poem to Lucrezia Borgia among this group seems a further indication of Bembo's intent to make the poems of the *Carminum libellus* chronologically accurate. "Ad Lucretiam Borgiam" (Poem XII) could never have been published in the duchess's lifetime, but with her long dead, Bembo could tell the world how (and when) he had been emotionally "shipwrecked" (48) by his passion for her. He could also suggest, in Poem XV, how nice it would be for someone in love with an older man's wife if that man would only turn a blind eye and allow his wife to find happiness where she would.

With Poem XVI we move to the world of Rome and of affairs both clerical and literary, a world without women, at least as far as the poems are concerned, and therefore a world without that feminine interplay which had so nourished Bembo's life up to this point. But it was not a world without friendship, and Bembo's warmth, his ability to admire with generosity and grace, and his love of words beautifully turned in the service of uniting the ancient past to the present find their expression in the twelve poems which make up the next group. These poems, particularly the "Hymn to St. Stephen," also illustrate a peculiar phenomenon of the humanist mentality: how easily permeable was the membrane between classical myth and the Christian religion. In Bembo's case there seems hardly to have been any distinction at all. God the Father is Jupiter, the Virgin Mary a "beauteous Nymph," Christ a "great-hearted Hero," all this appearing in the middle of a graphic account of Stephen's martyrdom. These are public poems. One, "To Sempronius," deals forthrightly with a question important to his humanist contemporaries: should one write in the vernacular? Another, "At the Tomb of Poliziano," pays tribute on behalf of all his fellow-poets to the acknowledged "arbiter" of Italian poetry.

Poem XXVIII, with its eulogy of the oak-tree, symbol of the Della Rovere family, marks the end of this section. The poems that follow, XXIX to the end, are with one exception all epitaphs, giving the book's last section a "dying fall." While the opening poems were set in an Arcadia of nymphs and shepherds, the final poems live in the real world of mortality. They are bracketed by two epitaphs, elegantly turned, but full of pain. These are the epitaphs for his younger brother, Carlo, dead untimely at thirty, and for his son, Lucilius, who lived only to the age of nine. In between these are ten epitaphs, including ones for his dear friend Ercole Strozzi, his old teacher Niccolò Leonico Tomeo, his fellow-humanists Filippo Beroaldo and Jacopo Sannazaro, and even his little dog, appropriately named Bembino. They create the portrait of a man who has had a life rich in important friendships, but who now, near the end, constantly feels the weight of bereavement. Like the Roman matron Septimiana of Poem XXXIX, Bembo, full of years, seems to be wishing for death.

The poems in the Appendices are divided as follows: the first four are youthful compositions which Bembo chose to omit from the manuscript he prepared for printing; the next three are ones which the manuscript tradition suggests are almost certainly Bembo's. These seven are all to be found in Codex 635 of the Biblioteca Antoniana in Padua. The last ten, however, though Bembesque in character, leave some editors in doubt about their authenticity. (See the Note on the Text.) Of those which are almost certainly Bembo's the seventh, "Ad Lycorim," is the most intriguing. When it first appeared in print in 1887, it was described as an epithalamium and was indeed published as a gift for a couple on the occasion of their wedding. In presenting to "Lycoris" the figure of Penelope as the faithful wife, this poem is a mirror image of Poem XIII which presents to "Gallus" the figure of Aeneas as the unfaithful lover. The poem also suggests that the two years Bembo passed in Messina studying Greek with Lascaris were not just spent in climbing Mt. Etna. He had absorbed his Homer well.

The last ten poems are an interesting mix, gathered from a number of different manuscript sources and presenting a number of poetic styles. "Echo" first appeared tentatively attributed to Bembo in 1563 in a Venetian MS entitled *Carmina illustrium poetarum*. Despite the early attribution the rhymed lines have made it seem suspect to all later editors except Seghezzi. The wit of the next two poems, "Petri Bembi Carmen" and "Lycda," however, suggests Bembo's hand, the ending of the "Carmen" recalling that of Poem XI "Ad Telesillam" and the text of "Lycda" reminding the reader how well its author knew his Catullus. The fourth poem, "Ex Bembo" is found in a MS in the Vatican library and is, in fact, a translation into Latin of one of Bembo's Italian sonnets, "Si come suol, poi che 'l verno aspro e rio." It is a single image contained in a single sentence beautifully laid out in sixteen delicate lines.

The fifth poem, "Ad Angelum Gabrielem gratulatio," is found with six of Bembo's early poems in a MS in the Biblioteca Universitaria of Bologna. It reads like the other poems from Bembo's youth — hyperbolic, a little disjointed, but full of wit and affection. If it is not Bembo's, it must be from the pen of someone who knew and loved Angelo Gabriel equally well. The next four poems are epitaphs of the sort at which Bembo excelled. As we saw, he had already included one for Sannazaro in the book he had prepared for publication. This one, "Quid moror?" along with "Echo" and "Lycda," are described as of uncertain authorship in a book entitled *Carmina poetarum nobilium* which was published in Milan in 1563. The epitaph for Raphael first appeared in print as attributed to Bembo in *Carmina illustrium poetarum italorum* which was printed in Paris in 1576. If, indeed, Bembo did write the epitaph for Raphael, it is unwittingly the most famous verse he wrote, for thousands of visitors to Raphael's tomb in the Pantheon struggle to translate it every year. The final one, for Foglietta, reads like something Bembo composed out of affectionate duty, somewhat formulaic, but published as Bembo's in 1574 by Uberto Foglietta, Agostino's son.

Finally, there are the 619 lines of "Sarca" (Appendix A, Poem VIII), Sodano's text (which we have otherwise followed in this volume) contains an expurgated version which was printed in Rome in 1842 in the *Spicilegium Romanum* as being derived from a MS in Vienna. In 1994 a German scholar, Otto Schönberger, published the text of the Viennese MS in full with a German translation. His is the text printed here. Schönberger argues quite convincingly that the poem is Bembo's both for stylistic reasons and reasons inherent in the MS itself. The title, *P. Bembi Sarca*, is followed by the amplifying words *P[etri] B[embi] Secretar[ii] Ven[etarum] Sarca*, indicating that Bembo wrote the poem after he had become historian of Venice, but before he had been made a cardinal. During those years in Padua he was at work on many different projects, among which were editing his love-letters to Maria Savorgnan and Lucretia Borgia and preparing various of his works for posthumous publication. To remake "Benacus" (Poem XVIII) into a full-fledged myth of his native countryside while at the same time paying expressive homage to Catullus LXIV and to his idol, Virgil, seems completely appropriate to that moment in Bembo's life.

"Sarca" begins in precise geographical definition. A glance at a modern-day atlas of northern Italy will enable the reader to see exactly what rivers, mountains, towns, and cities Bembo is describing. After a call to the Muses to preside over the telling of the story, as if to alert the reader to the fact that "Sarca" is more than a tale of love, the poem, like the mountain river it first depicts, rushes headlong into Sarca's impetuous wooing, Garda's flight, and Benacus's acceptance of the marriage proposal on his daughter's behalf. Then the hexameters move into a stately processional mode, first in a lengthy description of Sarca's dwelling and the preparation of the marriage bed, then in an extended catalogue of the groups gathering for the ceremony. The resemblance to the organization and pace of Catullus LXIV is everywhere apparent, culminating in the prophecy of Manto, the blind Theban priestess, who unfolds to the newly married couple what the Fates have in store for them. Out of the lake named Garda, which will result from the merging of the river Sarca and the river Benacus (here Bembo takes a modest liberty with geographical fact), will flow the river Mintius (Mincius, or Mincio in Italian). This is the river which flows by the city of Mantua, and out of Mantua comes Virgil. The next hundred lines of the poem are an encomium to Virgil, beginning with a summary of the *Eclogues*, the *Georgics*, and the *Aeneid*, and ending with a brief description of the poems of famous poets who made Virgil their model — Statius, Pontano, and Sannazaro. The poem ends with Manto wishing all "the joys of lawful love" to the newly married pair.

There is much that indicates "Sarca" as Bembo's work. Jacob Burckhardt called it the "masterpiece" of the Renaissance humanist desire "to expand and complete Graeco-Roman mythology,"[6] and in its sweep and erudition it rises beyond everything else Bembo wrote. Its homage to Virgil lies not only in the overt praise of the final lines but also, as Schönberger points out, in the progression of the action "from . . . bucolic-erotic to mythic-historic,"[7] emulating the sequence of Virgil's works. Unlike the earlier poem on which he draws, here Bembo is freed from the need to flatter and extol Giberti, a need which constrained "Benacus" and impelled Bembo to publish it as soon as it was written. Finally, the praise of Virgil, which seems to flow seamlessly out of the flowing of the river Mintius, merges without pause into praise for Bembo's older contemporaries whom we know meant much to him. Like the epitaphs at the end of the book he prepared for publication, this praise seems rightly to be Bembo's final gift to Pontano and Sannazaro, who shared his life's passion.

Why, then, did Bembo not acknowledge and celebrate this special child of his mind? There are several possible reasons. "Sarca" is really an epyllion and as such would not have fit comfortably into the *Libellus*, the longest of whose poems is only 195 lines. More importantly, by the time "Sarca" was finished, Bembo was again purposefully angling for a cardinal's hat, and to Paul III, eager for a reform council and anxious about the abuses and lapses that had made the Church so vulnerable to criticism, "Sarca" might well have appeared unseemly. Finally, once Bembo had been raised to the cardinalate, the strict, reformist, pre-Tridentine atmosphere would have inhibited his publishing a work which looked like so much "playing among the woods" and enjoying the "frolicking of nymphs," as Toffanin put it.[8] But, thanks to Schönberger's efforts, we now have "Sarca" in its unexpurgated entirety, a monument and an epitaph to a writer whose love of the past made it alive in the present. As a contemporary, Cosmus Anysius, wrote just after Bembo's death:

> Bembe, iaces, tecumque iacent Tritonia, Musae,
>   Religio, Charites, Phoebus, Atlantiades.
> Sed vivunt potius tecum, nam tempora foetus
>   Ingenii poterant nulla abolere tui.

> Bembo, you lie dead and with you lie Minerva, the Muses,
>   Religion, the Graces, Apollo, and Mercury.
> But yet with you they live, for no amount of time
>   Can wipe away the creations of your genius.

De Aetna, published when Pietro Bembo was only twenty-five, is full of the youthful exuberance which characterizes the Faunus poems and the "Song of Congratulation to Angelo Gabriel," both of which are mentioned in the course of the dialogue. Springing as it does from Bembo's recent sojourn in Sicily, the work radiates the joy of his just completed studies and the satisfaction of being in possession of information which everyone wants to hear. Though it is ostensibly about the father's desire to learn about the fires of Etna and the son's desire to describe his trip up the mountain, it has as its subtext young Bembo's absorption in learning and his father's dedication to Venetian politics.

Pietro gives to the two characters of Bembo *père* and *fils* a relaxed formality of speech, each one having a chance to voice both his private concerns and his warm feelings for the other. The young Bembo's ardent nature and generosity of heart are readily apparent, both in his solicitude for his father's health and in the deference with which he puts into his father's mouth the dialogue's final disquisition on the nature and source of volcanic fires. This explanation, though much abbreviated, is drawn from the first century poem *Aetna*, once attributed to Virgil.[9]

Bembo also pays homage to his poetic idol in other ways. Though the dialogue's pages are laced with quotations from the Greek authors the young Pietro had just finished studying, its time span—a passage from midday to late afternoon—and its form—two characters engaged in thoughtful conversation—are modeled on Virgil's *Eclogue* 1. Here, in his first published book, Bembo is already acknowledging his debt to the poet whom, in his last long poem, he calls the "glorious wellspring" (*clara origo*) of Latin poetry.

Many have helped bring this project to fruition; in particular Barbara Post and Maria Arroyo were generous guides to languages other than Latin. I am grateful to all my children for their encouragement and support. Heartfelt thanks go to Virginia Brown for her careful reading and to James Hankins for seeing me through. Charles Chatfield and Michael Putnam were the angels on either side.

NOTES

1. Hugh Shankland, *The Prettiest Love Letters in the World* (Boston: David Godine, 1987), Letter XV.

2. Baldassar Castiglione, *The Book of the Courtier*, tr. Charles P. Singleton (New York: Doubleday, 1959), p. 351. For an analysis of Bembo's speech in Book IV, see James Hankins, "Renaissance Philosophy and Book IV of *Il Cortegiano*," in *Baldesar Castiglione: The Book of the Courtier*, ed. Daniel Javitch (New York: Norton, 2002), pp. 377–388.

3. Carlo Dionisotti, "Pietro Bembo," in *Dizionario biografico degli italiani*, Rome: Treccani, 1966), p. 140.

4. Shankland, *Love Letters*, Letter XXXV.

5. To be published in the *I Tatti Renaissance Library*, edited and translated by Robert W. Ulery.

6. Jacob Burckhardt, *The Civilization of the Renaissance in Italy*, tr. S. G. C. Middlemore (New York: Albert and Charles Boni, 1935), p. 261.

7. Otto Schönberger, *Sarca: Petrus Bembus: Einleitung, vollständiger Text, erste Übersetzung und Anmerkungen* (Würzburg: Königshausen und Neumann, 1994), p. 23.

8. Giuseppe Toffanin, *La fine dell' umanesimo* (Turin: Fratelli Bocca, 1920), p. 28, as cited in Marco Pecoraro, *Per la storia dei carmi del Bembo. Una redazione non vulgata*, (Venice: Istituto per la Collaborazione Culturale, 1959), p. 40.

9. W. V. Clausen, F. R. D. Goodyear, E. J. Kenney, and J. A. Richmond, eds., *Appendix Vergiliana* (Oxford: Clarendon Press, 1966), p. 65f., ll. 445f. Although the attribution of *Aetna* to Virgil began to be doubted as early as Donatus's fourth century life of the poet, Bembo seems to have believed the poem authentic.

LYRIC POETRY

ETNA

CARMINUM LIBELLUS

Pastorum Chorus

Pastores tua turba te rogamus,
 Seu tu nomine Pan arundinator,
 Seu Faunus dubii potens futuri,
 Barbatus capripesque cornigerque,
5 Seu malis, Pater, Incubus vocari:
 Nos et res tueare, Dive, nostras.

En iam ver redit et dies rebellem
 paulatim sibi vendicat teporem;
 Iam collis viret et sinu soluto
10 Florentes tibi porrigit genistas.
 Pastores tua turba te rogamus,
 Nos et res tueare, Dive, nostras.

Nunc annus puer et tenellus orbis;
 Nunc sol purior et colora tellus;
15 Nunc ludit Venus alma, nunc sorores
 Festas Gratia poscit ad choreas.
 Pastores tua turba te rogamus,
 Nos et res tueare, Dive, nostras.

Novum montivagae thymum capellae
20 Tondent, et cytisi comam arbutique
 Pascunt purpureos oves per agros,
 Et pugnam cupidi cient mariti.
 Pastores tua turba te rogamus,
 Nos et res tueare, Dive, nostras

LITTLE BOOK OF POEMS

: I :

Choral Prayer of the Shepherds

We, your shepherds, your followers, entreat you,
    Whether you are Pan the Fluteplayer by name
    Or Faunus, master of the doubtful future,
    Hairy-faced and goat-footed and horn-bearing,
    Or you wish, Father, to be called Incubus,   5
    Watch over us and our doings, divine one.

See how spring returns and little by little
    The growing light reclaims the rebellious warmth.
    Now the hill grows green and in its softened folds
    It blossoms forth the yellow broom flowers for you.   10
    We, your shepherds, your followers, entreat you,
    Watch over us and our doings, divine one.

Now the year is youthful and the world tender;
    Now the sun is purer and the earth abloom;
    Now fostering Venus makes merry, now Grace   15
    Calls her sisters to the festival dances.
    We, your shepherds, your followers, entreat you,
    Watch over us and our doings, divine one.

The mountain-wandering she-goats nibble at
    The new thyme, and the ewes pasture on the shoots   20
    Of clover and arbutus in the bright fields,
    Their ardent mates eagerly provoking fights.
    We, your shepherds, your followers, entreat you,
    Watch over us and our doings, divine one.

25   Nunc o nunc opus est, Pater, volenti
       Aspires genio, et gregem revisas,
       Dum liber stabulis: tibi dicatum
       Ne qua sors populum gravis fatiget.
       Pastores tua turba te rogamus,
30   Nos et res tueare, Dive, nostras

     Tu fures, avidum genus, coerce;
       Tu morbos abige atra saevientes;
       Tu bellum iubeas, bonus, famemque
       Ignotis procul exulare terris.
35   Pastores tua turba te rogamus,
       Nos et res tueare, Dive, nostras.

     Defendat saturas nemus capellas;
       Fida non egeant oves canum vi;
       Audaces lupus inter erret agnos,
40   Cumque hoedis Libyci accubent leones.
       Pastores tua turba te rogamus,
       Nos et res tueare, Dive, nostras.

     Absit fraus scelerum comes, suoque
       Se livor miser imbuat veneno;
45   Et lis cedere discat, et solutam
       Devinctus metuat furor quietem.
       Pastores tua turba te rogamus,
       Nos et res tueare, Dive, nostras.

     Sit pax candida, sit beata, plena
50   Pomis copia frugibusque cornu:
       Qualis cum positum recenter orbem
       Saturnus Iove sanctior regebat.
       Pastores tua turba te rogamus,
       Nos et res tueare, Dive, nostras.

Now, o now, Father, with a willing spirit   25
    You must again favor and visit your flock,
    While it is free from winter quarters: lest some
    Heavy lot trouble those who call themselves yours.
    We, your shepherds, your followers, entreat you,
    Watch over us and our doings, divine one.   30

Do you keep within bounds thieves, that greedy race;
    Banish all diseases that rage direfully;
    May you, in goodness, order war and hunger
    Far away into exile in unknown lands.
    We, your shepherds, your followers, entreat you,   35
    Watch over us and our doings, divine one.

Let the thicket protect the sated she-goats;
    Let the sheep not need a trusty pack of dogs;
    May the wolf wander among the daring lambs,
    And the Libyan lion lie down with the kids.   40
    We, your shepherds, your followers, entreat you,
    Watch over us and our doings, divine one.

Let deceit, companion of crime, be absent,
    Let wretched envy steep in his own poison;
    And let contention learn to give way, and let   45
    Wild madness, in chains, learn to fear unbound peace.
    We, your shepherds, your followers, entreat you,
    Watch over us and our doings, divine one.

Let there be peace, bright and blest, a plenteous
    Abundance of apples and cornel-berries;   50
    Just as when Saturn, holier even than Jove,
    Wielded the power in the newly-made earth.
    We, your shepherds, your followers entreat you,
    Watch over us and our doings, divine one.

55 Audis nos, Pater? an novam per agros
     Suspiras Venerem et preces recusas?
     Ah cur nos fugis? hi tui poetae:
     Haec olim tibi ducitur chorea.
     Pastores tua turba te rogamus,
60   Nos et res tueare, Dive, nostras.

     Scimus quid sit amor, quid obstinata
     Defigi tacitum iecur sagitta;
     Adsis tu tamen, ipse dum laboro
     Coepti carminis explicare pensum.
65   Pastores tua turba te rogamus,
     Nos et res tueare, Dive, nostras.

     Et ver pulvereum, humidam et vehat sol
     Aestatem pecori laborioso;
     Neu laxent pluviae, vel impotenti
70   Sydus ubera comprimat calore.
     Pastores tua turba te rogamus,
     Nos et res tueare, Dive, nostras.

     Tum fons vitreus, et perennis unda
     Festinans placido sonet susurro,
75   Quo sitim veniat meridiemque
     Umbrosa pecus elevare ripa.
     Pastores tua turba te rogamus,
     Nos et res tueare, Dive, nostras.

     Gregi haec poscimus: at gregis magistros
80   Praesens perpetua leves iuventa,
     Quam lusus comitetur et voluptas
     Et nudos Venus osculans amores.
     Pastores tua turba te rogamus,
     Nos et res tueare, Dive, nostras.

Do you hear us, Father? Or are you sighing   55
   Through fields over a new love and spurn our pleas?
   Ah, why do you flee us? We are your poets:
   From all time past it is yours to lead this dance.
   We, your shepherds, your followers, entreat you,
   Watch over us and our doings, divine one.   60

We know what love can be, how that obdurate
   Arrow is planted deep in the silent heart.
   Nevertheless, be present now, while I work
   To spin the length of this song I have begun.
   We, your shepherds, your followers, entreat you,   65
   Watch over us and our doings, divine one.

Let the sun carry with it a dusty spring
   And a dampened summer to the toiling flocks;
   Do not let the rains relax, nor the Dog-Star
   Hinder the rich milk with its powerful heat   70
   We, your shepherds, your followers, entreat you,
   Watch over us and our doings, divine one.

Let the glass-green fountain and the running wave
   Hasten to murmur with their gentle whisper
   Where the flock comes to slake its thirst and lighten   75
   The heat of noontime on a shadowy bank.
   We, your shepherds, your followers, entreat you,
   Watch over us and our doings, divine one.

We ask these things for our flock; moreover may
   You, at hand, refresh the keepers of the flock   80
   With youth eternal, whom sport and joy attend
   As well as Venus kissing naked cherubs.
   We, your shepherds, your followers, entreat you,
   Watch over us and our doings, divine one.

85   Sic te nec fatuae petant puellae,
            Nec Nymphae fugiant meticulosae,
            Dum fessae gelidi nemus Lycaei,
            Et gratum tibi Maenalon revisunt.

                        : II :

                Faunus ad Nympeum fluvium

                    Fictum pro antiquo

        Quid tibi nobiscum est, fluviorum infamia, Nympeu?
            Flecte alio cursus, perniciose, tuos.
        Flecte procul, removeque meo vestigia luco:
            Impurum sacra non decet ire via.
5   Quantum Baianas fregit lascivia villas,
            Criminis articulus parsque pusilla tui est.
        Huc veniunt mixtae pueris de more puellae,
            Inque tua, posita veste, natatur aqua.
        Lusibus interea duxisse procacibus horas
10   Nequitiaque iuvat continuare diem:
        Cumque libet, mediis passim iunguntur in undis,
            Lascivum femori conseriturque femur.
        Tu tamen haec pateris, nec te mea numina tangunt,
            Ante oculos fieri turpia probra meos.
15   Quin etiam si quid specto, et spectare necesse est,
            Illi se improbius liberiusque petunt.
        Permolitur pueroque puer, pactique vicissim
            Obscaenos agitant nostra sub ora modos;
        Meque vocans uda media inter savia lingua,
20   Crissat ab imposito fixa puella mare.

                            8

So, let not empty-headed maidens seek you,   85
    Nor let the apprehensive nymphs take to flight,
    When, exhausted, again they visit your groves
    On cold Lycaeon or Maenalos so dear.

: II :

Faunus Speaks to the River Nympeus

A fiction in the manner of antiquity

What have we to do with you, Nympeus, disgrace of rivers?
    Turn your course elsewhere, destructive one.
Turn far away, and remove all traces from my grove:
    It becomes not the unclean to go by the holy way.
The degree to which wantonness destroyed the villas of Baiae   5
    Is but one tiny part of your crime.
Hither come girls and boys, together by custom,
    To swim in your water, their clothes laid by.
And they have passed hours thus in saucy games
    And in wantonness they delight to spend the day: 10
And when they please, they couple everywhere in the midst
    Of the waves, thigh entwined with wanton thigh.
Yet you allow these things, and my divine power affects you not,
    Virtue becoming vice right before my eyes.
Indeed, even if I see aught (and one has only to look),   15
    They keep pursuing each other more wickedly and more freely.
Boy rubs against boy, and bound each to each
    They perform their obscene thrustings before my very eyes.
Calling out to me with her wet tongue in the midst of kisses,
    A girl grinds her hips beneath a penetrating male,   20

9

At mihi tum mediae saliunt tentigine venae,
    Surgit et in cornu spina recurva suum.
Omnia sed parvi facerem tamen: hoc mihi magno est,
    Hoc dolet, hoc aequa non ego mente fero:
25   Adsueti longa cum sint in crimina culpa,
    Concubitus fugiunt qualibet arte meos,
Sive Lycam puerum coepi mollire precando,
    Seu tacitus, qua se fert Telesilla, sequor.
Ille preces non audit amantis, at illa sequentem
30   Praevolat, et tardum ludit, ut aura, senem.
Non tu parva meo praebes alimenta furori,
    Amnis moeche, et vos insidiosa vada:
Nam neque nos olidi vincunt pruritibus hirqui,
    Nec sum Lampsacio castior ipse Deo.
35   Quod si me Cybele curat iustissima mater,
    Quam penes est bruti fasque nefasque soli,
Invisi latices fundo pereatis ab imo,
    Vosque petant sicci traiiciantque pedes.

: III :

Faunus ad nymphas

Dicite cur nostros, Nymphae, fugiatis amores:
    Quid Faunus, quo sic despiciatur, habet?
Cornua si mihi sunt, sunt et sua cornua Baccho:
    Inque sinus vocat hunc Cressa puella suos.
5   Ignea si frons est, an non frons ignea Phoebo est?

And then from its center my member leaps up, outstretched,
    And my curving prick rises into a horn.
But still I would make all of little account; yet this thing is great
      to me,
    This grieves me, and this I cannot bear with a serene mind:
Although by long wickedness they are hardened to depravity,   25
    By some deceit or other they continue to flee my embraces,
Whether I begin to melt the boy Lyca by my entreaties,
    Or I am quietly following where Telesilla betakes herself.
He hears not a lover's prayers, and she flees before me, following,
    And they tease, like a breath of wind, this tired old man.   30
You offer no small food for my madness,
    You adulterous stream, with your deceitful shallows;
For the stinking he-goats do not outdo me in sexual cravings,
    Nor am I more chaste myself than the Lampsacian god.
But if mother Cybele, most just as she is, cares about me,   35
    She in whose power lies what is and is not allowed to the
      brute earth,
May your hateful waters perish from their lowest depths,
    And may travellers seek out and pass over your bed dry-shod.

: III :

Faunus Speaks to the Nymphs

Say why you flee my love-making, Nymphs:
    What does Faunus have that he is so despised?
If I have horns, Bacchus, too, has his horns:
    And yet the Cretan maid calls him to her bosom.
If I have a fiery aspect, is not Phoebus' face fiery, too?   5

Hoc tamen est Clymene facta parente parens.
Barba riget suffusa genis? dedit improba saepe
    Oscula barbato Deianira viro.
Intonso densoque tegor praecordia villo?
10   Nil ideo Marti est Ilia questa suo.
Capripedem arguitis: quid claudo turpius? at tu
    Nupsisti claudo, Cypria pulchra, Deo.
Denique si qua meae pars est non bella figurae,
    Exemplum a coelo, quod capiatis, habet.
15 Sed vos nimirum mortalia facta sequutae,
    Omnis quando auro conciliatur amor,
Pastorum et pecoris tenui custode repulso,
    Quaeritis a magnis munera magna Deis.

: IV :

Iolas ad Faunum

Mollibus Alcippe vernantia serta genistis
    Collis ab usque iugo fert tibi, Faune, sui.
Ut vidi, huc amens summo de monte cucurri:
    Aspice perculso quam tibi corde loquor.
5 Nunc adeo si saepe tuos cantavimus ignes,
    Affer opem flammae tu quoque, Dive, meae.
Formosi cum te floris velabit honore,
    Haec illi dicas, ut tua verba, precor:
'Alcippe, miserum fastu quae perdis Iolam
10   Teque simul tacito fallis inepta dolo,

Yet nonetheless submissive Clymene made him a father.
Does a spreading beard make my cheeks rough?
    Deianira often gave mischievous kisses to her bearded
        husband.
Is my chest covered with a thick and shaggy pelt?
    Ilia did not complain thus of her Mars.   10
You charge me with goat's feet: What is baser than being lame?
    Yet you, lovely Venus, were wed to a lame god.
Hence if there is any part of my appearance which is not
        beautiful,
    Heaven offers an example for you to take.
But doubtless you are following human ways   15
    Since among them all love is won over by gold,
And having driven off the lowly guardian of shepherds and
        sheep,
    You then demand great gifts from the great gods.

: IV :

Iolas Speaks to Faunus

Alcippe is bringing you first-blooming garlands of tender broom
    All the way from the ridge of your hill, Faunus.
Seeing this, I ran hither wildly from the mountaintop;
    Look how I speak to you with beating heart.
If I have often sung of your fires of passion,   5
    Do you now bring comfort to my flame, divine one.
When she crowns you with the tribute of a lovely flower,
    I beg that you will say these words to her as yours:
"Alcippe, you who are destroying wretched Iolas through pride
    And at the same time stupidly deceiving yourself with silent   10
        guile,

13

Munera, quae portas, bene si tibi nota fuissent,
    Damni te poterant admonuisse tui.
Nec reflorescunt, quae iam cecidere, genistae,
    Nec redeunt, qui iam praeteriere dies.
15   Quod si nulla mei tangit te cura poetae,
    Ah saltem formae parce, puella, tuae.'

: V :

Thestylis ad Faunum

Thestylis Alconis lectum pressura mariti,
    Numinis et cultus semper amica tui,
Ipsum, Dive, suae tibi virginitatis honorem
    Solvit, adhuc nulli vincula tacta viro:
5   Utque ea zona tuam pinum complexa tenebit,
    Sic se animo, sic se vinciat ille, rogat.

: VI :

Daphnis ad Faunum

Hac tibi, Faune, tua quae pendet fistula pinu,
    De victo grates Thyrside Daphnis agit.
Quod si etiam illius dederis superare magistrum,
    Caedetur festis alba capella tuis.

If you had marked well, the gifts you bring
    Would have warned you of your loss.
The blossoms of broom which now have fallen will not flower
        again,
    Nor will those days return which now have passed by.
But if no concern for my poet touches you,   15
    Ah, maiden, at least have a care for your own beauty."

∶   V   ∶

Thestylis Prays to Faunus

Thestylis, about to lie upon the couch of her husband Alcon,
    But always a devotee of your power and your worship,
Loosens for you, oh deity, her girdle, the very honor of her
        virginity,
    Which till now has been touched by no man's hand;
And as her girdle is about to clasp your pine in its embrace,   5
    She prays that thus, O thus, he may bind himself in spirit.

∶   VI   ∶

Daphnis Prays to Faunus

With this reed-pipe, Faunus, which hangs on your pine tree,
    Daphnis returns thanks for the defeat of Thyrsis.
But if you grant that he beat his teacher too,
    A white she-goat will be slain on your festival day.

: VII :

Galatea

Pana Deum Siculi per iniquas littoris undas
    Eludit tarda dum Galatea fuga,
Seque adeo spe provectus studioque sequendi
    Plus medium infido tingueret ille mari:
5   'Quo fugis, o Galatea? mane, mane o Galatea:
    Non ego sum, dixit, non ego, Nympha, Cyclops,
Qui flavum avulsis iaculatus rupibus Acin,
    Saevitiae liquit tristia signa suae.
Pastorum pecorisque Deus, cui garrula cera
10   Prima dedit varios fistula iuncta modos,
Quem gelidi frondosa colunt pineta Lycaei
    Laetaque Maenalio Parrhasis ora iugo,
Unam de cunctis te diligo Neptuninis:
    O Galatea, mane, o iam Galatea mane',
15   Ille loquebatur; fundo declive maligno
    Littus erat: gressum non tenuere pedes.
Sed pelagi dum caeca urget male cautus, et instat
    Qua refugit pendens, subtrahiturque solum,
Labitur, et summas dorso converrit arenas:
20   Labentem intortis obruit unda fretis,
Utque deam, 'Galatea' iterans 'Galatea', vocabat,
    Implerunt tenues ora vocantis aquae.
Tum primum latices epotavisse marinos
    Pana ferunt, ponti nec latuisse Deum,

: VII :

Galatea

While Galatea with hesitant flight slipped from the god Pan's
    grasp
    Among the harsh waves on Sicily's shore,
And he, still carried on by hope and eagerness to follow,
    Soaked himself above his waist in the treacherous sea,
He said, "Whither do you flee, O Galatea? Stay, stay,   5
    O Galatea: I am not, I am not the Cyclops, nymph,
Who, after hurling boulders at golden Acis,
    Left on him the sad traces of his savagery.
I am the god of shepherds and sheep, for whom the speaking
    flute
    Held tight by wax, first gave forth a mix of melody,   10
He whom the leafy pinewoods on chill Lycaeon worship
    And whom the joyful people of Arcady worship on the
        Maenalian ridge,
I love thee alone, out of all the daughters of Neptune:
    O Galatea, stay, O Galatea, do stay."
So he spoke; the seashore was steep with   15
    Treacherous ground: his feet could not hold their place.
But he presses forward heedless of the dark waves, and leaning
    forward
    Is almost upon her as she flees, when the ground slips out
        from under him,
He slips, and grazes the topmost sands with his back,
    And the waters of the twisting sea rush over him as he slips.   20
And as he called, "Goddess, Galatea, Galatea," again and again
    A mist of water filled his mouth as he called.
They say that then Pan first drank the waters of the sea,
    But did not go unnoticed by the ocean god,

25   Sed quia Nereidas ibat vexare puellas,
      Offensum fluctus non tenuisse suos.
   Ergo illum nandi insuetum glauca excipit alto
      Unda sinu: exultant irrequieta vada.
   Marmora ter superare manu conatus amara,
30   Ter circumfusis est revolutus aquis;
   Nympha Dei lapsum cupidis spectabat ocellis,
      Gratior et pulchro risus in ore fuit.
   Spectarant, sparsi ut steterant per littora, Fauni,
      Pan, comites Fauni, grataque turba tua,
35   Et mixtus Faunis, cordi cui semper amores
      Nympharum et querulo tibia rauca sono,
   Incubus, et Satyri, et coniferae Sylvanus
      Arboris agresti cinctus honore caput.
   Qui simul atque ipsum gentis videre parentem
40   Pana sub impuris mergier aequoribus:
   'Nympha redi, Galatea redi, neu desere amantem,'
      Ingeminant omnes, 'candida Nympha redi.
   Ah tantum ne admisse tuis sit dedecus undis,
      Quod taceant nulli post, Galatea, dies',
45   Ingeminant Divi; clamoribus icta resultat
      Arida pumiceum qua lavit Aetna pedem.
   Illa metum fallax simulare et tendere in altum
      Et vanas surda reiicere aure preces;
   Quo magis ii tristes moesti versare querelas,
50   Et pelagi expertes dicere amore Deos.

But because Pan's purpose was to harm the Nereid maids,   25
    Neptune was angered and did not hold back his waters.
Thus did a a grey-blue wave, high-arching, sieze the god,
    unused to swimming, in its restless surge.
Three times he tried to surmount the bitter flood by hand,
    Three times he was rolled back by the all-surrounding waves;   30
The nymph took in greedily the spectacle of the god as he
      slipped down,
    And pleasant was the laughter from her lovely mouth.
The Fauns, companions of Faunus, and your pleasing throng
    Watched you, Pan, as they stood scattered along the shore,
And mingling with the Fauns—he to whose heart the loves   35
    Of the Nymphs are dear, and the piercing flute with its song
      of complaint,
Incubus, and the Satyrs, and Sylvanus, his head
    Bound with the rustic emblem of the cone-bearing tree.
Who all, as soon as they see Pan himself,
    The parent of their race, sinking under the ugly waters,   40
Redouble their cries. "Nymph, come back, Galatea, come back;
    Do not abandon your lover, bright Nymph, come back.
Let not such a disgrace be permitted to your waters,
    About which none in after-days, Galatea, will be silent."
The deities cried out again and again, and barren Etna,   45
    Struck by the shouts, resounded where it washes the pumice
      at its foot.
She, deceitful, pretends to be frightened and moves out into the
      deep
    And disdains their useless pleas with a deaf ear;
Wherefore saddened, they continue their sorrowful plaints all the
      more
    And say that the gods of the sea have no share in love.   50

Pectora pars pulsare manu, pars currere in undas
    Cedit, et argutos tardat arena pedes.
Omnia quae obliquo, lente nans, respicit ore,
    Unaque tot gaudet fallere Nympha Deos.
55   Utque satis lusit: 'Certe sat lusimus, inquit,
    Successuque mei non caruere doli.'
Atque ita iactatis relegit freta versa lacertis,
    Pronaque non longum vincere tendit iter.
Summa secant pulsae fluctu saliente papillae,
60   Spumea sub niveo murmurat unda pede.
Tum summo apprehensum cornu sustollit: at illi
    Clauserat insolitus lumina victa sopor.
Ut rediit cum luce animus: 'Quo percitus oestro
    Coniugium affectas, dixit, inepte, meum?
65   Perque ausus vada salsa sequi regna invia vobis,
    Invitam pergis sollicitare Deam?
Numen aquae gaudet tumidarum numine aquarum,
    Conveniunt votis vota propinqua meis.
Tu pete montivagas, quarum es de gente, capellas,
70   Parte tui, et nostros linque, proterve, toros.'

Some resort to beating their breasts with their hand, some run
    Into the waves, and the sand slows their splashing feet.
The Nymph, swimming slowly, looks back with sidelong glance,
    And rejoices that she alone has cheated so many gods.
And when she has played at this enough, she says: "Truly I have   55
    Played enough, and my stratagems have not been without
        success."
And so turning about, she went back through the sea with strong
        strokes
    And stretching forward she made to master the short space to
        shore.
Her breasts, beaten by the leaping billows, cleave the tops of the
        waves,
    And the sea hisses, churned to foam by her snowy foot.   60
Then having caught him, she raised him up by the tip of his
        horn,
    But an unwonted sleep had closed his vanquished eyes.
When with the light his life returned, she said, "Struck by what
        frenzy,
    Absurd creature, do you aspire to join yourself to me?
Through the salt sea, a kingdom pathless to you, do you dare to   65
        follow me,
    And persist in troubling a goddess who is unwilling?
A deity of the waters delights in her power over the swelling
        waves,
    My kinfolk's prayers agree with my own.
You, go seek the mountain-treading goats, to whose race you
        belong,
    They are your folk, and leave our couches alone, shameless   70
        one."

: VIII :

Priapus

Ante alias omnes, meus hic quas educat hortus,
    Una puellares allicit herba manus:
Quam rapiunt, non ut capiti dent ferre corollas
    Et niteat multo flore revincta coma;
5   Laeta nec ut festi velentur limina templi,
    Cum facit ad patrios plebs venerata Deos;
Nec phiala ut molles capiat conclusa maniplos
    Guttaque supposito stillet odora foco.
Atque ea non beta est, non brassica, non amaranthus,
10   Non quae flaventi lumine caltha micat;
Lubrica non lapathus, non est Cereale papaver;
    Adiuvat aut medicas quae panacea manus;
Nec Baccho cynara et mensis accepta secundis,
    Artificum nec qui surgis, acanthe, labor;
15   Nec quae cum rapidi vertit se lumine Phoebi,
    Nec quae de pueri nomine nomen habet.
Longe alia est longeque alios aptatur in usus,
    Nam primum bifido nititur illa pede.
Enodem tenta in caulem, resupinaque tota,
20   Et patulum minio sparsa rubente caput,
Est eadem, gelidis albet cum terra pruinis,
    Est, cum sydereo finditur usta cane.
Nil refugit, nulloque potest non tempore pangi,
    Nullis non apte conseriturque locis.
25   Certa nec ulla soli ratio est, cultusque serendae:

: VIII :

Priapus

Before all the others which my garden here brings forth,
    One plant entices the hands of girls.
They seize it, not to make circlets for their heads,
    That their hair might glow, bound up with many flowers;
Nor that they might adorn the joyous threshold of a festal   5
      temple,
    When the people offer worship to their fathers' gods;
Nor that a closed vial might hold soft handfuls
    And a fragrant distillation might drip onto the hearth
      beneath.
Nor is it a beet, nor a cabbage, nor amaranth,
    Nor yet a marigold gleaming with its golden light;   10
Nor is it the smooth sorrel, nor the poppy of Ceres;
    Nor panacea which aids the doctors' hands;
Nor is it the cynara, welcome with wine and dessert,
    Nor you, acanthus, who spring up as a labor for artists
Nor that plant which turns itself to the light of fiery Phoebus,   15
    Nor that which has its name from the name of a boy.[1]
It is different and apt for different purposes,
    For first it rises from a twofold foot;
Tightened into a smooth stalk, and fully bent back,
    And its spacious head spread with a red like cinnabar,   20
It is the same, when the ground is white with icy frost,
    And when the earth cracks open, scorched by the dog-star.
It flees from nothing, nor is there any time in which it cannot be
      planted,
    There is no place into which it does not aptly twine itself.
It has no need of a particular soil, nor a particular manner of   25
      planting;

23

Foecundum, subigas tu modo, semen habet.
Semina seu mandes sulcis, seu fossa feraces
    Accipiat plantas, utraque tuta via est.
At cum iam prima coepit pubescere sylva,
30   Exaltatque opibus luxuriatque suis.
Tum vero lachrymae summo de vertice manant,
    Mella quibus cedant, Sicelis Hybla, tua.
Quin etiam digitis contrectarique superne
    Gaudet et attactu crescit ab ipsa tuo.
35 Nec minus hanc (quae cuncta mihi licet usque tueri,
    Nam me posse loqui foemina nulla putat)
Quamlibet ingenuae gaudent tetigisse puellae,
    Et mediam tenera continuisse manu;
Saepe iuvat summae prono dare basia vultu,
40   Lentam sollicita saepe fovere mora.
Dumque fovent, tenues planta risere tumente
    Per tunicas agilem surgere, perque manus.
Tum mirata novam faciem non rustica virgo,
    Praegrandesque toros insolitumque decus:
45 'Te veneror, gramen magni mihi numinis instar,
    Teque meum columen, te mea sceptra puto.'
Dixit; nec cunctata diu vestemque reducit
    Et bibulam inducto sedula fonte rigat.
Illa madet fusa circum sua vimina vena,
50   Quasque haurit, largo foenore reddit aquas,

It is teeming with seed, if only you rub it.
Whether you entrust the seed to a furrow, or a deeper trench
   Receives the fruitful plants, either way is safe.
And at the time when the first forest growth has begun to show
      itself,
   It leaps up and revels in its own richness.   30
Then indeed tears drip from its topmost part,
   To which even your honey, Sicilian Hybla, yields.
Indeed, it rejoices to be handled on top by the fingers,
   And itself grows from your touch.
Likewise it is this plant (the whole of which it is given to me to   35
      watch over,
   For no woman realizes that I can speak),
Above all that tender maidens rejoice to have touched,
   And to have held right round in a soft hand.
Often it pleases them, with face leaning forward, to kiss its tip,
   Often to fondle its stalk with stimulating delay.   40
And while they are fondling it, as its stem swells, they laugh to
      see
   It rise up nimbly through its thin tunic, and through their
      hands.
Then the clever maiden marvels at its new appearance,
   Its huge protuberance and unusual glory:
"I worship you, a plant like a great god to me,   45
   I think of you as my pillar, I think of you as my rod of office."
She spoke no more; and hesitating not a bit she draws back her
      robe
   And busily moistens her thirsty self with the fount which has
      entered her.
With watercourse streaming, she dampens her flower basket all
      about,
   And those waters which she drinks, she gives back with ample   50
      interest,

Cultricumque sinus laetis proventibus implet,
　　Perfugium in multis una reperta malis.
Nam quae, longiquas sponso volitante per undas,
　　Carpitur indigno sola relicta situ,
55　Et macet in viduo pertabescitque cubili,
　　Fibra se multum graminis huius alit.
Molle iecur tacita quae deperit icta sagitta,
　　Plurimam in epoto semine sentit opem.
Cui facies pallet, caulem si prandet opimum,
60　Prandenti gratus serpit in ora rubor.
Et quae turgidulos flendo corrumpit ocellos,
　　Ut temere in lachrymas hoc genus ire vides,
Rore inspersa levi, summa qui prosilit herba,
　　Laetitias animo luminibusque facit.
65　Et quam nigra malis terrent insomnia visis,
　　Admorso placidus germine somnus habet.
Dudum habilis tum si qua viro est, materque vocari
　　Expetit, ignavos conqueriturque dies,
Olim ne sterilem postrema redarguat aetas,
70　Auxilium radix, tempore sumpta, venit.
Denique si qua suo mulier male culta marito est,
　　Hanc vorat atque assis non sua damna facit.
Quamque magis digitos implet capientis et ore
　　Manditur oppleto, tam magis illa placet.
75　In molli latet umbra aliis, mihi semper aperta est:
　　Tam bona non debet graminis herba tegi.

And that plant fills the laps of lady-gardeners with rich produce,
    And is found to be a place of refuge in the midst of many
        evils.
For the woman whose husband has flitted across far-away seas,
    Who is left all alone, weakened by undeserved neglect,
And who grows thin in bereavement and pines away in her   55
        chamber,
    The fiber of this plant nourishes greatly.
When she melts in her soft heart, stricken by the silent arrow,
    She feels enormous strength from the seed she has drunk.
She whose appearance is pale, if she eats of this fat stem,
    A pleasing flush creeps into her face as she eats.   60
And she who spoils her dear little eyes, swollen with weeping,
    (For you see this sort burst rashly into tears),
When she has been sprinkled with the dew that leaps from the
        tip of this plant,
    Rejoices in her heart and in her eyes.
And she, whom black nightmares frighten with evil visions,   65
    Calm sleep holds, once she has nibbled this bud.
If any woman has been for a long time apt to a husband, and
        longs
    To be called mother, and complains loudly of idle days,
Lest Time's finality not prove her barren,
    The root of this plant comes to her aid, if she takes it in time.   70
Finally, if there is any woman who has been badly tended by her
        husband,
    She devours this plant greedily and deems her losses not
        worth a farthing.
And the more she fills her grasping fingers and eats
    With a full mouth, so much the more does it please her.
Some conceal it in the soft shade, but I have it always in the   75
        open:
    The stem of so good a plant ought not to be covered over.

Nomine si cupias cognoscere, Menta pusilla est.
  Rides? Sic illam Roma diserta vocat.
Sed quae, docti homines cum dicunt, Menta pusilla est,
80   Haec mihi non docto maxima vel nimia.
Parcite Romulidae, verbo sum lapsus in uno:
  An cuiquam nimium tale quid esse potest?

: IX :

Leucippi et Alconis tumulus

Fer casiam et flores et odori balsama trunci,
  Quanta super tumulos integat umbra duos.
O Pan, Pan, periere tui Leucippus et Alcon:
  Fer casiam, et plena balsama carpe manu.
5   Carpe manu flores, ipsaque volente Thalia,
  Nympharum sectis sparge sepulchra comis.
Illi, proh, tantum quos tu laudare solebas,
  Musa quibus cordi semper amorque fuit,
Proh facinus, periere; nec est revocabile damnum:
10   Aspice, composito fletur uterque rogo.
O Pan, Pan, seu te gelidi montana Lycaei,
  Seu tenet umbrosa Maenalis ora nape,
Huc ades, et tepidam lachrymis resperge favillam:
  Dedecet hic lachrymas continuisse, Pater.
15   Ipsa Venus flevit: teneri flevistis Amores:
  Fleverunt Dryades, Nereidesque Deae.
Phoebus adest, repetensque suos mala fata poetas
  Vexat flebilibus saxa nemusque modis.

If you desire to know it by name, it is the "tiny Mint"
    You laugh? Thus Rome, the eloquent, calls it.
But that plant which is "tiny mint", according to the speech of
        the learned,
    To me, the unlearned, is the greatest, or even too great.   80
Spare me, sons of Romulus, I have erred in one word:
    For to anyone can such a thing ever be too great?

:   IX   :

The Tomb of Leucippus and Alcon

Bring sweet marjoram and flowers and balsam with fragrant bark,
    Shade enough to shelter their two graves.
O Pan, Pan, your Leucippus and Alcon have perished:
    Bring sweet marjoram, and gather balsam with a full hand.
Gather flowers in your hand and, since Thalia herself is willing,   5
    Scatter over these graves the severed hair of the nymphs.
Those, alas, whom you were wont so much to praise,
    Who ever took delight in poetry and love,
Oh, outrage! they have perished; and the loss is irrevocable;
    Look, with their funeral pyre built up together, we weep for   10
        both.
O Pan, Pan, whether the ridge of chill Lycaeon holds you,
    Or the region of Maenalos with its shady glen,
Come hither, and sprinkle their still warm ashes with your tears;
    It is not fitting here to hold back tears, Father.
Venus herself has wept: you, gentle Loves, have wept;   15
    The Dryads have wept and the Nereid goddesses.
Phoebus is here, and recalling the wretched fate of his poets,
    He troubles the cliff and grove with his tearful songs.

Atque ait haec: 'Periere mei Leucippus et Alcon:
20   Estque adeo, qui me numen habere putet?
En facinus, rapuere meos mala fata poetas,
      Quaque sequar raptos, non datur ulla via,
Quos alui, quorum ipse pio cantabar ab ore,
      Et dederam laurum crinibus ire meam.
25 Sume fidem: cornu celeres intende sagittas,
      Nimirum ut fugiant te bona prima tua.
Rumpe fidem: cornu celeres infringe sagittas,
      Nominis illa tui gloria, Phoebe, iacet.
Nymphae, terrarum praesentia numina, Nymphae,
30   Quae colitis Thusci littora curva maris,
Phoebus ego: Phoebi testes estote doloris,
      Quanquam etiam vester debuit esse dolor.
At vos ulla mei tangit si cura doloris,
      Quanquam etiam vester debuit esse dolor,
35 Pastores, tumulo Phoebi decorate poetas,
      Et memorem in tumuli caedite fronte notam:
'Hic geminae Phoebi curae, Leucippus et Alcon,
      Pastores ovium, pastorum et uterque magistri.'

:   X   :

Ad Melinum

Quid dominam assiduis vexas, Meline, querelis?
      Frangitur iniusto laesa timore fides.
Simplicitas magis ipsa iuvat, cum lege soluti

And he speaks thus: "My Leucippus and Alcon have perished;
    That being so, would anyone think I have divine power?   20
Behold the outrage! Evil fates have snatched away my poets,
    And whereby I might follow them, torn from me, no way is
        given.
I nourished them, I myself was praised by their dutiful voice,
    And I gave them my laurel for their hair.
Seize your lyre; stretch swift arrows on your bow,   25
    Since it is all too true that your good things flee first from
        you.
Crush your lyre; break the swift arrows of your bow,
    The glory of your name, Phoebus, lies dead.
Nymphs, O nymphs, ever-present divinities of the earth,
    You who dwell on the curved shore of the Tuscan Sea,   30
I am Phoebus: be witnesses to Phoebus' grief,
    Although you must have been grieving, too.
Yet if any concern for my grief touches you,
    Although you must have been grieving, too,
Shepherds, honor these poets of Phoebus with a tomb,   35
    And carve on the face of the tomb a sign of remembrance:
"Here lie twin objects of Phoebus' love, Leucippus and Alcon,
    Shepherds of their sheep and each a teacher of shepherds."

: X :

To Melinus

Why do you trouble your mistress, Melinus, with constant
        complaints?
    Trust once injured is shattered by baseless fear.
Simplicity herself delights the more, when, with strictures
        loosened,

Iungitur in tacito foemina virque toro.
5   Mitem animum dedit infirmis natura puellis,
      Fecit et ad blandas mollia corda preces.
Culpam in amore suae qui nullam agnoscit amicae
      Novit qua melius arte perennet amor.
Mulciber aeternos Venerem tenuisset in annos,
10   Usa minus duro si foret illa viro.
Ah pereat, quicunque suae peccata puellae
      Obiicit et flentem sustinuisse potest.
Ipse ego si videam, nollem vidisse fateri,
      Gaudia ne flendo dissipet illa mea.
15   Tu quoque, quod nolles fieri, desiste vereri:
      Non erit: innocuos ipse tuetur amor.

: XI :

Ad Telesillam

Ne valeam, Telesilla, tuo ni semper in ore
      Saevus Amor facibus cum pharetraque sedet.
Nam quoties mala verba moves, toties mihi pectus
      Vapulat heu pueri de pharetra et facibus.
5   Sed peream, Telesilla, tuo ni semper in ore
      Blanda Venus violis cum casiaque sedet.
Oscula nam quoties mihi das auferre petita,
      Das toties Veneris et casiam et violas.
Quid Siculis ingrata favis absynthia misces?
10   Sive mihi tantum sis bona, sive mala,

A man and woman are united on a quiet couch.
Nature has given a gentle soul to weak maidens,   5
    And has made their hearts responsive to flattering pleas.
He who perceives no fault in the love of his darling
    Knows by what art love better endures over the years.
Vulcan would have held Venus for all time,
    If she had found him a less harsh husband.   10
Ah, let him perish, whoever he is who exposes the faults of his
      lady-love
    And is able to withstand her weeping.
If I myself should see a flaw, I would not want to confess having
      seen it,
    Lest she destroy all my joys by weeping.
You, also, cease to fear what you do not wish to happen: 15
    It will not happen; love himself watches over the blameless.

: XI :

To Telesilla

May I lose my health, Telesilla, if fierce Amor does not
    With torch and quiver sit always in your countenance.
For as often as you say evil words, so often is my heart
    Buffeted, alas, by the torch and the quiver of that boy.
But may I die, Telesilla, if gentle Venus does not sit always   5
    In your countenance with marjoram and violets.
For as often as you give me the kisses I ask of you
    Just as often do you give me the marjoram and violets of
      Venus.
Why do you mix displeasing wormwood with Sicilian honey?
    Whether you are ever so good to me or ever so bad,   10

33

Altero uti superem laetus, dum te mea vita
    Placata potior, altero uti moriar.

      : XII :

Ad Lucretiam Borgiam

Tempore, quo primam miscens fluvialibus undis
    Iapetionides rite animavit humum,
Scilicet hac teneras oneravit lege puellas
    Natura, in nostris parca tenaxque bonis:
5   Ut speciem et clarae ferret quae munera formae,
    Ingenii nullas quaereret illa vias;
Quaeque animi decus indueret, cultumque per artes
    Pectus Apollineas ingeniumque ferax,
Illa sibi nullum formae speraret honorem:
10   Atque omnes pacto iussit adesse Deos.
Plurima cumque novo crevisset foemina mundo,
    Eventus certam sustinuere fidem,
Namque ut habent mala rura valentes saepe colonos,
    Pigraque, qui bonus est, otia sentit ager,
15   Sic non formosae cultu nituere puellae,
    Et quae pulchra, eadem desidiosa fuit.
Prima, meum atque aevi sydus spectabile nostri,
    Tantum animo, quantum, Borgia, fronte micas:
Et tibi cum facie non certet Agenore nata,
20   Non Helene Idaeo rapta Lacaena Pari,
Te tamen in studia et doctas traducis in artes,

In the one case I am happy to live on, so long as you, my life,
    Are content; in the other, I am happy to die.

: XII :

To Lucrezia Borgia

Long ago, when Prometheus, son of Iapetus, mingling soil
    With river water, in due form first created life,
Nature, sparing and frugal as to our good things,
    Burdened tender young women with this rule:
That she who possessed loveliness and the gifts of bright beauty   5
    Should not pursue the ways of the mind;
And she who wore adornments of the mind and a soul cultivated
    By Apollonian arts and a fruitful intellect,
Should hope for no distinction of beauty;
    And Nature commanded all the gods to agree.   10
And when many had grown to womanhood in the young world,
    The results justified the sureness of the compact.
For just as harsh terrain often has need for strong farmers,
    And the field that is rich experiences lazy leisure,
So girls who are not beautiful shine through cultivating   15
      themselves
    And she who is pretty, that same is given to idleness.
You are first, a brilliant star for me and my time,
    As you sparkle in soul, Borgia, so do you also in appearance;
Even Europa, the daughter of Agenor, could not match you in
      loveliness,
    No, nor Spartan Helen who was carried off by Trojan Paris.   20
Moreover, you excel in studies and in the learnèd arts,

Nec sinis ingenium splendida forma premat.
Sive refers lingua modulatum carmen Hetrusca,
  Crederis Hetrusco nata puella solo;
25 Seu calamo condis numeros et carmina sumpto,
  Illa novem possunt scripta decere Deas.
Naulia seu, citharamve manu percurrere eburna,
  Et varia Ogygios arte ciere modos,
Seu revocare Padi vicinas cantibus undas,
30   Mulcentem dulci flumina capta sono,
Seu te nexilibus iuvat indulgere choreis,
  Et facili ad numerum subsiluisse pede,
Quam timeo, ne quis spectans haec forte Deorum
  Te praedam media raptor ab arce petat,
35 Sublimemque ferat levibus super aethera pennis,
  Detque novi coelo syderis esse Deam.
Quicquid agis, quicquid loqueris, delectat: et omnes
  Praecedunt Charites, subsequiturque decor.
Ipse decor sequitur: sed, si modo vera fatemur,
40   Hei mihi, quam multis est decor ille malo.
Nam minus Aetneas vexant incendia rupes,
  Quam quibus est facies, Borgia, nota tua;
Nec facies modo, sed docti quoque pectoris artes;
  Ah pereat, si quem forma sine arte movet!
45 Atque ego, qui miseros olim securus amantes
  Ridebam et saevi regna superba Dei,
Spectabamque mari laceras de littore puppes,
  Nunc agor in caecas naufragus ipse vias.

And you do not allow your gleaming beauty to conceal your
    intellect.
If you set a song in the Etruscan tongue to music,
    One would believe you a girl born on Etruscan soil;
If, taking up your flute, you compose songs and their lyrics,   25
    These could fittingly have been written by the nine Muses.
Whether you strike the naulia or the lute with your white hand,
    Or summon up Theban melodies with varied skill,
Whether you call back the neighboring waves of the Po with
    your songs,
    Soothing the river in thrall to your sweet sound,   30
Or whether it delights you to indulge yourself in intertwining
    dances,
    And to leap to the beat with facile foot,
How I fear lest some one of the gods, watching this by chance
    From the middle of high heaven, will, like a thief, seek you as
    booty,
And carry you on light wings aloft to heaven's height,   35
    And allow you to be goddess of a new star in the firmament.
Whatever you do, whatever you say, is delightful; and all
    The Graces walk before you, and comeliness follows after.
Yes, comeliness itself follows; but, if I merely confess the truth,
    Ah me, how terrible to many is that comeliness.   40
For flames are less harassing to the rocky slopes of Etna
    Than is the sight to them, Borgia, of your well-known face;
And not just your face, but also the skills of your learnèd mind;
    Ah, let that man perish if beauty without knowledge move
    him!
And I, who safe, once, used to laugh at wretched lovers   45
    And at the proud rule of that savage god,
And who used to watch from the seashore the storm-torn ships,
    Am now myself, as one shipwrecked, driven into blind-dark
    ways.[1]

: XIII :

Amica ad Gallum

Galle, meum sydus, mea lux, mea summa voluptas,
  Quo levis ille tuus tam cito fugit amor,
Lusibus ut metam cupias imponere nostris,
  Teque meo properes eripuisse sinu?
5   Siccine tot nostri de te meruere labores,
  Et mea non ullo crimine laesa fides?
Haeccine tu nobis olim promissa dedisti,
  Iuratus Paphiae numina magna Deae,
Cum te nunquam alia caliturum, Galle, puella,
10   Sed fore dicebas tempus in omne meum?
Heu male consultas veri quaecunque putamus
  Ullius in verbis pondus inesse viri,
Et miseras, quae, more meo, vitamque necemque
  Atque omnes ponunt spes in amante suas.
15   Nutat ut in summis vento leve culmen aristis,
  Fluxa labat vestro sic in amore fides;
Utque undam premit unda sequens pellitque priorem,
  Sic vos usque novus versat et urget amor;
Atque ita tu, bone Galle, novo male captus amore,
20   Qua me destituas, pergis inire viam.
Interea ficto velas tua crimina vultu,
  Accumulasque malis perfida facta dolis:
Quaeque potes melius campo committere aperto,
  Bella per insidias dissimulata moves.

: XIII :

A Lady-Friend Speaks to Gallus

Gallus, my star, my light, my uttermost pleasure,
    Whither does that light love of yours flee so fast,
That you wish to put a finish to our love-games,
    And hasten to snatch yourself away from my embrace?
Have my many efforts deserved thus from you,   5
    And my good faith, which has never been violated by any
        fault?
Once, did you not give these promises to me,
    Having sworn by the divine power of Venus, goddess of
        Paphos,
When you said that you would never warm to another girl,
        Gallus,
    But would be mine for all time?   10
Alas, you ponder the truth poorly, whoever of us women think
    That there can be weight in the words of any man,
And are pitiable who, following my example, place
    Both life and death and all their hopes in a lover.
Just as when the light top of the highest grainstalks nods in a   15
        breeze,
    So trust in your love, once it has wavered, slips away.
And just as when a following wave presses and strikes on the
        wave before,
    So new love constantly turns you and urges you on.
And so you, good Gallus, unhappily seized by a new love,
    Hasten to enter on the way by which you might desert me.   20
Meanwhile you hide your guilt with a false face,
    And you heap up perfidious deeds through wicked guile.
Through pretense you make secret wars
    Which you might better join on an open field.

25   Nam mihi nulla facis querula convitia lingua,
        Nec rapit ira meas ungue notare genas,
     Ac neque turbatos abstergere flentis ocellos,
        Figereque abstersis oscula luminibus,
     Nec piget illapsos fronti componere crines,
30   Et dare compositae florea serta comae:
     Atque illos laudas, atque hanc, et colla manusque
        Exiguosque pedes virgineumque latus:
     Utque prius, videorque tibi te digna, proborque,
        Meque tuos oculos, corque animamque vocas.
35   Sed te iam totam culpari, Galle, per urbem
        Fingis, et a populo non bona verba pati,
     Plus aequo facilem quia des te semper amanti,
        Meque animo nimium perpetiente feras;
     Quaelibet et praesto venias in iussa, nec umquam
40   Abscedas lateri longius ungue meo;
     Quoque tui plures attavi gessere triumphos,
        Et proprio quo plus decore micas;
     Hoc inquis magis indignum et deforme videri,
        Te Veneris laqueis implicuisse caput,
45   Atque dies totos dominae parere puellae,
        Quae tua foemineo sub pede colla premat.
     Haec mala ne serpant, curam te velle parumper
        Nominis et famae dicis habere tuae.
     Ista tui nova cura venit tibi nominis unde,
50   Me nisi quod miseram linquere, Galle, paras?
     Namque in amore movent propriae quem incommoda vitae,
        Damna potest famae quique timere suae,

For you offer me no reproof with a complaining tongue,   25
    Nor does anger drive you to mark my cheeks with your nails.
It does not shame you to wipe my eyes swollen with weeping,
    And plant kisses on those eyes once dried,
And smoothe back tousled locks from my forehead,
    And place garlands of flowers on that smoothed-back hair;   30
And you praise those locks and this hair, my neck and hands,
    And tiny feet and maidenly figure;
And, as before, I seem to you worthy of yourself and am
      approved of,
    And you call me your eyes, your heart, your soul.
But you make yourself blameworthy, Gallus, throughout the   35
      whole city,
    And are enduring hard words from the populace,
Because you always give yourself far too easily to a lover,
    And indulge me with long-suffering heart,
To my every command attending promptly, never
    Departing by a finger from my side;   40
And the more triumphs your ancestors have celebrated
    And the more you shine in your own glory,
The more unworthy and shameful it seems, you say,
    For you to have wrapped your head in Venus' snares
And to obey your mistress all day and every day,   45
    So that she presses your neck beneath her womanly foot.
Lest these evil things gain ground, you say that for a little while
    You wish to care for your name and fame.
Whence comes that new concern for your good name
    Unless it is that you, Gallus, are preparing to leave me   50
      wretched?
For as far as love goes, he who is moved by the disadvantages
    To his own life and who can fear injury to his reputation,

Atque novas leges moerenti dictat amicae,
    Subtrahit hic laxo iam sua colla iugo:
55   Quosque canit titulos speciosaque nomina rerum,
    Dissidii causas quaerit habere sui.
Aeneas donec miseram dilexit Elisam,
    Fatorum et nati mentio nulla fuit.
Sed sive ille novam muris praecingeret urbem,
60   Haerebat Phrygio pulchra Libyssa viro;
Seu vexare feras cursu iaculisque pararet,
    Vecta comes celeri Sidonis ibat equo;
Seu daret e solio populis sua iura vocatis,
    Iura simul populis quae daret, uxor erat.
65   Verum ubi cessit amor, tum spe surgentis Iuli
    Ducitur et fatis lintea danda putat;
Tum videt intrantem muros et multa monentem
    De Maia genitum, de genitumque Iove;
Ostia tum Lyciae Tyberina capessere sortes
70   Grynaeaque iubet cultus in aede Deus,
Et patris Anchisae in somnis super urget imago,
    Debita Troianis Itala regna sequi.
Galle, adeo non ora gerit mendacia, cuius
    Legitimi pectus aestuat igne Dei.
75   Albis nigra bonus confundere nescit amator,
    Vertereque ambigua fasque nefasque via.
Tam purum nihil est veri quam sensus amoris,
    Indigeatque ulla quod minus artis ope.
Ille nihil didicit fictis componere verbis,
80   Qui, quod amat, certa novit amare fide.

And imposes new injunctions on his grieving lady-love,
    Is already withdrawing his neck from her loosened yoke.
The honors that he proclaims and the specious repute of his   55
    affairs,
    He seeks to hold as an excuse for his departure.
As long as Aeneas loved pitiable Dido,[1]
    There was no mention of the fates and his son.
For whether he were girding the new city with walls,
    The lovely Libyan clung to her Trojan husband;   60
Or whether he prepared to harass wild beasts in a javelin hunt,
    The Sidonian woman went as his companion on a swift horse.
Or whether, with the people summoned, he gave his laws from a
    throne,
    She who gave laws to the people at the same time was his
    wife.
But when love ceased, then he is drawn by the hope of the   65
    growing Iulus,
    And thinks that because of his destiny their sails must be
    raised.
Then he sees the son of Maia, the offspring of Jupiter
    Entering the fortifications and warning of many things.
Then the Lycian prophecies and the god worshipped
    In the Grynaean temple order him to seize the Tiber's mouth;   70
And the image of his father Anchises presses him in dreams
    To seek the Italian kingdoms owed to the Trojans.
Gallus, that man does not possess lips that lie,
    Whose breast burns with the fire of the true God.
The good lover does not know how to confuse black with white,   75
    Or to alter what is right and not right in an ambiguous way.
There is nothing so pure as the feeling of true love,
    And nothing needs less help from any artifice.
He who knows how to love his lover with sure faith,
    Has not learned to make up anything with false words.   80

Nec quaerit furtis, bene sed placuisse merendo,
    Et tantum pollens simplicitate sua est.
Adde quod est Amor ipse puer, nec convenit illo
    Versutum pectus militis esse duce.
85   Utque Deus nullo velat sibi corpus amictu,
    Sic nudis animis vult sua bella geri:
Quemque videt non insidiis, non artibus uti,
    'Hic bonus est', inquit, 'miles, eritque mihi'.
At contra incerti et malefidum vulgus amantes,
90   Illita felle malae pectora fraudis habent.
Nam semper magnis se dicunt ignibus uri,
    Ardet ut in summo Sicelis Aetna iugo:
Sed modo se patriae, modo se causantur amicis,
    Nunc dare principibus imperiisque diem,
95   Nunc famae spectare viam, nitique per ora
    Ire virum, atque astris inseruisse caput,
Dum fallant astu miseras perdantque puellas:
    Quos inter magnum tu quoque nomen habes.
Atque utinam vanis in te, mea vita, querelis
100   Invecta et falsa dicerer usa nota:
Constantique fide tu nos, ut fingis, amares,
    Adversi ferrent nec mea vela Noti.
Sive tamen nostri perstas in amore fideque,
    Arcessis propera cur mea fata via?
105   Seu tuus ille prior menti deferbuit ardor,
    Ah cur me miseram linquere, Galle, paras,

He does not seek to have pleased by slyness, but by deserving
    well,
    And he is so much the stronger because of his candor.
Add to this that Love himself is a boy, and it is not fitting
    Under his command that the soldier's breast be crafty.
And as the god of love does not cover his body with any   85
    garment,
    So he wishes his love battles to be waged with naked souls.
When he sees a man refraining from treachery or artifice,
    "This man," he says, "is a good soldier and he shall be mine."
But by contrast fickle lovers are a faithless throng,
    They have hearts smeared with the poison of wicked deceit.   90
For always they say they are burning with a great fire,
    Just as Sicilian Etna burns along its highest ridge;
But at one moment they plead they must give time to their
    country,
    At another to their friends, now to princes and empires,
Now to look out for the way to fame, and to strive to make their   95
    way
    Before the gaze of men, and to lift their heads among the
    stars,
While they deceive and ruin wretched maidens with their
    cunning;
    Among such men you, too, have a great reputation.
Would that I could be said to have attacked you, my life,
    With groundless complaints and false accusations,   100
And would that you had loved me with a constant faith, as you
    pretend,
    and that contrary winds did not bear my own sails away.
Nevertheless, if you are persevering in love and faith with me,
    Why are you summoning my doom along this hurried path?
Or if that earlier ardor of yours has cooled in your mind,   105
    Why are you, Gallus, preparing to abandon me in my misery?

Quae te uno semper colui male sana tenore,
    Quae sum per longas usque sequuta vias?
Ipsa quidem non defugio tua iussa, nec ulla
110   Parte tuus nobis dissimulatur honos.
Sed cave, ne titulos dum vis augere, perempta
    Infirmet laudes una puella tuas.

: XIV :

Ad Lygdamum

Heu diversa tuis quam sunt mea, Lygdame fata:
    Ut nos non uno versat in orbe Deus!
Tu, quod amas, crebro invisis, longumque tuendo
    Aegrum animum atque avidos pascis amore oculos;
5   Et lateri admissus iocundos aure susurros
    Pendulus et fragrantem excipis ore animam;
Summa vel auratae suspendis basia mitrae,
    Dum loqueris vacuam blandus ad auriculam;
Levibus aut raptum digitis, teretive lacerto
10   Molle decus domina non renuente geris;
Et trahis a prima serus convivia nocte,
    Dum sol frenatos ad iuga poscat equos.
At mihi longiquae gentesque urbesque petuntur,
    Ut toto a domina separer orbe mea;
15   Et modo nimbosas mannis transmittimur alpes
    Saxaque vix ipsis exuperanda feris;
Nec caeci nemorum tractus suspectaque lustra,

I who always worshipped you madly with single-minded course,
    I who ever followed you through way upon way?
Indeed, I have not shirked your commands, nor
    In any way is your good name ignored by me.   110
But beware, lest while you wish to augment your distinctions,
    One woman, thwarted, may shake your reputation to its base.

: XIV :

To Lygdamus

Alas, how different is my lot from yours, Lygdamus,
    As if God does not turn us about in the same world!
You often visit the object of your love, and with long gazing
    Feed your sick soul and eager eyes with love;
And, admitted to her side, you allow merry whispers in your ear   5
    And, hanging over her, take in a fragrant breath from her
        mouth;
Or you drop kisses on the top of her golden turban,
    While you speak caressingly into her open ear;
Or you steal the soft grace from her smooth fingers
    And sleek arm, with your mistress making no objection;   10
And you draw out entertainments from early evening until late,
    Till the sun demands his horses be harnessed to his chariot.
But I must seek faraway peoples and cities,
    So that I am separated from my mistress by the whole world;
And even now I am carried by ponies across the cloud-covered   15
        Alps
    And over rocks scarcely to be climbed, even by wild beasts;
Neither pathless stretches of forest nor treacherous bogs

Nec tardant nostras flumina adaucta vias.
Interdum audaci vastum trabe currimus aequor,
20   Velaque nostra iidem venti animamque ferunt.
Qua tamen in terra est mea lux, convertor ad illam,
      Et frustra Eurydices nomen in ore meo est:
Atque ita coniunctorum animis et amore duorum,
      Alteri adest semper quod cupit, alteri abest.

⁙ XV ⁙

De Amica a viro servata
diligentissime

Non tua nequicquam mediis sitientis in undis,
      Tantale, flumineus respuit ora liquor;
Nec frustra esurientem eludunt arbore ab alta
      Semper verticibus pendula poma tuis.
5   Nempe haec damnatos exercet fabula amantes:
      Huic nos poenarum debita turba sumus.
En ego, cui domina est, quae me mihi charior ipso est,
      Pro qua non metuam, vivat ut illa, mori;
Quae me prae dulci germana et fratribus aureis,
10   Praeque suo sese dicit amare viro;
Cum teneant nos iidem ambo intra tecta penates
      Una eadem, atque uno pene etiam in thalamo,
Saepe ut nuda sinus et qualis surgit ab ipso
      Mane toro veniat conspicienda mihi;
15   Non tamen huic possumve meos narrare labores,
      Atque aliquam adversis poscere rebus opem;

Nor swollen rivers may stay our journey.
Sometimes we hurry over vast waters in a daring boat,
    And the same wind drives our sails and carries my life.   20
Nevertheless wherever on earth the light of my life is, I am
        turned towards her,
    And, though in vain, the name of my Eurydice is on my lips.
And so, of we two conjoined in spirit and in love, to one
    What he desires is always present, to the other always absent.

: XV :

Concerning a Lady-Friend Guarded Most Carefully
by Her Husband

The river water did not reject your lips without good reason,
    Tantalus, thirsting in the midst of the waves;
Nor did the fruit hanging from the lofty tree always above
    The top of your head elude your hungering to no purpose.
Truly this tale troubles those condemned to love;   5
    We are the throng due such punishments as these.
Look at me; she is my mistress, dearer to me than my very self,
    For whom I would not fear to die that she might live;
Who says she loves me more than her sweet sister
    And her golden brothers, more than her husband;   10
Although the same household gods watch over us both
    Under the very same roof, and almost even in the same
        chamber,
So that she often comes forth from her own bed
    In the morning, bare-breasted, for me to watch her;
Nevertheless I cannot tell her of my sufferings   15
    And demand some aid in this cruel affair;

Nonve sedere una, non dextrae iungere dextram,
  Non dare lacteolis basiolum digitis:
Omnia quae possunt alii, qui tam nec amantur,
20   Nec quorum tantus concutit ossa Deus.
Atque haec non patior, quia magnos impia Divos
  Laeserit acta gravi lingua furore mea;
Aut violarim audax proavorum sancta sepulchra
  Et fraterna piis eruerim ossa locis;
25 Aut reserans Italas Gallis venientibus urbes
  Intulerim Veneta barbara signa manu.
Sed neque sopiti Alecto intentavit in ora
  Luridam ab inferno stans Phlegethonte facem;
Foemina devotum nec me ulla potentibus herbis
30   Prodidit, et magici docta ministra doli,
Infecitque dapes et diris pocula succis,
  Quales Circaeos imbuerant cyathos
Tunc, cum hominum e facie remex patientis Ulyssei
  Induit in varias pectora versa feras.
35 Quippe horum nihil est, tantum tuus ille maritus,
  Eurydice, annosis durior ilicibus,
Observat te meque simul prohibetque vel uno
  Cedere te lateri longius ungue suo.
Ille tuae raptum fronti decus et mea nuper
40   Misit in Adriacas dona scelestus aquas.
Quamque mihi telam pingebas nexibus aureis,
  Igni non ipso mitior igne dedit.

Nor can I sit with her, nor join my right hand to hers,
    Nor even give the tiniest kiss to her milk-white fingers;
Others can do all these things, those who are not so loved,
    And whose bones the powerful God does not shake.   20
And I do not suffer these things because my disloyal tongue,
    Driven by a grievous madness, has offended the great gods;
Because I dared to violate the holy tombs of my ancestors
    And dug up my brother's bones from their sacred resting-
        place;
Or, unlocking the cities of Italy to the oncoming French,   25
    I have borne barbarian standards in my Venetian hand.
But neither has Alecto, from hellish Phlegethon, standing before
        me,
    Stretched out her ghastly torch towards my face as I sleep;
Nor has any woman or her attendant, learnèd in magical deceit,
    Betrayed me, accursed, with powerful herbs,   30
And poisoned my food and drink with dreadful juices,
    Such as tainted Circe's drinking cups
At the time when the crew of long-enduring Ulysses changed
    Their twisted bodies from the likeness of men into various
        wild beasts.
Indeed, nothing of these is my lot, only that that husband of   35
        yours,
    Eurydice, harder than aged oaks,
Watches you and me together and forbids you
    To leave his side any farther than a nail's breadth.
Only recently that wicked man consigned to the waters of the
        Adriatic
    My gift, a jewelled adornment, which he snatched from your   40
        forehead.
And the cloth, which you were variegating with knots of gold,
    He consigned to the fire, he no gentler than the fire itself.

Ille tibi, si quando aliquo diversus abire
    Cogitur et regis castra viasque sequi,
45   Imponit legem exosus, ne quod mihi verbum
    Dicas, ne ve in me lumina coniicias,
Neve aliquem auscultes, de me quicunque loquatur,
    Neve legas digitis scripta notata meis.
Utque pater bimae, gestit quae incedere, natae,
50   Sic custode tuum munit utrumque latus.
Interea querulo plenas sermone tabellas
    Dat tibi, iuratos commemoratque Deos
Et Venerem matrem et, cui vincla iugalia curae,
    Saturni magnam progeniem atque nurum:
55   Et modo quae in nostro capiantur, scribit, amore
    Comperta esse tibi singula consilia.
Nunc si comperiet quicquam, mala multa minatur,
    Teque absens etiam ferreus excruciat.
Ne valeas unquam insanos finire dolores,
60   Nullaque sit miserae non gravis hora tibi.
Proh superi, Eurydice, tune haec tam tristia, tamque
    Perdita facta animo perpetiente feres?
Tune ullis sine deliciis poteris, mea vita,
    Cum tibi tam ingrato consenuisse viro?
65   Adde quod exuperat cornicum saecla vetusta,
    Natus et is multo est, quam pater ante tuus:
Quasque vides, ipso non sunt in vertice: canos
    Occulit adscitis calvitiumque comis;
Immundamque animam et late graveolentia odoro

If he is compelled on occasion to depart for someplace else,
    And follow the encampments and journeys of his king,
Filled with hatred, he imposes his command that you speak   45
    No word to me nor even cast your eyes on me,
Nor even listen to anyone whosoever might speak about me,
    Nor read any piece of writing inscribed by my fingers.
And like the father of a two-year-old daughter, who is starting to
        walk,
    He in like wise provides you with a guardian on each side.   50
Meanwhile he sends you letters full of complaining talk,
    And reminds you of the gods you both have sworn oaths by
And of mother Venus, and the daughter-in-law and powerful
        offspring
    Of Saturn, in whose care are the bonds of marriage;
And he writes to you that all the plans   55
    Which have been made in our love are known.
And if he should find out anything from now on, he threatens
        many evils,
    And absent, but still hard as iron, he tortures you,
Lest you should ever be strong enough to end these mad sorrows
    And no hour not be weary to you in your wretchedness.   60
Ah, by the gods above, Eurydice, will you bear such a mass of
        sorrows,
    Such destructive deeds, with an ever-enduring spirit?
Will you ever be able, my life, without any joys
    To grow old with a husband so displeasing to you?
In addition he surpasses the crow in the length of his years,   65
    And he was born much before your own father;
Those hairs which you see are not growing from the top of his
        head;
    He hides his white hair and baldness with someone else's
        locks;
He tends to his foul breath and evil-smelling lips attentively

70   Flore Arabum et multis artibus ora fovet.
         Parcite custodes: non est mea digna puella,
             Quae senis impuri perferat imperium;
         Et me si videat quis vestrum accedere ad illam,
             Avertat se, aliam dissimuletque viam;
75   Aut niveam dum tango manum, dum mollia carpo
             Oscula, vos somno lumina victa date.
         Si piget hoc, dura tum me vincite catena,
             Et contusa gravi compede crura sonent,
         Mille vel inclusum dubiis perplexibus error
80   Detineat, tecti Creta superba tui;
         Innixi aut ferro muri atque adamantina turris,
             Cocyti aut triplici sepiat unda lacu,
         Dum servet nostram custodia nulla puellam.
             Ah pereant, quos haec tam mala cura movet!
85   Tum primum Eurydices cupiam periisse maritum,
             Illa sit ut duro libera servitio:
         Quemque velit, cuicunque velit, spectetque loquaturque,
             Acclinetque humero languida molle caput.
         Cur tamen ipse miser pereas? sine me tua tantum
90   Uxor amet: tunc te mi superesse velim,
         Tunc te laudabo, tunc te mea Musa per aevum
             Praesentum et venturum omnium in ora feret;
         Tunc quos nunc habeo et quos sum olim habiturus amicos,
             Omnibus ipse mihi charior unus eris.
95   Diliget illa etiam plus te, mitescere si te
             Senserit: immites ipse repellit amor.
         Peccabitque minus, modo si peccare libebit,
             De te cum sibi nil, unde queratur, erit.
         Obsequio tenerae vincuntur corda puellae,
100   Obsequium magni numinis instar habet.

With redolent flowers of Arabia and much artifice.   70
Lay off, you guardians; my girl does not deserve
    To endure the rule of a vile old man.
And if any of you should see me approach her,
    Let him turn away and pretend to be on another path;
Or while I touch her snowy hand, while I snatch   75
    Her soft kisses, pretend to be asleep.
If this annoys you, then bind me with hard chains,
    And let my bruised legs rattle with heavy fetters,
Or let your twistings, O Crete, proud of your palace,
    Hold me in their thousand uncertain entanglements;   80
Or let iron-bound walls and a tower of adamant surround me,
    Or the waters of Cocytus with its three-fold stream,
Provided no guardian keep watch on my girl.
    Ah, let them die, whom such an evil task impels!
Then best of all I would wish that Eurydice's husband perish,   85
    So that she would be free from her harsh servitude;
Let her look at, let her talk to, everybody she wants, anybody she
    wants,
    When tired, let her lean her soft head on my shoulder.
But why should you die, wretched man? Only allow your wife
    To love me: then I would wish that you survive me,   90
Then I will praise you, then my Muse will carry you
    Through time on the lips of all those now alive and to come;
Then, of those friends I have now and will have in time to come,
    You alone will be dearer to me than all.
She will love you even more, if she will feel you becoming mild: 95
    Love itself rebuffs the pitiless.
She will sin less, if only she be free to sin,
    When there will be nothing for her to complain of about you.
The hearts of tender maidens are conquered by compliance,
    Compliance is like a great divinity.   100

Obsequium blando paulatim assuescere amanti,
    Et Veneris multas ferre iugum docuit,
Quarum ante immodicos spirabant lumina fastus.
    Contra iusta malis instruit ira dolis:
105　Hos natura parens illis, ut cornua tauris,
    Alitibusque ungues rostraque longa dedit.
His se defendunt armis, laesaeque repugnant
    Scilicet: haec noceant ne tibi tela, cave.
Nec melius cavisse potes, quam si bene factis
110　Ingenium dominae promereare tuae.
Hae tibi sint artes, sic illam vincere tenta:
    Vinces, aut victus damna minora feres.
Nec tu foemineas irrites coniugis iras:
    Foemineus refugit crimina nulla dolor.
115　Nil metuunt violare, nihil pervertere parcunt:
    E coelo dederint praecipites superos,
Cum spe deiectaeque sua durique perosae
    Facta viri madidis ingemuere genis.
Traiecit rigido natorum pectora ferro
120　Isthmiaci Colchis victa dolore tori.
Apposuit natum patriis in prandia mensis
    Impia Bistonium Daulias ulta scelus.
Quot mare habet Libycum fluctus, quot littus arenas,
    Tot movet in laesa foemina corde dolos.
125　Sed quid ego haec repeto? me tantum utare magistro,
    Saevierit damno foemina nullo tuo.

Compliance has taught many girls to grow accustomed little by
    little
  To a gentle lover, and to bear the yoke of Venus,
Girls whose eyes previously breathed forth boundless pride.
  A just anger teaches girls to use many deceits in their defense;
Nature, our parent, gave women these, as she gave horns to bulls,   105
  Talons and long beaks to birds.
They defend themselves with these weapons and indeed when
    injured
  Fight back; beware, lest these darts harm you.
Nor are you better able to guard against such than if, by doing
    well,
  You deserve the goodwill of your mistress.   110
You have these skills, try thus to conquer her;
  You will conquer, or, being conquered, you will suffer smaller
    losses.
You should not stir up the womanly anger of your spouse:
  A woman's resentment does not shrink from any crime.
There is nothing they fear to injure, nothing they refrain from   115
    subverting;
  They would hurl the gods headlong from heaven,
When, with their hopes dashed and out of loathing for the deeds
  Of their harsh husbands, they have moaned with wet cheeks.
Medea, overcome by grief for her Corinthian marriage,
  Pierced the hearts of her sons with hard iron.   120
Wicked Procne, in vengeance for the crime of Tereus,
  Served up her son as the dinner at his father's table.
As many waves as has the Libyan sea, as many grains of sand its
    shore,
  That many schemes seethe in an injured woman's heart.
But why should I repeat these things? Only use me as your   125
    teacher
  And no woman will rage at an injury from you.

Tunc, quae te miserum mala nunc versantque trahuntque,
    Effluxisse tuo protinus ex animo
Dices, ut fracta fontis liquor effluit urna,
130   Gestatus flavo virginis in capite,
Si forte in triviis pueri dum praelia ludunt,
    Impulsus duri testam aperit silicis:
Atque haec dat gemitum et largo simul expluit imbri,
    Horridulos illi perluit unda sinus.
135 Pax aderit, pacisque Deus cum matre Cupido,
    Nudaque amabilibus Gratia mixta iocis,
Terque solum pellens tenero pede Lusus, ut olim
    Aurea cum faciles saecla tulere viros.
Nullae vexabant curae mortalia corda,
140   Libertas illo tempore magna fuit.
Dura nec inscriptis astabant legibus aera,
    Culpa scelusque aberant sollicitusque timor.
Nec vicina suis natam vetuere parentes
    Non observatos ferre per arva pedes.
145 Nec socias lecti mos custodire puellas,
    Liminaque obducta claudere firma sera.
Simplicitas magis ipsa iuvabat, tum bona passim
    Gaudia cum nullis iuncta habuere malis.
Haec et plura tibi contingent commoda: quae non
150   Regum spes alto nixa pedem solio,
Aerataeque acies constipatique manipli,
    Omnis et acta tuo terra sub arbitrio,
Omne mare exuperent: ipso te iudice felix,

Where now those evil deeds upset you and drag you, wretched
    man,
  Then you will say that straightway they have passed out of
    your mind,
Just as spring water flows out of a broken vessel,
  Carried on the head of a golden-haired maid, 130
If by chance, while boys are playing at war in the street,
  A blow from a piece of rough flint splits open the jar,
And it makes a cracking sound and at once pours forth water in
    quantity,
  The flow drenching the girl's shivering breast.
Peace will come, and Cupid, the god of peace, along with his 135
    mother,
  And the naked Graces entwining in their lovely play,
And Dalliance thrice striking the ground with soft foot, as once
  When the golden age bore easy-going husbands.
No cares used to trouble the hearts of mortals,
  Freedom was bountiful at that time. 140
Hard bronze tablets, inscribed with laws, did not exist,
  Blame and crime were absent, as was anxious fear.
Parents did not forbid a daughter to walk unsupervised
  In fields neighboring their own.
Nor did custom keep watch on girls who were bed-companions 145
  And close a stout door with bolt drawn tight.
Simplicity herself was ever ready to do good, and honest joys,
  Not joined to any evil, held sway all about.
These gifts and more will fall to you, which no hope,
  Resting her foot on the high throne of kings, 150
And bronze-armed battlelines and close-packed companies of
    soldiers,
  And the whole world driven under your rule,
And the whole ocean can surpass; but blessed by your own
    judgment,

Ditior et votis esse ferere tuis.
155 Des modo te nobis curare volentibus aegrum,
    Vulnera tractari sustineasque tua.
Promere opem egregios Podalirion et Chirona
    Vincam ego tam doctas non habuisse manus:
Ipse tibi adsistat medicae Deus arbiter artis,
160   Illa non poteris convaluisse via.
At si, quae moneo, surda contempseris aure,
    Verbaque do rapidis nunc mea turbinibus,
Irrita post paulo spreti praecepta poetae
    Flebis, teque mihi non habuisse fidem.

: XVI :

De Galeso et Maximo

Magni viri iussu versiculi conscripti: cum reliqui etiam,
qui Romae erant poetae, eiusdem viri iussu conscripsissent

Increpat admissi tenerum dum forte Galesum,
    Et queritur fluxa Maximus esse fide;
Dumque malos pueri mores incusat, et ipsi
    Dura lacessitus verba ministrat amor:
5 Non ille urgenti sese purgare magistro,
    Non multa offensum conciliare prece,
Inficias non ire et testes poscere divos,
    Largo purpureas imbre rigante genas;

You will be called richer than you could desire.
May you only grant to us, who are willing, to care for you when   155
    ill,
    May you endure to have your wounds treated by us.
I shall prove that Podalarios and Chiron,[1] outstanding in giving
    help,
    Did not have hands as learned as mine.
Though the god and master of the healing art himself stand by
    you,
    You will not be able to return to health by that means.   160
But if you despise my warnings with a deaf ear,
    I do now give my words to the wild whirlwinds,
And in a brief while you will bemoan the unheeded counsels of a
    poet
    Whom you scorned, and weep that you did not have faith in
    me.

: XVI :

About Galesus and Maximus

Modest verses written by the order of a great man: since all the other
poets in Rome had also written by order of the same man

When by chance Maximus rebukes gentle Galesus of a lover's
    crime
    And complains that he is wavering in his fidelity;
And when he finds fault with the bad habits of the boy,
    And exasperated love supplies him with hard words;
The boy doesn't clear himself, though his master urges it,   5
    He doesn't conciliate his offense with many a prayer,
He doesn't repudiate it and summon the gods to witness,
    Bedewing his glowing cheeks with a flood of tears;

Non etiam irasci contra, iustique doloris
10   Accensam in laesa promere corde facem.
Nil horum aggreditur: sed tantum ingrata loquentis
      Implicitus collo dulce pependit onus.
Nec mora, cunctanti roseis tot pressa labellis
      Oscula coelitibus invidiosa dedit,
15   Arida quot levibus flavescit messis aristis,
      Excita quot vernis floribus halat humus.
Maxime, quid dubitas? Si te piget, ipse tuo me
      Pone loco: haec dubitem non ego ferre mala.
Sed neque iam dubitas, nec te piget, inque volentem
20   Basia mellitus contulit illa puer.
Macte tuo damno et pueri, bone Maxime, culpa,
      Macte tua culpa nequitiaque, puer.
Nam veneror, quorum placidi non pectora mores
      Composuere minus, quam face torret amor.
25   Crediderim in sancto dentur si iurgia coelo
      Inter se faciles non secus esse Deos.
Ex omni vobis mollissima vellere fila
      Nevit docta colo ducere fata soror.
Quis sortem magis optandam sibi poscat amoris,
30   Maxime, sive tua, sive, Galese, tua?
Tene tui faciunt pueri peccata beatum?
      Tune tuo peccans gratior es domino?
Sic o saepe meus peccet, sic laedat amorem,
      Sic mihi se laeso praestet amore puer.

He isn't even angry with the man, nor does he display
   The flame of a justified sorrow burning in his injured heart.   10
He does none of these things; but wrapping himself around the
     neck
   Of him who is saying such unpleasant things, he hung like a
     sweet burden.
Straightway, he gave the hesitating man kisses pressed
   By rosy lips the gods above must envy,
As many as the dry harvest that grows golden with light ears of   15
     grain,
   Or as the awakened earth breathes out in spring flowers.
Maximus, why do you hesitate? If you are ashamed, put me
   In your place: I would not hesitate to endure such evils.
But now you do not hesitate, nor are you ashamed, and it is
   On a willing man the honeyed boy has conferred those kisses.   20
A blessing, good Maximus, on your injury and on the fault of the
     boy,
   A blessing, boy, on your fault and your wantonness.
For I am less in awe of those whose hearts calm habits
   Have kept in control than of him whom love burns with its
     torch.
I would believe that if strife were to arise in holy heaven   25
   The affable Gods would not behave otherwise among
     themselves.
The sister, learnèd at drawing the fates from her distaff,
   Has spun for you both the softest threads from every fleece.
Who could ask for himself a lot in love more to be desired,
   Than yours, Maximus, or yours, Galesus?   30
Do not the sins of your boy make you happy?
   Are not you in sinning more pleasing to your master?
Thus, oh often thus, may my boy sin, thus may he violate my
     love,
   Thus, though my love be outraged, may he offer himself to me.

: XVII :

Ad Sempronium

a quo fuerat reprehensus, quod materna lingua scripserit

Non quod me geminas tenere linguas,
 Et Graiam simul et simul Latinam,
 Semproni, reputem, mei libelli
 Materna tibi voce sunt loquuti,
5 Ut tanquam saturum hinnuloque aproque
 Vilem iuverit esse me fasellum:
 Quod tu carminibus tuis venustis
 Permirum tibi dixeras videri.
 Sed famae veritus malae periclum,
10 Campo versor in hoc loquutionis:
 Quod dicam tibi, quem proboque amoque
 Quantum pignora vix amant parentes,
 Ut cum noveris id, cavere possis.
 Nam pol qua proavusque avusque lingua
15 Sunt olim meus et tuus loquuti,
 Nostrae quaque loquuntur et sorores,
 Et matertera nunc et ipsa mater,
 Nos nescire loqui magis pudendum est,
 Qui Graiae damus et damus Latinae
20 Studi tempora duplicemque curam,
 Quam Graia simul et simul Latina.
 Hac uti ut valeas tibi videndum est:
 Ne dum marmoreas remota in ora
 Sumptu construis et labore villas,
25 Domi te calamo tegas palustri.

: XVII :

To Sempronius

By whom he was rebuked because he had written in his mother tongue

Not because I consider myself to have two languages,
    Both Greek and Latin at the same time,
    Sempronius, do my little books
    Speak to you in the language of my mother,
    As if it gave me pleasure to be a homely bean   5
    Satisfying the hunger of a donkey and a pig:
    Something that you said with your charming songs
    Seemed astonishing to you.
    But fearful of the danger of a bad reputation,
    I concern myself with this form of speech: 10
    Something I will tell you, you whom I cherish and love,
    Almost more than parents love their offspring,
    So that when you had knowledge of it, you could be on your
        guard.
    For by Pollux! it is more to be regretted
    That we do not know how to speak with the tongue   15
    Which our great-grandfathers and grandfathers, yours and
        mine,
    Once spoke, and with which both our sisters
    And my aunt and my mother herself now speak,
    We who give to Greek and Latin studies
    Hours of study and double the effort,   20
    As much in Greek as in Latin.
    While you live, you, too, should use this tongue,
    Lest while you are building marble palaces
    On remote shores at great cost and trouble,
    You roof over yourself at home with swamp reed.   25

: XVIII :

Benacus

Te Giberte cano, purus dum templa sacerdos
    Ingreditur, cupioque tuas attingere laudes.
    Sit modo non impar tanto sub pondere, quae me
    Musa vocat: nec eam ventura redarguat aetas
5   Obscurae carmen claro tibi condere famae,
    Et magnum brevibus voluisse intexere chartis.
Nuntius ut vitreas Benaci vectus ad undas,
    Muscoso subter pendentia fornice tecta,
    Atque Dei laetis implevit vocibus aures
10   Advenisse diem, quo formosissima terrae
    Ausoniae Verona sacris templisque regendis
    Demissum coelo et magnis virtutibus auctum
    Acciperet iuvenem, qualem vix ipsa petebat,
    Forte Pater gelido in luco sylvaque virenti
15   Fontibus et rivis cubito subnixus et urnae
    Iura dabat: cui carbasei mollissima fili
    Stamina pingebant fuco, vestemque parabant
    Caeruleam, innumerae nodis ac retibus aureis
    Collectos comptae crines tempusque decorum,
20   Incinctaeque auro surasque sinusque fluentes
    Vestibulo in thalami natae, niveosque lacertos
    Nudabant operi: quo pulchro ex agmine Sirme
    Docta lyrae digitis percurrere fila canebat
    Carmen, quod totidem numeris Gardeque Saloque
25   Reddebant; sol aestivos circumvagus orbes

: XVIII :

Benacus

I sing of you, Giberti, while a pure priest
    Enters the holy precincts, and I wish to compass your praise.
    Only may I be not unequal to such a burden
    As the Muse calls me to, lest the age to come convict me
    Of writing a song of insignificant repute for your fame   5
    And of wishing to enfold your greatness in modest pages.
When the message arrived at the glass-green waters of Benacus,
    Beneath its hanging roofs with their mossy arches,
    And filled the ears of the God with the joyful tidings
    That the day had come, when Verona, most beautiful   10
    Of the Ausonian places, would receive for the ruling
    Of its rituals and holy places a young man, sent from heaven,
    Endowed, too, with great virtues, of the sort she was hardly
        daring to seek,
    By chance the Father, in his cool grove and forest fresh
    With springs and rivulets, leaning upon his elbow,   15
    Was giving laws from his urn; for him his daughters painted
        with dye
    The softest thread of flaxen cord and fashioned a sky-blue
        garment,
    His countless daughters, at the entrance to his dwelling,
    Their hair handsomely arranged with knots and golden nets,
    Their foreheads beauteous, their ankles and their flowing   20
        garments
    Girded with gold, were baring their snowy arms
    For the work; from that lovely band Sirme, learned at
    Running her fingers along the strings of her lyre, sang
    A song, which in like notes Garda and Salò
    Re-echoed; the wandering sun, rubbing his summertime   25

Axe terens medio currum librabat Olympo.
Ergo avidis allata Deus postquam auribus hausit,
Promissosque olim fatis sibi laetus honores
Agnovit, tangens haerentem uligine barbam,
30   Demulcensque manu iussit vicina vocari
Flumina; dein sese placidum convexa sub alta
Speluncae senior solitaque in sede recepit.
Postera iam coelo stellas noctemque fugarat
Lustrabatque dies multo terrasque fretumque
35   Lumine, cum nitidis venit Ticinus in undis,
Piscosusque altas involvens Lambrus arenas.
Venit et indigenis foecundans Ollius arva
Deductus rivis, et cultos Abdua campos
Amne secans, fulvo ripasque interlitus auro.
40   Nec rapidus fluvioque Athesis spectandus amoeno
Defuit, aut Patavi circumque intraque pererrans
Moenia Meduacus triplici circumdata muro:
Moenia, quae positor pugnas et bella perosus
Musarum Iliacus studiis Phoeboque sacravit.
45   Populiferve Padus genitor, qui flumina centum
Ipse suo accipiens vasto latissimus alveo
Ubera terrarum cursu per pinguia lapsus
Portat, seque mari septenis amnibus infert.
Quos tunc atque alios velatus harundine crinem
50   Mintius excepit venientes limine primo
Obvius atque in tecta parentis saxea duxit,
Laetifico cordis non celans gaudia vultu.
Qui simul ac udos posuere sedilibus artus
Cristallo rigida fultis et iaspide glauca,

Wheels on their axle, was balancing his chariot in heaven's
    midst.
Then after the god had drunk in the tidings with eager ears,
And joyfully acknowledged the honors long ago promised him
By fate, touching his beard dripping with moisture,
And smoothing it with his hand, he ordered the neighboring   30
    rivers
To be called; then the aged one calmly betook himself
Underneath the lofty vault of his cave and to his wonted seat.
The next day had then put to flight the stars and night from
    the heavens
And was brightening the lands and seas more and more
With its light, when Ticinus[1] came in his shining waters,   35
And Lambrus, teeming with fish and rolling his deep sands.
Escorted by his native streams, Ollius also came,
Enriching the plowland, and Abdua, colored with tawny gold,
Cleaving with his waters the furrowed fields and banks.
Nor did swift Athesis, a sight to see with his charming stream,   40
Fail to come, nor Meduacus wandering around and among
The ramparts of Padua, surrounded by a threefold wall,
A city which its Trojan builder, deeply hating battles and wars,
Consecrated to the activities of the Muses and to Apollo.
Poplar-bearing father Padus himself came, who, gathering   45
One hundred rivers into his huge belly, carries them gliding
Far and wide through the earth's fertile richness,
And betakes himself to the sea in sevenfold streams.
These, then, and others Mintius received, his hair veiled in
    reed,
Meeting them as they arrived at his outer threshold   50
And led them into the rocky dwelling of his parent,
Openly showing in his happy countenance the joy of his heart.
As soon as they had placed their wet limbs on the benches
Braced with stiff crystal and blue-green jasper,

55   Continuo Nymphae mensas ante ora Deorum
          Speluncae in medio niveis mantilibus apte
          Consternunt, dapibusque onerant, Dictaeaque plena
          Vina ferunt referuntque manu, calicesque madentes
          Praecingunt myrto atque implexis flore coronis,
60   Purpureoque rosae, Medorumque arboris albo:
          Medorum quondam, sed quae nunc plurima laetas
          Benaci vestit ripas, non illa caduca
          Fronde virens, suavique auras permulcet odore.
          Post ubi prima quies epulis, Deus ipse magister
65   Undifragi domitorque lacus, praesentia circum
          Numina respiciens, his vocibus ora resolvit:
       'Quod votis toties nequicquam optavimus unum
          Vobiscum, Divi, fausto modo sydere luces,
          Vertentes luces fatorum orbisque ministrae,
70   Advexere: vehit pleno bona copia cornu,
          Largaque pomifera praetendit munera dextra.
          Quare vos primo longaevi a semine mundi,
          In mare fluctisonum prono labentia cursu,
          Volvite maiores, vaga flumina, volvite lymphas.
75   'Flos etenim iuvenum, longa formidine saecla
          Perdita qui solvat, quique agglomerata malorum
          Agmina tot bellique faces, quas vidimus ipsi,
          Bactra ultra, Thylemque ultra Scythiamque releget,
          Quique urbes, quique arva colat, Iove missus ab ipso est.
80   Volvite maiores, vaga flumina, volvite lymphas.

Straightway in the middle of the cave nymphs fittingly spread   55
Before the gods tables covered with white clothes
And loaded them with a banquet and brought and brought
    again
Wine from Crete with a lavish hand, and they bound
The dripping goblets with garlands intertwined with myrtle
    flowers,
With the deep red of roses and the white of Medean trees: 60
Once of the Medus, but now the greatest part clothe
The joyful banks of Benacus, vigorous with leaves that never
    fall,
And soothe the breezes with their sweet odor.
After the first quiet came upon the feast, the god himself,
Master and tamer of the wave-crashing lake, looking at   65
All the divinities present, opened his lips with these words:
"That single thing we had asked of you, gods, in vain
    With many and many a prayer, the days, the passing days that
        are
    Servants of the fates and of the world, have now brought
    With a lucky star. Plenty offers good things from her full horn   70
    And with her fruit-bearing right hands holds out abundant
        gifts.
    Wherefore you, from the first seed of the ancient world,
    Slipping in downward course to the sonorous sea,
    Roll on, great rivers, wandering streams, roll on.
"For the prince of young manhood, who looses from a long fear[2]   75
    The lost ages, and who banishes the heaped-up masses
    Of evils and the torches of war which we ourselves have seen,
    Beyond Bactria and Thule, beyond Scythia,
    And who fosters cities and farms, has been sent by Jove
        himself.
    Roll on, great rivers, wandering streams, roll on.   80

'Hic primum miseris viduatas civibus urbes
Accipiens, vacuosque suis cultoribus agros,
Replebit numerum exaequans augensque priorem:
Oppidaque ingenti multum quassata ruina
85   Prostratisque solo late moerentia tectis
Restituet, pulchroque dabit splendescere vultu.
Volvite maiores, vaga flumina, volvite lymphas.
'Magno namque pii iuvenis devinctus amore
Hetruscus Pater, excelsas qui Tybridis arces
90   Possidet et nutu Romanum temperat orbem,
Illius eximias virtutes claraque docti
Ingenii monumenta et sancti pectoris artes
Suspiciens, obitosque invicto corde labores,
Hoc dedit, has illi rerum permisit habenas.
95   Volvite maiores, vaga flumina, volvite lymphas.
'Quid memorem ut tener et primae sub flore iuventae
Ingentem ad ludum properaverit auspicibus Dis;
Indole dein quanta nixus, quam fortibus ausis,
Robore ceu firmo ventorum flamina quercus,
100   Aut scopulus fluctus saxo excurrente marinos,
Sic undas rerum excipiens et plena pericli
Multa diu casus victor superaverit omnes.
Volvite maiores, vaga flumina, volvite lymphas.

"This man, first paying heed to the cities bereft of their wretched
 citizens,[3]
 And the fields empty of their farmers,
 By equaling and increasing will again fill out their former
  number;
 He will restore towns greatly shattered by a vast destruction
 And grieving because their buildings lie overthrown far and   85
  wide
 Upon the ground, and he will make them shine with a noble
  aspect.
 Roll on, great rivers, wandering streams, roll on.
"For the Tuscan Father,[4] bound fast by the great love of his
 devoted son,
 He who occupies the lofty citadels of the Tiber
 And with a nod keeps the Roman world under his sway,   90
 Looking upon the exceptional virtues of that man and
 The monuments of his learnèd wit and the skills of his blessed
  soul,
 And the toils met with an unconquered heart,
 Has granted this and relinquished control of affairs to him.
 Roll on, great rivers, wandering streams, roll on.   95
"Why should I recall how he, young and in the first flower of
 youth,
 Hastened to the mighty contest under the auspices of the
  gods;
 Then, relying on his great excellence, on deeds bravely done,
 As an oak with its trunk steady in the wind's blast,
 Or a crag with its protruding rocks attacked by the sea,   100
 So he, having taken to himself for a long time the flood of
  affairs
 And the full beating of danger, has conquered, a victor over
  every mischance.
 Roll on, great rivers, wandering streams, roll on.

'Saepe illum abruptis in vallibus Apennini

105   Versantem, luctantis equi cum frangeret armos

Praecipitansque viam obstrueret torrentibus imber,

Poeninas vel per fauces tractusque volantem

Aerios, summo miseratae e vertice, Nymphae

Optavere graves cohiberent nubila nimbos.

110   Volvite maiores, vaga flumina, volvite lymphas.

'Saepe illi ad magnos reges mandata ferenti

Astitit unigena proles Iovis, ut bona mater:

Ut mater bona, quae charo timet omnia nato

Et cupit in duros comitem sese addere casus.

115   Tum pueri mirata oculos et verba loquentis,

"Ipse meas artes iam nunc tibi, dixit, habeto."

Volvite maiores, vaga flumina, volvite lymphas.

'Testis adest triplices magnas discreta per oras,

Fluviorum nemorumque ferax pecudumque virumque

120   Gallia, non auri, pictae non indiga vestis;

Diversosque iugo ad ventos interque cadentem

Surgentemque diem longo protenta Pyrene,

Altis quae geminas despectat frontibus undas.

Tum dictis factisque potens illa inclyta bello

125   Lataque et in latas Hispania dissita terras.

Volvite maiores, vaga flumina, volvite lymphas.

'Hae nam te insolita orantem, aversasque suorum

Flectentem regum mentes, Giberte, videbant,

"Often while he was maneuvering in the steep valleys of the
    Apennines,[5]
  When a rushing rainstorm battered the flanks of his struggling   105
    horse
  And blocked the way with its torrents,
  Or when he was racing through the passes and high regions of
    the Alps,
  The Nymphs, pitying him from their lofty peak,
  Desired the clouds to restrain their heavy downpours.
  Roll on, great rivers, wandering streams, roll on.   110
"Often when he was bearing orders to great rulers,
  The only-begotten offspring of Jove stood nearby, like a good
    mother,
  Like a good mother who fears everything for her dear son
  And desires that she be a companion to him in such harsh
    circumstances.
  Then, marvelling at the eyes and words of the boy as he   115
    speaks
  Said, 'Now, yes now, you have my skills for yourself.'
  Roll on, great waters, wandering streams, roll on.
"Present as a witness is Gaul, divided into three great regions,
  Fruitful in rivers and forests, in cattle and men,
  Needing neither gold nor embroidered garments;   120
  And Pyrene,[6] with her long ridge stretched to the different
    winds
  Between the falling and the rising day,
  She who looks down on two oceans from her lofty brows.
  Next, Hispania, powerful in words and deeds, renowned in
    war,
  Broad herself and laid out in broad regions.   125
  Roll on, great rivers, wandering streams, roll on.
"For all of them saw you, Giberti, asking for unwonted things
  And bending the hostile minds of their kings,

Acceptos conversa sonos cum vocis imago
130   Redderet, et dociles iterarent nomina ripae.
Volvite maiores, vaga flumina, volvite lymphas.
'Testis et Adriacus, parvo qui flumine Rhenus
Lambit humum; testis Thuscis haud maximus undis,
Maior prole virum, et divinos Arnus honores
135   Promeritus, coelum divisque recentibus augens,
Pulchros qui colles, pulchramque intersecat urbem:
Gens quorum imperio dispar, nec legibus aequa,
Illius in studiis iam dudum et amore quiescit.
Volvite maiores, vaga flumina, volvite lymphas.
140   'Tu vero tu Roma, tui genus ecquod alumni
Iam non curarum, non commemorare laborum
Una potes? tolle egregium per saecula nomen,
Tolle decus daque alta virum volitare per ora.
Volvite maiores, vaga flumina, volvite lymphas.
145   'Quantum Trinacriae vertex se sustulit Aetnae,
Aut cinctus stellis Atlas, aut Caucasus ingens,
Tantum clara virum Romae se nomina tollunt.
Illa novos tibi coelestum concessit honores
Antiquis cumulans: at tu praesentia saecla
150   Firmabis veterumque abolebis damna malorum.
Volvite maiores, vaga flumina, volvite lymphas.
'Ecce tibi laeto vestit se gramine tellus
Et tibi sylva comas nutrit, tibi pabula surgunt;
Foecundus mites implet tibi pampinus uvas,
155   Palladis et nigrum tibi ducit bacca colorem;

When the returning likeness of a voice re-echoed the sounds
It has received, and the dutiful banks said your name again   130
    and again.
Roll on, great rivers, wandering, streams, roll on.
"The Adriatic is also a witness, and the Reno which washes the
    earth
    With a modest stream; a witness, too, is Arno, hardly the
      greatest
    Of Tuscan rivers, but greater in her manly offspring and fully
      deserving
    Of divine honors, and enlarging heaven with fresh divinities,   135
    Which cuts between lovely hills and a lovely city,
    Whose people, unlike in empire and unequal in laws,
    Have for long ages lived peacefully in its study and love.
    Roll on, great waters, wandering streams, roll on.
"You, truly you, Rome, what kind of cares, what kind of tasks   140
    On the part of your nursling are you not now uniquely
    Able to recall? Extol his admirable name through the ages,
    Extol his glory, and grant that it fly high upon the lips of men.
    Roll on, great rivers, wandering streams, roll on.
"As much as the peak of Sicilian Etna lifts itself up,   145
    Or Atlas, girt by the stars, or huge Caucasus,
    So much do the bright names of the men of Rome raise
      themselves.
    She has granted to you new honors of the gods,
    Heaping them upon the old; but you will strengthen
    This present age, and wipe away the damage of ancient evils.   150
    Roll on, great rivers, wandering streams, roll on.
"Lo! the earth is clothing herself with joyful greenery for you,
    And for you woods nourish their leaves, for you pasturage
      springs up;
    For you burgeoning vine-branches fill up with soft grapes,
    And Athena's berry takes on for you its dark color;   155

Tum spisso quem rete trahant vel harundine longa,
Flexivagus nostris crescit tibi piscis in undis.
Volvite maiores, vaga flumina, volvite lymphas.
'Accipe quae tibi Parnasi de colle sorores
160   Dona ferunt, sacram lauri de fronde coronam,
Et plectrum, et citharam, scriptasque ab Apolline chartas,
Aeternum quas ediscant celebrentque minores.
Volvite maiores, vaga flumina, volvite lymphas.
'Accipe quae calathis porgunt tibi munera Nymphae,
165   Luteolum calthae florem casiamque virentem,
Liliaque violasque et purpureos hyacinthos.
Haud porxisse prius poterant: bella, horrida bella,
Pertulimus, dulces et deformavimus agros.
Volvite maiores, vaga flumina, volvite lymphas.
170 'Ut cum lethiferos accendit Syrius ignes,
Rivus aquas, hortus flores, pratum invidet herbas;
Pallet humi nullo facies depicta colore,
Ipsa suos sitiens foetus non educat arbos,
Intereunt fruges siliqua labente perustae;
175   Arva colit nemo siccis arentia glebis,
Vomeris et durum non admittentia dentem:
Cuncta iacent nimio coeli contusa calore:
Tristia sic nostris aderant prius omnia terris.
Volvite maiores, vaga flumina, volvite lymphas.
180 'At postquam laetos effudit Iuppiter imbres,
Rivus aquas, hortus flores, pratum explicat herbas;
Ipsa viret tellus, ripae collesque nitescunt.

Whether they drag it in with a thick net or a long pole,
The flexuous fish grows for you in our waters.
Roll on, great rivers, wandering streams, roll on.
"Receive the gifts which the sisters bring to you
   From their Parnassian hilltop, a sacred crown of laurel fronds,   160
   A lyre, a lute, poems written by Apollo,
   Which our descendants might forever learn and treat with
      honor.
   Roll on, great rivers, wandering streams, roll on.
"Receive the gifts which the Nymphs extend to you in their
      baskets,
   The yellow blossom of the marigold and the greening   165
      marjoram flower,
   Lilies, and violets, and purple hyacinths.
   They could never make these offerings before, for we
   Have been enduring wars, dreadful wars, disfiguring our sweet
      fields.
   Roll on, great rivers, wandering streams, roll on.
"As when the Dog Star kindles his death-dealing fires,   170
   The river begrudges water, the garden its flowers, the meadow
      its grasses;
   The face of the earth, painted with no color, grows pale,
   The thirsty tree does not produce its fruit,
   The crops perish, completely scorched with husks falling off;
   No one cultivates the parched fields with their dried-up clods,   175
   For they will not even admit the hard tooth of the plow;
   Everything lies prostrate, struck by the intense heat of the sky:
   Thus were all things grieving in our lands before.
   Roll on, great rivers, wandering streams, roll on.
"But after Jupiter poured out joyful rainstorms   180
   The river spreads out its waters, the garden its flowers, the
      meadow its grasses;
   The earth itself flourishes, banks and hills start to glow.

Dant segetem sulci, nemus altas sufficit umbras;
Poma suos curvant crescentia pondere ramos;
185   Ruris turba Deam venerata ligonibus udam
Vertit humum et putres exercet vomere campos.
Cuncta vigent coeli foecundis roribus aucta:
Nostras sic iocunda manent nunc omnia terras.
Volvite maiores, vaga flumina, volvite lymphas.
190 At vos in septem discreti culmina montes,
Tuque, pater Tyberine, tuum qui flumen Olympo
Devehis, hunc olim vobis multosque per annos
Sic satis o tenuisse: meam mihi iam date partem.
Ipse dabo multis, ne sint mea gaudia sola:
195   Et tandem nostris iuvenem concedite terris.'

: XIX :

Pro Gorytio votum ad deos

quibus aediculam exaedificaverat

Sancta, quibus propriam posuit Gorytius aram,
Numina, perpetuosque arae sacravit honores:
Humani columen generis, divina puella,
Ipse sibi legit summi quam rector Olympi,
5   Et tu, divinae genitrix augusta puellae,
Felix sorte tua, felix nata atque nepote,
Aetereique puer magnum patris incrementum,
Arte boni quos egregia coeloque Savini
Spectari, Pario et spirare in marmore fecit:
10   Hac vos pro pietate illi, pro munere tali

The furrows give corn, the grove proffers deep shade;
Swelling fruits bend the branches with their weight;
The country folk, having duly worshipped the goddess, turn   185
The moist earth with their mattocks and work the crumbling
    soil with their plow.
Everything flourishes, enriched with the fertile dews of heaven:
Thus all things now stand joyful in our lands.
Roll on, great rivers, wandering streams, roll on.
"But you hills, separated into seven peaks,   190
    And you, father Tiber, who carry your river-waters down
    From Olympus, it is sufficient for you to have claimed this
        man
    In the past and for many years: now grant me my share.
    I myself will offer him to many, lest the joys be mine alone,
    And at last hand over the young man to our lands."   195

: XIX :

Prayer on Behalf of Gorytius to the Gods

for whom he had built a shrine

Sacred divinities, for whom Gorytius has placed a special altar,
    And consecrated perpetual offerings for that altar:
    Chief support of the human race, divine maiden,
    Whom the ruler of highest Olympus picked out for himself,
    And you, too, majestic mother of the divine maiden,   5
    Happy in your lot, happy in both daughter and grandson,
    The youth who is the great offspring of the father of heaven,
    Whom, by the splendid art and chisel of Sansovino,
    He fashioned to be viewed and to breathe in Parian marble,
    On account of this devotion and because of such a gift,   10

Reddite, si sacrorum unquam pia carmina vatum
Et castae movere preces coelestia corda,
Reddite quae posco, mea nec sint irrita vota:
Ut quos longa dies miseris mortalibus olim
15 Advectat varios senio veniente labores,
Aegrum animum et segnes effoeto in corpore sensus,
Inque solum pronos vultus nixisque bacillum
Poplitibus, tardosque gradus tremebundaque membra,
Tum crebras lachrymis causas, et dura suorum
20 Funera et eversos mutata sorte penates,
Quaeque alia ex aliis passim mala consternatas
Implerunt terras cupidi post furta Promethei:
Horum ille immunis totos centum expleat annos
Auspiciis, Superi, vestris, et numine vestro
25 Integer, ut nunc est, nec longae damna senectae
Sentiat: et charus patriae, iocundus amicis,
Dives opum, Roma incolumi Latioque fruatur.

: XX :

Hymnus ad divum Stephanum

Nam quae te culpae et sceleris tam dira cupido,
Infelix Solime et saeclis damnanda futuris,
Corripuit? tantas aut quis furor egit in iras?
Ut iuvenem patris aetherei praecepta canentem
5 Dicta tibi et veterum reserantem oracula vatum

Grant, if the pious verses of holy bards
And their chaste prayers can ever move heavenly hearts,
Grant him what I ask for, let not my prayer be vain,
So that the manifold troubles which length of days brings
Over time to pitiable mortals, as old age comes on,   15
A sick spirit and sense made sluggish in a weakened body,
A face bent toward the ground and a staff to support
One's legs, slow steps and trembling limbs,
And frequent reasons for tears, and the harsh funeral rites
Of dear ones and household gods overturned as his lot   20
    changes,
From the evils which have everywhere filled
The frightened earth after the theft of eager Prometheus:
That he, free from these ills, may fill out a hundred full years
Under your protection, O gods above, and by your divine power
May he be unscathed, as he is now, and never feel the losses of 25
    old age:
And dear to his country, delightful to his friends,
Rich in all he may want, may he take joy in a Rome and
    Latium at peace.

: XX :

Hymn to Saint Stephen

Pray, what dreadful desire for crime and wickedness,
    O cursed Jerusalem, a desire damned by future ages,
    Seized you? What madness incited you to such a rage?
    How is it you drove out the youth chanting the teachings of
        the heavenly father,
    Spoken to you, and revealing the foretellings of the ancient   5
        prophets

83

Praestanti eloquio, teque ad meliora vocantem,
Compita per mediasque vias e moenibus urbis
Illusum expuleris; tum caeca perdita mente
Concursu pressum ingenti, saxisque petitum
10 Nudatos artus, ceu quondam grandine densa
Iuppiter ingeminans terram quatit aethere ab alto,
Crudelis letho dederis nil tale merentem?
Ille quidem placido sustollens lumina vultu
Lustrabatque oculis coelum, intrepidusque pericli
15 Laudabat superos, et spe sua damna levabat:
Cui se, quantus erat, manifesta in luce videndum
Ipse pater Divum dederat cum compare nato
Sublimis, medioque illi fulgebat Olympo.
Quin etiam extremo cum iam sub fine laborum
20 Disiectus duro frontem et cava tempora nimbo
Iret iter propius lethi, tamen hostibus ipsis,
Pro scelere immani moriens, pro talibus ausis
Ah veniam superos anima fugiente rogabat:
Placabat superos hosti iam frigida lingua.
25 Salve, bis senis lectus parere magistris,
Macte animo, puer, egregio et praestantibus ausis,
Macte nece, et veris magnum decus addite Divis.
Tu princeps ignominiam plagasque cruentas,

With extraordinary eloquence, and calling you to better things,
Drove him in mockery through the crossroads and from the
   high walls
Of the city; how then, with thoughts dark and deadly, did you
   cruelly give him
Over to death (he deserving no such thing),
Overwhelmed by a huge crowd, his naked limbs   10
Attacked by stones, as once Jupiter, from the lofty heavens,
With redoubled vigor would shake the earth with thick hail?
He indeed with calm countenance, lifting up his eyes,
Traversed the heavens with his gaze, and undisturbed by his
   danger
Praised the gods above, and lightened his suffering with hope.   15
To him, the father of the gods had given a vision of himself,
Glorious as he was, seen in palpable light with his son as
   companion
On high, and he shone for him from the midst of Olympus.
Nay, even when now, at the last end of his sufferings,
His forehead and hollow temples shattered by a rain of hard   20
   stones,
He was approaching ever nearer to death, still on behalf of his
   enemies,
Though dying because of their savage crime, their great
   rashness,
Ah! even as his soul fled away, he asked for them to be forgiven.
His tongue, now lifeless, conciliated the gods for his enemy's
   sake.
Hail, youth, chosen to obey the twelve teachers,   25
Well done in your admirable spirit and glorious daring,
Well done in your death, and a great glory added to the true
   gods.
You are the first witness to the deed, the ignominy and bloody
   wounds

Et longum memoranda nepotibus aspera fata
30   Magnanimi post Herois, quem candida partu
Coelicolum regi tecto sub paupere Nympha
Non ullam venerem, nullos experta hymeneos
Ediderat patrii flavas Iordanis ad undas,
Testis ades facti: sacro tu primus ab illis
35   Sanguine palmiferae terram conspergis Idumes:
Et pulchrae insolitos decerpens laudis honores,
Purpurea gaudes frontem cinxisse corona:
Unde tibi grati nomen dixere minores.
Te colimus: certo tibi tempore sacra quotannis
40   Rite damus et thura tuis imponimus aris.
Quod si ulla o votisque hominum precibusque moventur
Numina, nec cunctis adeo stat perdere Divis
Ausoniam populosque Italos nomenque Latinum,
Atque malis prope iam confectae moenia Romae,
45   Sancte, veni, coetusque tuos tuaque aurea templa,
Laeti quae festa velamus fronde per urbes,
Dexter adi, placidusque animis illabere nostris.
Ac primum miseris bellorum et caedis amorem
Da, Pater, exuere et tercentum mittere in annos
50   Tigrimque Tanaimque ultra, et post ferre quietem
Sollicitos populi fasces, adiectaque regnis
Regna super, validoque undantia milite castra,

And the bitter fate, long to be remembered by those coming
    after,
Of the great-hearted Hero, whom the shining Nymph   30
Had borne under a poor roof for the king of the heaven-
    dwellers,
She untouched by any love-making, by any wedding rites,
Near the golden waters of her paternal Jordan;
You, as the first of them, sprinkled the soil
Of palm-bearing Judea with your holy blood   35
And, snatching the unaccustomed honors of lovely praise,
Rejoice to have bound your forehead with a gleaming crown,
Whence those who came later, grateful, have given you this
    name.
We venerate you; at the appointed time each year
We duly make holy offering and place incense on your altars.   40
But oh! if any divine beings are moved by the vows and
    prayers
Of humankind, and it does not stand fixed with all the gods
    to destroy
Ausonia and the peoples of Italy and the citizens of Latium,
And the fortifications of Rome, now near to ruination from
    her evils,
Come, holy one, and joining your throngs and your golden   45
    churches,
Which we are happily covering with festal garlands throughout
    our cities,
Come as a favorable omen, and serenely glide into our souls.[1]
But first, Father, grant us in our pitiable state to shed our love
Of wars and slaughter and send them three hundred years
Beyond the Tigris and the Don, and afterwards grant   50
To the magistrates concerned for their people to establish calm,
And cause kingdoms added to kingdoms and camps
    abounding

Et pacem venerari et mitia vertere duris:
Dein pestes scelerum tantorum, atque agmine longo
55 Multa odii concreta modis mala semina diris,
Infectasque diu labes et crimina purga
Heu solito graviora, irasque averte Deorum.

: XXI :

Armilla aurea Lucretiae Borgiae
Ferrariae ducis

in serpentis effigiem formata

Dypsas eram: sum facta, Tago dum perluor, aurum
Tortile Nympharum manibus decus: at memor olim
Eridani, auditaque tua, Lucretia, forma,
Heliadum ne te caperent electra tuarum,
5 Gestandum charae fluvius transmisit alumnae.

: XXII :

De Iulio puero

qui se ipsum pinxerat in tabula

Ut sol, cum placidis semet depingit in undis,
A te sic ipso picte puelle micas.

In powerful soldiery to reverence peace and turn from harsh
    acts to meekness;
Then drive away in long lines the plagues of such wickedness
And the many evil seeds of hatred hardened in dreadful ways;   55
Purge these stains long imbued and crimes
Graver, alas, than usual, and turn away the anger of the gods.

: XXI :

The Golden Bracelet of Lucrezia Borgia
Duchess of Ferrara

made in the form of a serpent

I was a poisonous snake: while bathing in the Tagus, I was made
    Into a golden bracelet to adorn the hands of nymphs; but
        mindful,
    Once, of the Po, and having heard of your renowned beauty,
        Lucretia,
    Lest the amber of your own poplars possess you,
    The river sent me to be worn by his dear foster-daughter.   5

: XXII :

Concerning the Boy Julius

who painted a self-portrait on a tablet

Like the sun, when he makes an image of himself in calm water,
    So you, too, shine by yourself, painted boy.

: XXIII :

Pegasus equus paternum insigne

Graecia cum celeres mihi daedala fingeret alas,
    Esse, homines, vobis dixit in astra viam.

: XXIV :

Cum cereis albis
dono missis Bernardo monacho

Vivat in Euganea reliquum tibi lumen oliva,
    Cera sed in sacris luceat alba tuis.

: XXV :

Camino inscriptum

Hanc nisi Phoebeo rapuisset ab orbe Prometheus,
    Ars homini flammae nulla, nec usus erat.

: XXVI :

Politiani tumulus

Duceret extincto cum Mors Laurente triumphum
    Laetaque pullatis inveheretur equis,
Respicit insano ferientem pollice chordas
    Viscera singultu concutiente virum.

: XXIII :

The Horse Pegasus, My Father's Insignia

When the skillful Greek made swift wings for me,
　He said: Humankind, this will be for you a way to the stars.

: XXIV :

Accompanying a Gift of White Tapers
Sent to the Monk Bernardo

May the rest of your light rise from the Euganean olive,
　But let a white wax taper gleam during your holy rites.

: XXV :

Inscription for a Forge

If Prometheus had not snatched it from Phoebus' orb,
　Man would have had neither art nor use from fire.

: XXVI :

The Tomb of Poliziano

When glad Death was leading the triumphal procession after
　　Lorenzo had died
And was being drawn by horses in mourning harness,
She looked back and saw a man striking with frenzied thumb

5   Mirata est, tenuitque iugum: furit ipse pioque
           Laurentem cunctos flagitat ore Deos.
       Miscebat precibus lachrymas lachrymisque dolorem;
           Verba ministrabat liberiora dolor.
       Risit, et antiquae non immemor illa querelae,
10   Orphi Tartareae cum patuere viae,
       'Hic etiam infernas tentat rescindere leges,
           Fertque suas', dixit, 'in mea iura manus.'
       Protinus et flentem percussit dura poetam,
           Rupit et in media pectora docta sono.
15   Heu sic tu raptus, sic te mala fata tulerunt,
           Arbiter Ausoniae, Politiane, lyrae.

: XXVII :

Galli epitaphium

       O fatis nimium duris exercita Roma,
           Ten decuit toties ultima damna pati?
       Ille tuus sanguis Gallus, tua magna voluptas,
           Gallus Aventini gloria prima soli,
5   Gallus Musarum et Phoebi gratissimus hospes,
           Donavit cithara quem pater ipse sua,
       Et cinxere Deae lauro et dixere poetam
           Melpomeneque suum, Calliopeque suum;

At the strings of his lyre while sobbing shook him to his
    depths.
She was amazed, and reined in the chariot; the man himself is   5
    frantic
    And importunes all the gods for Lorenzo with devout lips.[1]
With his prayers he mingled tears and with tears his grief;
    Grief supplied words all the more freely.
She laughed, and not at all unmindful of her ancient grievance,
    When the ways of the underworld opened up to Orpheus,   10
She said: "This man is trying to abrogate the laws of the lower
    world,
    And raises his hands against my rights."
Straightway harsh Death struck the weeping poet
    And broke his learned heart in mid-song.
Alas, thus you have been snatched away, thus wicked fate has   15
    borne you off,
    Poliziano, great master of Ausonian song.

: XXVII :

Epitaph for Gallus

O Rome, harassed by too harsh a fortune,
    Was it right that you suffer so often the utmost loss?
He, Gallus, your descendant, your great delight,
    Gallus, first glory of the Aventine land,
Gallus, most pleasing guest of the Muses and Phoebus,   5
    To whom father Phoebus himself gave his own lyre,
And whom the goddess Muses, his own Melpomene and
    Calliope,
    Bound with laurel and proclaimed their poet:

Cui lex et bene suadus honos, rectique cupido,
10   Et probitas cordi simplicitasque fuit.
Candida cui ridebat hianti copia cornu,
     Et faciles Nymphae semicaperque Deus;
Mater et incanos spicis evincta capillos
     Implebat laetis messibus arva Ceres;
15 Cui Nar sulfureus, nigra cui Farfarus unda,
     Et qui, Roma, tuas Fucinus auxit aquas,
Atque Almo, atque Anio Tybrisque paterque Numicus
     Flumina iusserunt largius ire sua:
Delitiae, mea Roma, tuae, lususque leporque,
20   Et spes, et senii remus et aura tui,
Gallus, per quem oblita tuorum es ante malorum,
     Occidit: heu sine amore et sine lege Deos!

: XXVIII :

Iulii secundi pontificatus maximus

Illa piis populis mundoque accepta recenti
     Sub Iove, cum nondum ferreus orbis erat,
Nec proscissa graves vertebant arva iuvenci,
     Vinea nec lachrymas falce resecta dabat,
5 Mella sed aeriae sudabant roscida sylvae,
     Et lac pro gelida flumen habebat aqua.

He held dear the law and eloquence, desire for the right,
　　Uprighr virtue and the simple life.　　　　　　　　　　　10
Fair Plenty smiled on him with wide-open horn,
　　As did the gracious nymphs and the half-goat god;
And mother Ceres, her graying hair bound round with spikes of
　　　　grain,
　　Filled his fields with joyful harvests;
For him the sulphurous Nar, for him the Farfarus with its black　　15
　　　　waters,
　　And Lake Fucinus, who augments your waters, O Rome,
And the Almo and the Anio and the Tiber and father Numicus
　　All ordered their waters to flow more bountifully;
Your favorite, my Rome, your wit and your charm
　　And hope, the strength and breath of your old age,　　　　20
Gallus, because of whom you have forgotten your troubles in
　　　　earlier times,
　　Is dead: alas for the gods bereft of love and law!

: XXVIII :

The Supreme Pontificate of Julius the Second

That tree was pleasing to devout people and to the new-made
　　　　earth
　　Under Jove, when the world was not yet iron,
Not yet were heavy bullocks turning the plowed fields,
　　Nor yet was the vineyard, pruned by the sickle, giving forth its
　　　　juices,
But the lofty trees were still dripping honey like dew　　　　　5
　　And the river ran milk instead of chill water.

Nunc o nunc redit ad primos bona quercus honores,
    Quos habuit, mundi cum tener orbis erat;
Quercus, glande sua quae quondam Heroas alebat,
10   Cura Deum quercus sancta piumque nemus,
Dignaque Cecropiae pinguis cui sylva Minervae
    Cedat, et Herculeis populus apta comis;
Cedat et ipsa suo laurus Phoebeia luco,
    Inflexaeque pedem Bacchica serta hederae,
15 Vel myrti Veneris, vel Sylvani cyparissi,
    Vel quae capripedi pinus amata Deo est.
Namque boni mores nostro rediere sub aevo,
    Ut primum posito constitit illa situ:
Simplicitasque inculta comam, rectique cupido,
20   Et lex et probitas et sine labe fides.
Nec redit ad primos tantum bona quercus honores,
    Quos habuit mundi cum tener orbis erat:
Sed provecta solo nitidis caput inserit astris,
    Quantum homines aluit, tantum alitura Deos.

: XXIX :

Caroli Bembi fratris epitaphium

Qualis honos coeli, puro cum surgit Olympo
    Lucifer et fessis clarum caput exerit astris:
Tale decus te, Bembe, tuis mala fata tulerunt.

Now, oh now, the virtuous oak comes back to the primal honors,
   Which it had when the circle of the world was young;
To the oak tree, which once nourished the demigods with its
      acorns,
   Sacred oak and holy grove, care of the gods,   10
Let the rich orchard worthy of Athenian Minerva give place,
   And the poplar suitable for the locks of Hercules;
And let Apollo's laurel itself give place in its own grove,
   And the Bacchic garland of curving ivy;
Let also the myrtles of Venus, and the cypresses of Sylvanus give 15
      place,
   And the pine-tree, beloved of the goat-footed god.
For good customs returned to our times,
   As soon as that tree stood positioned in its place,
Simplicity with her hair unadorned, and upright ambition,
   And law and honesty and faith without fault.   20
Not only does the virtuous oak return to the primal honors
   Which it had when the circle of the earth was young,
But carried far above the ground, it raises its head among the
      shining stars,
   And as it has nourished men, so also will it feed the gods.

: XXIX :

Epitaph for My Brother Carlo Bembo

Like the brilliance of the sky, when the day-star rises in the clear
      heavens
   And its bright head passes above the exhausted stars,
   Such was your glory, Bembo, when evil fates took you from
      your own.

97

: XXX :

Herculis Strozzae epitaphium

Te ripa natum Eridani Permessus alebat,
    Fecerat et vatem Marsque Venusque suum.
Iniecere manus iuveni et fatalia duris
    Stamina pollicibus persecuere Deae.
5   Uxor honorata manes dum conderet urna,
    Talia cum multis dicta dedit lachrymis:
'Non potui tecum dulcem consumere vitam:
    At iam adero amplexans te cinerem ipsa cinis.'

: XXXI :

Marci Antonii Gabrielis Veneti epitaphium

Demessam patriae segetem crescentibus herbis
    Morte tua, venerande puer, specimenque relinquis
Praereptum genti morum et virtutis avitae.
    Te Patavi colles, vitrea te Silis in unda,
5   Te Veneti flevere lacus, terque Hadria vastum
    Implevit gemitu moerens et questibus aequor.

: XXX :

Epitaph for Ercole Strozzi

Permessus nourished you, born by the bank of the Po,
    And Mars and Venus made you their bard.
The goddess Fates laid hands on you as a young man,
    And cut through your destined life-threads with hardened
        thumbs.
When your wife buried your remains in an honored urn,   5
    She spoke these words with many tears:
"I was not able to spend my sweet life with you,
    But soon I will be here, ashes myself, embracing your ashes."

: XXXI :

Epitaph for Marco Antonio Gabriel of Venice

By your death, revered boy, you are leaving behind the crop
    Of your country harvested while its blades still grew, and a
        pattern
Of morals and ancestral virtues has been snatched from your
        people.
    The hills of Padua weep for you, Silis weeps in its glassy
        waters,
The Venetian lagoons weep for you, and thrice has the Adriatic   5
    In its grief filled its watery expanse with groans and laments.

: XXXII :

Philippi Beroaldi minoris epitaphium

Felsina te genuit, colles rapuere Quirini,
    Longum audita quibus Musa diserta tua est.
Illa dedit rerum domino placuisse Leoni,
    Thebanos Latio dum canis ore modos.
5   Unanimes raptum ante diem flevere sodales,
    Nec Decimo sanctae non maduere genae.
Quae pietas, Beroalde, fuit tua, credere verum est
    Carmina nunc coeli te canere ad citharam.

: XXXIII :

Scythae poetae Feltrini epitaphium

Scythae oculos clausit Phoebus: flevere sorores,
    Fleverunt Charites, funera duxit Amor.

: XXXIV :

Certaldi philosophi epitaphium

Et terram et coelum ingenio Certaldus obibam,
    Quaeque fuere aliis clausa, reclusa mihi.

: XXXII :

Epitaph for Filippo Beroaldo the Younger

Felsina brought you forth, the hills of Rome snatched you away,
　　By whom your eloquent Muse was heard for a long time.
She granted that you pleased Leo, the master of our world,
　　When you sang Theban melodies with a Latin voice.
With one accord your comrades wept for you, carried off before 　　5
　　　　your time,
　　And the holy cheeks of Decimus[1] were streaming.
Such piety, Beroaldo, was yours, that one may truly believe
　　You are now singing your songs to a heavenly lyre.

: XXXIII :

Epitaph for Scytha, Poet of Feltre

Phoebus has closed the eyes of Scytha, the Fates have wept,
　　The Graces have wept, and Love has performed the funeral
　　　　rites.

: XXXIV :

Epitaph for the Philosopher Certaldo

I, Certaldo, traversed the earth and the heavens with my genius,
　　And those things which were closed to others, opened
　　　　themselves to me.

: XXXV :

Longolii epitaphium

Te iuvenem rapuere Deae fatalia nentes
  Stamina, cum scirent moriturum tempore nullo,
Longoli, tibi si canos seniumque dedissent.

: XXXVI :

Leonici epitaphium

Naturae si quid rerum te forte latebat,
  Id legis in magno nunc, Leonice, Deo.

: XXXVII :

Telesillae epitaphium

Quid mors tam pulchram rapuisti dura puellam?
  Nunquid, me miserum, te quoque tangit amor?

: XXXVIII :

Catelli epitaphium

Nil tibi non dominus tribuit, Bembine catelle,
  A quo nomen habes, et tumulum et lachrymas.

: XXXV :

Epitaph for Longolius

While you were yet a youth the Fates were spinning the thread
   Of your destiny, when they learned that you would never die,
Longolius, even if they had given you white hair and old age.

: XXXVI :

Epitaph for Leonico

If anything in all of nature was by chance hidden from you,
   You are reading it now, Leonico, in God's greatness.

: XXXVII :

Epitaph for Telesilla

Why, harsh death, have you snatched away a maiden so lovely?
   Could it happen, woe is me! that love touches you also?

: XXXVIII :

Epitaph for My Puppy

Your master gave you everything, little dog Bembino,
   From whom you have a name, a tomb, and tears.

: XXXIX :

Fictum pro antiquo

Aelia natorum manesque sequuta mariti,
    Usa sua iacet hic Septimiana manu.
Vir Turrinus erat, cum quo tria lustra peregit,
    Iurgiaque in sancto nulla fuere toro.
5   Binaque de primo suscepit pignora partu,
    Dein natam matris spemque metumque suae.
Crudeles Divi, proles adoleverat, at mors
    Iniecit tetricas perviolenta manus.
Post quae moerentem, ne quid superesset amanti,
10   Abstulit orbatae proxima luna virum:
Quem simul ac flamma vidit lambente cremari,
    'Ergo ibis, tecum nec tua', dixit, 'erit?
Eripies mihi tu nunquam hoc, fortuna: licebit
    Hoc saltem invita te potuisse mihi.'
15 Dixerat, et stricto fixit sua pectora ferro:
    Sic moriens charo nunc quoque iuncta viro est.

: XL :

Iacobi Synceri Sannazari Epitaphium

Da sacro cineri flores: hic ille Maroni
    Syncerus Musa proximus, ut tumulo.

: XXXIX :

A Fiction in the Ancient Manner

Aelia Septimiana, having followed the souls of her children and
    husband,
  Lies here by the work of her own hand.
Her husband was Turrinus, with whom she passed three times
    five years,
  And no quarrels existed in their blest marriage-bed.
At her first childbirth he received twin love-pledges,   5
  Then a daughter, her mother's hope and fear.
O cruel gods, the children grew, but violent death
  Laid on them its gloomy hands.
After that, lest anything remain to the loving woman,
  The next moon snatched her grief-stricken husband from her, 10
    already childless.
As soon as she saw him being consumed by the licking flame,
  She said: "Will you go, therefore, and your own wife not be
    with you?
Fortune, you will never snatch this from me; even with you
    unwilling
  This power will at least be permitted to me."
She stopped speaking, and stabbed her breast with a drawn sword: 15
  Thus was the dying woman now also joined to her dear
    husband.

: XL :

Epitaph for Jacopo Syncerus Sannazaro

Offer flowers to these holy ashes: here lies
  Syncerus, nearest to Virgil in inspiration as in his tomb.

: XLI :

Lucilii Bembi filii epitaphium

O multum dilecte puer, quae dura parenti
   Fortuna invidit te superesse tuo?
Quam producebam laetus te sospite vitam,
   Erepto peior morte relicta mihi est.

: XLI :

Epitaph for Lucilio Bembo, My Son

O much loved boy, what harsh fate
    Begrudged that you survive your parent?
The life which I used to lead in my happiness while you were
       safe,
    Once you were snatched away, remains worse to me than
       death.

APPENDIX A

: I :

De Fauno et Galatea

Cum fugeret summas Faunum Galatea per undas,
    Et se iam medio tingueret ille mari:
'Quo fugis, o Galatea? mane, mane o Galatea:
    Non ego sum', dixit, 'non ego, Nympha, Cyclops.'
5   Ignea tum roseo convertens lumina vultu:
    'Dii facerent esses nunc', ait illa, 'Cyclops:
Dummodo nulla truces Cyclopas terra habuisset,
    Heu non dum flumen cum meus Acis erat.'

: II :

De Christo marmoreo Pyrgotelis

Quales Asia nos apella vidit,
    Europae dabat artifex videndos;

Quales viximus in priore saeclo,
    Caelum Pyrgotelis dedit magistri
5   Longum posterioribus videri.

A quo Pyrgoteles vitam tulit; hunc etiam ipse
    Vivum, quo potuit, fecerat esse, modo.

POEMS EXCLUDED FROM THE CARMINUM LIBELLUS

: I :

About Faunus and Galatea

When Galatea was fleeing from Faunus through the crests of the
    waves,
    And he had then plunged himself in the midst of the sea,
He said, "Whither are you fleeing, O Galatea? Stay, stay,
    Galatea!
    I am not, no, I am not the Cyclops, Nymph."
Then turning towards him the fiery eyes in her rosy face,   5
    She said, "The gods have now made you a Cyclops to me:
If no land had ever held the savage Cylopes,
    My Acis would not now, alas, be a river."

: II :

On the Marble Christ of Pyrgoteles

Our living nature the way Asian Apelles saw it,
    The artisan made visible to Europe;

Our living nature as it was in an earlier time,
    The chisel of Pyrgoteles the master
    Gave to posterity to be seen for a long time to come.   5

He from whom Pyrgoteles took life, even him Pyrgoteles himself,
    In as far as he could, made alive.

: III :

Ficus ad Poetas

Exuperent cum iam vestri mea poma libelli,
　　Quae polycarpos eram, nunc polycarmen ero.

: IV :

Eadem

Carmina qui tulerit, pomis donatus abito,
　　Tot pomis, quot erunt sua carmina; carmina si me
　　Vestra manent, pueri, poma haec vos nostra manebunt.
　　Poma haec dulcia nostra magis, vel carmina vestra?
5　　Carmina dulcia vestra, et poma haec dulcia nostra.
　　Poma haec nostra legenda, an carmina vestra legenda?
　　Carmina vestra legenda; legenda et poma poetae.

: V :

De Pado exundante

Eridanus tumidis ripam quondam transilit undis,
　　Nil mirum: facit hoc, Borgia, te ut videat.

: III :

A Fig for the Poets

Since your little books have now surpassed my fruits,
    I who was rich in figs will now be rich in verses.

: IV :

The Same Subject

Let him who brought poems, leave, gifted with fruit,
    With fruits as numerous as his poems; if your poems
    Keep for me, these fruits of ours will keep for you.
    Are these apples of ours sweeter, or your poems?
    Your poems are sweet, and these apples of ours are sweet, too.   5
    Are these apples of ours to be plucked, or your poems to be
        read?
    Your poems must be read; plucked also must be the fruit of a
        poet.

: V :

On the Po in Flood

The Po at times leaps over its banks in swollen surges,
    No wonder: it does this, Borgia, that it might look at you.

: VI :

De Arione marmoreo

Messanae Delphini insidenti pro fonte,
quem Panormitani perfregerunt

Me fera per medium servavit Ariona pontum:
    Vos, Siculi, in vestra dilaniastis aqua.

: VII :

Ad Lycorim

Quale suo nunquam satiatus vellus in auro
    Attalus Idaeas pingere iussit acus;
Quale nec Idmonii fecerunt stamina fusi,
    Texere sed sola est Palladis ausa manus;
5   Talia vir tibi dona tuus dat habere, Lycori,
    Hermus Acidalia dona petenda Dea.
Et super his geminas forma praestante puellas
    Servitium dignas non nisi ferre tuum.
Altera Pelleo tibi venit ab usque Canopo,
10   Divite qua Nilus flumine culta secat;
Altera ab Eurotae campis, quam raptor Abydum
    Turca levis verso ferre volebat equo;
Navita sed propere nostram vecturus ad urbem
    Artibus et multa merce redemit Arabs.
15   Nec satis hoc: partes se se demittit in omnes,
    Officiumque pii coniugis Hermus agit.
Nam modo qua possis digitos incendere gemma

: VI :

On the Marble Statue of Arion

Sitting on a dolphin, in the form of a fountain at Messina,
which the people of Palermo broke in pieces

A wild creature saved me, Arion, in the midst of the high seas:
   While you, Sicilians, have torn me to pieces in your own
      springwater.

: VII :

To Lycoris

Such a fleece in its natural gold insatiable Attalus
   Ordered Phrygian needles to depict;
Such cloth the threads of Arachne's spindle did not fashion,
   But only the hand of Athena dared to weave;
Hermus, your husband, gives such gifts for you to have, Lycoris,   5
   Gifts worthy of being sought by the goddess Venus.
And besides these he bestows two maidens of glorious beauty
   Worthy to be in your service only.
The one comes to you all the way from Pellaean Canopus,
   Where the Nile cleaves the farmland with its rich waters;   10
The other from the fields of the Eurotas, whom the nimble
     brigand
   From Anatolia wished to carry off to Abydos on his retreating
     horse;
But an Arab sailor, on his swift course to our city,
   Bought them with cleverness and for a large sum.
Nor is this enough: Hermus is himself engaged in each detail   15
   And fulfills the duty of a loving spouse.
For now he seeks how your fingers can glow more beautifully

Pulchrius, aut flavas irradiare comas;
Nunc tua quo melius circundes colla monili
20   Quaerit, et in cultu plurimus ille tuo est:
Seu tu candiduli specie tangaris elenchi,
      Seu magis ire bono comptam adamante placet.
Foelix, cui talem contingit habere maritum,
      Tamque suo cara est, si qua puella viro.
25   Si tua coniugii tibi sors optanda fuisset,
      Quem potius cuperes, non habuisse potes.
Ille bonam faciem cultu torpere maligno
      Non sinet, et taciti damna subire situs:
Sed tibi quae placido tribuerunt Numina vultu,
30   Defendet placida perpolietque manu.
      Quam bene, quod facies haec tam bona contigit illi;
      Cultori facies haec data nempe suo est.
Vivere quo posses multos formosa per annos,
      Sic tibi crediderim consuluisse Deos.
35   Si minus hic mitis, vel tu formosa fuisses,
      Alterius poteras forsitan esse viri.
Talis at huic uni fueras nuptura marito,
      Iampridem et formae debitus ille tuae est.
Utque tuae pietas illius debita formae,
40   Sic illi fuerat debita forma tua.
Novi ego: vos Charites primis iunxere sub annis,
      Et manibus tedas conseruere suis:
Quasque ita venturo possem proferre sub aevo,

With a gem, or your golden hair shine;
Now he asks how you might better surround your throat with a
    necklace,
    And he is especially attentive in the matter of your adornment: 20
Whether you would be touched by the beauty of a white shiny
    pearl,
    Or it should please you to go about adorned with a fine
    diamond.
Happy she to whose lot falls such a husband,
    And she is as dear to him as any young wife to her husband.
If you had been obliged to choose your own lot in marriage,   25
    You cannot have possessed anyone whom you would rather
    desire.
That man will not allow an attractive face to lie untended
    Through niggardly sloth, and suffer the injuries of silent
    neglect;
But that which the gods have granted to you with a serene glance
    He will defend and perfect with a serene hand.   30
What a good thing, that this most lovely face fell to his lot;
    This face was surely given to one who would cherish it.
So I should think that the gods had taken council on your behalf
    How you can live on, beautiful, through many years.
If he had been less gentle, even if you had been less beautiful,   35
    Perhaps you might have belonged to another man.
But, being such as you are, you were to be the bride of this
    singular husband
    And now for a long time he has been a debtor to your beauty.
And just as his devotion is due to your beauty
    So your beauty is due to him.   40
This I know: the Graces have united you from your earliest years,
    And have entwined your marriage torches with their own
    hands:
One of the three gave me these words

Has ibi tum voces e tribus una dedit:
45 'Conveniunt placidi pulchro cum pectore mores,
      Et formosa pio danda puella viro est.'
    Sed cave ne nimio subeant mala gaudia fastu,
      Quamque decet, placeat plus tua forma tibi.
    Et dolet, et dicam: vellem quoque falsa monere:
50   Exiguum formae gaudia tempus habent.
    Est aliud maius multoque potentius istis,
      Sub nulla positum conditione bonum,
    Quod neque fallenti carpit pede curva senectus,
      Ipsa nec invisi flamma maligna rogi;
55 Cui neque Erithreos possis conferre lapillos,
      Nec bis Getula vellera tincta manu:
    Quod neque dat facies vobis, neque cura, puellae,
      Sed casti mores ingenuusque pudor.
    Illud habet quaecunque proba est, quaecunque pudica,
60   Quaeque virum, debet qualiter uxor, amat.
    Haec tibi forma prior potioraque gaudia sunto:
      Hic tibi sit cultus, hic tua cura decor.
    Nam quo compta magis, vel quo speciosior ulla est,
      Hoc citius petimus, num sit et illa proba.
65 Nec cultus, nec forma placet sine pondere morum:
      Plus etiam morum pondera laudis habent.
    Aspice quam vivat totum cantata per orbem
      Exemplum casti Penelopea tori.
    Pergama corruerant decimo servata sub anno,
70   Et Danaum Phrygias hauserat ignis opes.
    Iamque lares patrios Pelopeia turba tenebat,
      In media multo flore iacente via.

Which I can thus convey to the coming age:
"Gentle behavior most suits a beautiful heart   45
    And a lovely maiden should be given to a devoted husband."
But beware lest evil joys follow upon excessive pride,
    Lest you become complacent with your beauty.
It is painful, but let me say it: and would that my warnings be
        false:
    The joys of beauty have but little time.   50
There is something else greater and more powerful than that:
    Goodness placed under no stipulation,
Which neither bent old age takes away with its faltering step,
    Nor the spiteful flame itself of the hateful funeral pyre;
It may not be compared with the pearls of Erithrea   55
    Nor fleece twice-dyed by Afric hand:
Neither primping nor a pretty face gives that to you, maidens,
    But only chaste behavior and natural modesty.
Whoever is virtuous, whoever is modest has that,
    And she loves her husband just as a wife ought.   60
Let this kind of beauty be paramount, and these joys more
        potent for you:
    Let this refinement, this grace, be your care.
For the more adorned a woman is, the more beautiful,
    The more quickly do we ask, whether she be also virtuous.
Neither comeliness nor beauty please without the weight of   65
        character,
    For weight of character earns much more praise.
Look at how the example of Penelope's chaste marriage-bed
    Lives, a theme of song throughout the world.[1]
Troy, kept safe for ten years, had collapsed
    And Greek fire had swallowed up Phrygian wealth.   70
And now the Greek warriors were claiming again their ancestral
        homes,
    With many a flower strewn before them in their path.

Oscula quisque suae dederat repetita puellae
    Atque expectato solverat ora sono;
75   Narraratque suos illa pendente labores,
        Pinxerat et minimo castra ratesque mero;
Spectaratque viri positas ex ordine praedas
        Uxor et audaci parta trophaea manu.
Forsitan et lateri pugnacem aptaverat ensem
80   Et galeae longas presserat orbe comas.
Sola viri reditum votis operata pudicis
        Penelope surdos flebat habere Deos:
Cumque darent aliae pexis in crinibus aurum
        Et tegeret Graias splendida palla nurus,
85   Ipsa suos non compta sinus, non compta capillos
        Stabat, et in vultu signa dolentis erant.
Dixerat Icarius: 'quid te, mea nata, fatigas?
        Quid quereris lentum non rediisse virum?
Dum bene tu longas consumis frigida noctes,
90   Et potes in vacuo stulta cubare toro,
Quis scit an externam prudens amet ille puellam
        Interea, et siccos non sinat ire dies,
Castaque Penelope mentem non tangat Ulissis,
        Decideritque viri nomen ab ore tuum?
95   Certe ego dudum illam timui, quam fortibus herbis
        Fama est Argolicos detinuisse viros:
Et modo quaerenti quaedam mihi dicta Calypso est
        Naufragium passo concubuisse duci.
Ominer incassum: sed me tamen omnia tangunt,
100   Veraque nescio quo sunt mala cuncta modo.

Each one had given sought-after kisses to his girl
    And had loosened his tongue with long-awaited words;
He had told the story of his trials as she hung there,   75
    And had depicted both camp and ships in a splash of wine;
His wife had looked at the booty of her husband laid out, piece
        by piece
    And the trophies gained by his daring hand.
Perhaps she had fitted the combatant's sword to her side
    And pressed down her long locks with the circle of his helmet.   80
Only Penelope, laboring with pious prayers for the return of her
        husband,
    Wept that she had deaf gods.
And when others put gold on their well-combed hair
    And a shining cloak covered the young matrons of Greece,
She, with garments disarrayed and hair uncombed,   85
    Stood still, with signs of sorrow on her face.
Icarius had said to her: "Why do you weary yourself, my child?
    Why do you complain that your tardy husband has not
        returned?
While you pass the long nights unwarmed,
    And foolishly allow yourself to sleep on an empty couch,   90
Who knows whether that cunning man is making love to a
        foreign woman
    In the meantime, and does not let his days be arid,
And whether he even thinks of chaste Penelope
    And whether your name ever falls from his lips?
Indeed I have long feared that woman, whom rumor says   95
    Has held Greek men prisoners by means of strong herbs,
And lately, when I inquired, a certain Calypso was said
    To have slept with their leader when he suffered shipwreck.
May I prophesy to no purpose: still, everything comes home to
        me:
    Somehow or other all evil prophecies come true.   100

Dum tamen hoc tantum nostras pervenit ad aures,
  Causa tui luctus quaelibet esse potest.
Quamlibet ille potest de se fecisse parentem,
  Quosque pater dicat, quamque maritus habet.
105 Possidet et carae dotalia coniugis arva,
  Inque peregrino moenia magna solo,
Oblitus miserique patris natique tuique.
  I nunc et co⟨n⟩stans dicier uxor ama!
Nempe mihi tanti non est faciendus Ulisses,
110   In viduo maneas semper ut ipsa toro.
Nec tam dura mihi fuerat sperata senectus,
  Esset ut a lachrymis illa gravanda tuis.
Eia age, rumpe moras vacuumque relinque cubile:
  Quod tibi vir nunc est, te licet esse viro.
115 Elige de multis, cui sis iungenda marito:
  En ultro veniunt ad tua vota proci.
Nec praescire labor tibi, quem nolimve velimve est,
  Dum tibi quis placeat, iam mihi quisque placet.
Tantum ne dubita: quid enim dubitabile verum est?
120   Hora tibi melior non reditura fugit.
Heu nimium propere subit erumnosa senectus:
  Cur fraudas annos, filia dura, tuos?'
Dixit et amplexus carae dedit oscula natae,
  Et patriae lachrymas non tenuere genae.
125 Illa sub haec oculos aegre demissa tenebat,
  Candida purpureus tinxerat ora pudor.
Quid faciat? cedat ne patri laesura maritum,

Yet provided this tale reaches our ears alone,
    You can have any cause you like for your grief,
Whatever woman he has made pregnant,
    Whatever children he has, whatever wife.
He possesses, too, the dowered lands of his dear wife,   105
    And great fortresses in a foreign land,
Forgetful of his wretched father, his son, and you.
    Go now and love being called a constant wife!
Certainly I would not value Ulysses at such a rate
    That you yourself should always rest in a widow's bed.   110
Hoped-for old age had not been so hard for me,
    That it had to be weighed down by your tears.
Ah me, go now, break off delay and leave your empty chamber,
    Because now there is a husband for you, you are allowed a
        husband.
Choose from the crowd the husband to whom you would wish to   115
    be joined;
    Look at the suitors who come willingly according to your
        wishes.
Do not trouble to know beforehand whom I wish or do not wish,
    Provided someone pleases you, he pleases me also.
Only do not have doubts: for what doubtful thing is true?
    Your better hour is fleeing, never to return.   120
Alas, wretched old age comes on with great speed:
    Why are you cheating your years, unyielding child?"
He finished speaking, and embracing his dear daughter, he kissed
    her,
    And tears overflowed the father's cheeks.
In response to these words she with difficulty kept her eyes   125
    downcast,
    And a blush of modesty tinged her pale face.
What should she do? Should she yield to her father and injure
    her husband,

An neget et duro vulneret ore patrem?
Hinc pietas aetasque sui lachrymaeque parentis,
130   Inde maritalis obstat et urget amor.
Plus tamen urget amor superatque in coniuge coniux;
    Sed timet affectum sollicitare senem.
Dumque timet, radii manibus cecidere pudicis,
    Atque oblita suum dextra reliquit opus.
135 Stamina tum relegens revolutaque pensa reponens,
    Per causam tacito tempora fronte terit.
Ah, etiam rupit lenti bona litia fili,
    Ut traherent certas illa plicanda moras:
Ruptaque cum posset firmo connectere lino,
140   Infirmo vanum callida fecit opus.
Quid te parva iuvat mora temporis, Icarione?
    Ad tibi fallendos nil facit illa dies.
Tela erat ante oculos, tibi quam texebat, Ulisses:
    Ad telam sensus contulit illa suos.
145 Protinus et tenui, 'faveas mihi,' murmure dixit,
    'Iniice tu longas officiosa moras.'
Inde hilari moestum vultu solata parentem,
    Talia composito pectore verba refert:
'Tela haec caepta mea cum perficietur Ulissi,
150   Ipsa libens veniam sub tua iussa, Pater.'
Accipit Icarius promissaque tempora servat,
    Spargit et in tepidos thura merumque focos.
Dumque parat natae thalamos taedasque maritas,
    Producit pactam tela retexta moram.

Or refuse and wound her father with a stubborn expression?
On this side stands duty and the age and tears of her father,
    On the other marital love remains a barrier and weighs upon   130
      her.
Still love weighs more heavily, and in the wife the role of wife
      conquers;
    But she fears to give anxiety to the troubled old man,
And while she is fearful, the shuttles fall from her chaste hands,
    And her forgetful right hand lets go its work.
Then picking up the distaff again and replacing the unwound   135
      wool,
    Under this pretext, with silent brow, she uses up time.
Ah! she even breaks good lengths of supple thread,
    So that the need to retie them might ensure further delay,
And though she might have woven the broken fabric with strong
      thread,
    She cunningly made the work vain with weak.   140
Of what advantage is brief mourning to you, daughter of Icarius?
    It is of no use to you in whiling away your days.
The cloth which she was weaving for you, Ulysses, was openly
      displayed:
    To the cloth she devoted all her feelings.
Straightway, with a faint murmur, she said,   145
    "Be dutiful, O loom, and impose long delays."
Thereupon, comforting her sad father with a cheerful countenance
    She replied in these words with a calm heart:
"When this cloth, begun for my Ulysses, is finished,
    I will gladly follow your orders, father."   150
Icarius accepts, and awaits the promised moment,
    And he sprinkles incense and wine onto the warm hearth.
And while he readies a marriage bed and wedding torches for his
      daughter,
    The unwoven cloth creates the agreed-upon delay.

155 Sic illa invitoque parente, ultroque petita
    Absenti potuit casta manere viro.
    Et ne forte putes paucos mansisse per annos,
    Quatuor huic spatium lustra fuere morae.
    Sed legitur nunc illa omnique legetur ab aevo:
160   Haec merces tanto digna labore fuit.
    Tu quoque perpetuo celebrabere, pulchra Lycori,
    Tu quoque venturo nomen ab orbe feres;
    Si modo Penelopen castasque imitata maritas,
    Materiem dederis laudibus ipsa tuis.
165 Hoc tamen ut facias, non expectandus Ulisses,
    Icariusve tibi decipiendus erit.
    Prona via est, qua carpis iter: tibi cura marito
    Sit tantum ut placeas conveniasque tuo.
    Ille quidem nostro iuvenis rarissimus aevo est:
170   Convenies isti nec nisi rara viro.
    Nec quia non praestes, te nos nunc ista monemus:
    Sed potes hortatu pronior esse meo.
    Hoc tibi pro tanto debemus coniuge, qui nos,
    Thesea Pirithous sic ut amavit, amat,
175 Cui tu sera tuos iungas foeliciter annos
    Comprecor, o digno iuncta puella viro.

: VIII :

Sarca

Pierides magno genus ab Iove, quis labor alto
Asserere interitu clarorum gesta virorum,

Thus, though her father was unwilling and herself sought after,   155
    She was able to remain chaste for her absent husband.
And lest you might think that few were the years she remained
      thus,
    The extent of her waiting was four times five years.
But now she is read about and will be read about in every age:
    This was a prize worthy of such long suffering.   160
You, too, will be ever renowned, lovely Lycoris,
    You, too, will have a name in the world to come;
If only you imitate Penelope and other chaste wives,
    You yourself will provide material for your praises.
Moreover, when you do this, you will not have to await a Ulysses   165
    Nor deceive an Icarius.
The way is easy, by which you make this journey: let your care be
    Only that you please and live in harmony with your husband.
He indeed is a young man most rare in our time:
    Nor will you live in harmony with such a husband unless you   170
      too are rare.
Not because you are not excellent do I now warn you this way,
    But because, at my urging, you can be even more well-disposed.
This I owe you for such a spouse, who loves me
    Even as Pirithous loved Theseus.
To him, I pray, may you, late ripening, join with joy the years of   175
      your life,
    O maiden united to a worthy man.

: VIII :

Sarca

Muses, sprung from great Jove, you who make it your work
To protect from ultimate loss the deeds of famous men,

Longaque consulere involvant ne saecla tenebrae,
Neu subeant animos priscarum oblivia rerum;
5   Linquere si gelidas Permessi fluminis undas,
Murmuraque Aonii fontis rupemque potestis,
Alato quam excussus equo sacer abluit amnis;
Huc, precor, huc non sit grave concessisse: fluenta
Hic quoque sunt virides inter labentia ripas,
10 Hic quoque perspicui fontes et amoena vireta
Nec procul umbrosae valles tacitique recessus,
Prataque nec pictis distincta coloribus absunt.
Benaci ad ripam dulces captabimus umbras,
Antiquos donec Sarcae referamus amores
15 Et Gardae liquidas translatum nomen ad undas.
Sunt ignota quidem et multis haec obsita saeclis;
Vos meminisse tamen, vos et memorare potestis.
Eia agite, ipse lacus sternit cantantibus undam,
Nec fremitu assurgens nec fluctu concitus ullo.

20   Sarca erat Alpinos inter clarissimus amnes,
Qui montana ruens inter fragmenta sonanti
Gurgite praecipiti spumans delabitur unda.
Hic dum forte Arci per vallem et pinguia culta
Mitior allapsu leni rigat arva suasque
25 Attenuans vires per prata virentia fundit,
Tectus harundinea madidum caput extulit umbra
Gurgite de medio, circumspectansque subinde
Hinc atque hinc laevae deflexit lumina ripae.
Atque hic umbrosam prope morum visa fluentes
30 Pectere nympha comas ad solem, quas modo fontis

126

And take counsel lest darkness enfold past ages,
And forgetfulness of ancient matters take over our minds,
If you are able to leave the cool waves of the Permessus river,   5
And the murmuring of the Aonian spring and its rock,
Which the sacred stream struck by the winged horse washes,
Hither, I pray you, hither may it be no trouble to have come:
Here also are streams gliding between green banks,
Here also are clear springs and delightful glades.   10
Not far off are shadowy valleys, and silent retreats,
And meadows adorned with hues of many colors.
On Benacus' bank we will seek sweet shade,
While I tell the story of the long-ago passion of Sarca,
And how the name of Garda was transferred to these clear   15
    waters.
Indeed, these things are unknown and have been hidden for
    many ages;
You, however, have the power to remember and relate them.
Come now, bestir yourselves, the lake itself calms its waters
For your singing, neither rising with a roar, nor stirred by any
    wave.
   Sarca was brightest among the Alpine rivers,[1]   20
Which, while rushing among the mountains' crumbled roots,
Flows foaming with resounding flood in headlong surge.
Here, while by chance he was carrying his waters more gently
And with a milder current through the Arcus valley and its rich
    farmlands,
And, diminishing his force, was flowing through the greening   25
    meadows,
He raised his moist head, covered with reedy shade,
From the middle of the current, and looking all around,
Again and again he turned his eyes to the left bank.
And here, near a shady mulberry tree, a nymph was to be seen
Combing towards the sun her flowing hair which she had washed   30

Egelidi intingens secreta laverat unda.
Has illa interdum per lactea colla reflectens
Siccandas Phoebi radiis praebebat apertas,
Interdum ante ora et pulchros effundit ocellos
35 Nunc manibus mulcens, nunc pectine sedula eburno.
Linea vestis erat, sed quae potuisset Arachnes
Texta manu credi aut flavae labor esse Minervae.
Candida lina obiter tenuis disterminat auri
Virgula purpureis utrinque coercita filis.
40 Zona sinum gremio disterminat; at vaga lax
Vestis turgidulum pectus cohibebat amictu,
Pectus, quod geminis tunc primum exstare papillis
Coeperat et plenos ostendere virginis annos.
Benaco hanc olim rapta de Baldide nympha
45 Progenitam dici Gardam voluere parentes,
Cedentem nulli vultus formaeque nitore,
Quae nemora alta colunt fontesve aut stagna dearum.
Sed tunc non magno saliens Benacus ab ortu
Rivus erat, modico qui stagnans gurgite laevam
50 Vallis ad apricae partem secesserat, alta
Dum timet ad dextram labentis flumina Sarcae.
Huius ut ad roseos defixit lumina vultus,
Protinus caeruleas per venas concipit ignem
Sarca. Non assuetos meminit iam volvere cursus;
55 Ardet amans, stupet aspectu sic fixus in uno

Even now by dipping it in the hidden waters of the chilly spring.
At times bending back her milk-white neck
She spread apart her hair to dry in the sun's rays,
At times she let it fall in front of her face and lovely eyes,
Now smoothing it with her hands, now carefully with an ivory   35
    comb.
Her garment was of linen, but of the sort one could believe
Woven by the hand of Arachne or the work of golden Minerva.
A thin strip of gold runs through the white linen
And it is fastened on both sides by purple threads.
A maiden's girdle separates her bosom from her lap;   40
But her loosely shifting garment confined in its curve her swelling
    breasts,
Breasts which had only then begun to show with their twin
    nipples
And to make plain the fullness of her virgin years.
This nymph, daughter of Baldus, who had been carried off by
    Benacus,
Her parents wished to name Garda,   45
Yielding to none in the brightness of her face and form among
    those
Who dwell in the high groves and springs and pools of the
    goddesses.
But at that time Benacus, springing from humble origins,
Was a river, which, flowing from a modest pool,
Kept himself to the left side of the sunny valley,   50
While he fears the flowing waters of Sarca gliding to the right.
As he fixed his eyes on her rosy countenance,
Straightway Sarca begins to feel a fire throughout his dark blue
    veins.
Then he does not remember to flow in his usual course;
Being in love he burns, he is stunned, transfixed thus by one   55
    glance

Ut qui Gorgoneis riguit spectatus ocellis
Aut si qua in gelidis stat montibus aspera cautes.
Tunc omnem—domini quis credere possit ab igne?—
Fervere vicini fluvium stupuere coloni

60 Ireque cunctantem per campos mollius amnem
Mirati ignotas nequeunt ediscere causas.
Heu stolidae mentes et corda ignara, volucris
Quam magnae pueri vires, quam immensa potestas!
Non Phoebi caluere, sed igne Cupidinis undae.

65 Ille suo variat naturae numine leges
Ille gravi domat imperio mare, sidera, terras.
Ergo ubi dilapsi rediere ad pectora sensus
Atque sui factus compos, vestigia torsit
Paulatim Sarca ad dominam propiorque puellae

70 Adnatans: 'Salve', dixit, 'Iove digna marito,
Aut si aliquis maior Iove sit deus. En tibi meo
Pectore facta tuis sanandaque vulnera ocellis
Offero, Achilleae vulnus ceu Telephus hastae.
Sed tu non tantum meo medicina furori

75 Esse potes, verum potes ipsi aequare Tonanti,
Si me, virgo, tuis non dedignabere taedis.
Ne tamen ipsa erres de nobis nescia: Non te
Nunc aliquo credas ima de plebe rogari.
Ille ego sum aereis qui nascor in Alpibus, in quem

80 Innumeri exonerant nivium sua pondera montes;
Qui convulsa trahens non uno ex vertice saxa
Vorticibus vallem rapidis hanc Sarca pererro.

As one who having looked into the Gorgon's eyes stiffens
Or as a rough-pointed rock stands among the frozen mountains.
Then the neighboring farmers were astounded that the whole
    river boiled —
For who could believe its lord's fiery passion was the cause?
And the hesitating stream went more gently through the fields   60
And they marveled, unable to learn the hidden cause.
Alas for foolish minds and ignorant hearts, how great
Is the strength of the winged boy, how great his power!
It was not the heat of the sun which warmed those waters,
But the fire of Cupid. He alters the laws of nature by his divine   65
    power
And with his forceful command he tames the sea, the stars, and
    the earth.
Therefore when his scattered senses returned into his breast
And he was himself once more, Sarca turned his course
Little by little towards his mistress, and swimming nearer
To the girl said: "I greet you, maiden worthy to be married to   70
    Jove,
Or to a god greater than Jove if such there be. See, I lay
Before you the wounds made in my heart and healed by your
    eyes,
Like the wound Telephus received from Achilles' spear.
But you can be not just the healing of my torment,
Truly you can be equal to the Thunderer himself,   75
If, maiden, you do not disdain me for your marriage rites.
Still you may err, unaware of who I am; you should not
Now believe that you are importuned by someone of base birth.
I am one who is born in the Alpine air, into whom
Numberless mountains unburden their weight of snow;   80
I am he, Sarca, who, dragging rocks torn from many a peak,
Pass my wandering course through this valley with whirling
    foam.

Omnia cum libuit sterno sata, votaque spemque
Agricolarum eludo; at cum libet, arva remisso
85 Flumine perlustro, et florentia rura peragro,
Humorem glebis tacitum atque alimenta ministrans,
Ut poma evincant ramos atque horrea messes,
Efficio; sic finitimis dominamur in agris'.
Dicere plura parabat, at illa rubore decentes
90 Interfusa genas, veluti perfuderit ostro
Siquis ebur, roseis vel candida lilia sertis,
Effugit et medio haerentem sermone reliquit.
Non tamen idcirco desistit Sarca, sed illam
Pollicitis pariter sequitur precibusque fatigans.
95 Verum ubi dicta nihil sua proficientia cernit,
'Non sim Sarca', inquit, 'non amans ego, si meus intra
Verba precesque ignis cohiberi possit; inibo
Qua possim ratione meae succurrere flammae.
Ad vim confugiam; saepe est vis grata puellis:
100 Non exorari, sed vinci, ut honestius, optant'.
Haec dicens rapido attollit vestigia gressu,
Pone sequens; illa ut propius cognovit amantem
Adventare, fugit trepidanti exterrita cursu,
Non secus ac pavitans urgente indagine cervus.
105 Acrius ille instat, veluti cum lapsus ab alto
Accipiter penna sequitur stridente columbam;
Illa pavens tam praecipiti secat aera lapsu,
Quam quod Achaemenio telum propellitur arcu.
Tandem ubi visa fugae minui spes, quippe labantes
110 Deficiunt vires et utroque in poplite nervi,
Auxilium acclamans patrias deflectit ad undas.

When it has pleased me, I lay flat all the crops, and I mock
The prayers and hopes of the farmers; but when it pleases me, I
    glide
Through the fields with lessened force and roam the flowery   85
    countryside;
Dispensing quiet water and nourishment to the soil and crops,
I cause the fruit to subdue the tree-branches, and the harvest
The granaries; thus I hold dominion in the fields nearby."
He was preparing to say more, but she, her modest cheeks
Suffused with red, just as if someone had steeped   90
Ivory in purple, or white lilies in garlands of roses,
Fled away, and left him checked in the middle of his speech.
However Sarca does not cease on that account, but follows,
Wearying her with promises and pleas alike.
But when he sees his words are profiting nothing,   95
He says, "I would not be Sarca nor a lover, if my ardor
Could be confined to words and prayers; I will begin
To assist my passion by whatever plan I can.
I will have recourse to force; force is often pleasing to maidens:
They do not desire to be won over, as it is more honorable   100
To be conquered." Saying these things he turned his steps with
    swift pace,
Following behind her; when she realized her lover was
    approaching nearer,
Terrified, she fled with anxious haste,
Not unlike a deer trembling before the hurrying beaters.
He presses on more fiercely, as when, gliding down from on high   105
On whistling wings, a hawk seeks out a dove;
She in dread cleaves the air with a headlong downward flight,
Like a dart which is shot from a Persian bow.
At length when hope in flight seemed to diminish —
Indeed her strength and the sinews of each knee were faltering   110
    and failing —

Sed dum terga comasque afflatu sentit anhelo
Praedonis tangi, paulum conversa parantem
Hunc videt eductis iam iam sua colla lacertis
115   Nectere. Continuo exclamans: 'Pater, o pater', inquit,
'Affer opem natae, tua si tibi pignora curae,
Si de me generum, si legitimos hymenaeos,
Si gremio tenuisse unquam de coniuge natos
Sperasti nostro, non de raptore, nepotes!'
120   Nondum haec finierat, saltu cum corpus in undas
Misit et ima petens patriis complexibus haesit.
Diriguit primum tanta spe lusus amator;
Inde solo figens oculos et mente moratus
Paulisper: 'Praeda est in nostris cassibus', inquit;
125   'Vicimus; optato iam iam potiemur amore'.
Dixit et in vitreas Benaci proruit undas
Atque illum his audens compellat vocibus ultro:
'Quam mihi legitimis fungi tua filia taedis
Desposco, illa tuis poterat divellier ulnis
130   Atque ante ora rapi. Si qua olim lege maritus
Factus es ipse, mihi fieri libuisset eadem.
Nec desunt vires — tu testis — ad omnia; verum
Ex aequo tecum est animus, Benace, pacisci.

Calling aloud for help, she turns away towards her father's waters.
But when she feels her back and her hair touched
By the panting breath of him who would carry her off, turning a
    little,
She sees him ready with arm thrust out now, even now
To grasp her neck. Straightway crying out, she says: "Father, O   115
    father,
Bring help to your daughter, if your child means aught to you,
If you hope for a son-in-law from me, if you desire proper
    wedding rites,
If ever you want to hold in your lap grandchildren
From my lawful husband, not from a rapist!"
She had barely finished when with a leap she flung her body   120
Into the water and seeking the depths, fastened herself in her
    father's embrace.
Her lover, cheated of his great hope, at first stood rigid;
Then fixing his eyes on the ground and having stilled his mind
    for a moment,
He said, "The prize is in my snare;
I have won; at this very instant I am in possession of my chosen   125
    love."
So he spoke and rushed headlong into the glassy waves of
    Benacus,
And of his own accord daringly addressed the river with these
    words:
"Though I demand to perform a proper marriage with your
    daughter,
I have the power to snatch her from your arms
And carry her off before your face. Since you yourself once   130
Became a husband on that principle, I willingly would do the
    same.
I do not lack the strength—you are my witness—to do anything;
But my resolve is to make a fair bargain with you, Benacus.

Legitimos Gardae, divos quod tu ipse precari
135 Nunquam ausus, nunquam tibi quod contingere posset
Sperasses, thalamos peto: pacem aeternaque tecum
Foedera percutiam: inter nos satis hactenus esto
Ira certatum atque odio. Quam ferre maritis
Consuevere nurus dotem, non ferre recuso
140 Ipse meae sponsae. Mansuri pignus amoris
Confundam mea regna tuis, discrimen aquarum
Sit nullum inter nos, nomen cedamus uterque,
Tu natae ut dotem exsolvas, ego munera nuptae.
Garda tui simul et nostri sit gurgitis heres.
145 Atque hic praecipue nostro qui flumine cretus
Hanc vallem implebit magni lacus aequoris instar,
Ventura ut posthac connubia nostra loquantur
Saecula et aeternum nostros testentur amores,
Signetur placet egregio de nomine Gardae,
150 Garda sit ut nullo per me non nobilis aevo'.
        His pater auditis fugat omnem mente timorem
Atque odium; bene consultum nataeque sibique
Esse putat vel coniugio vel munere tanto.
Moxque manum iuveni intendens haec insuper addit:
155 'Non haec, Sarca, deum veniunt sine numine; mentem
Caelicolum pater hanc tibi summo inspirat Olympo,
Qui statuens odiis ut res utriusque sepultis
Laetius assurgant, paribus communia regna haec
Auspiciis iubet et sceptris moderemur eisdem.

I seek a legitimate wedding with Garda, something for which you
    never
Dared pray to the gods, something which you never hoped   135
Could happen; I will fashion an eternal compact of peace
With you; let us put an end to strife,
Anger and hate. The dowry which girls
Are wont to bring to their husbands, I myself do not refuse
To bring to my betrothed. As a pledge of my lasting love   140
I will mix my realm with yours; let there be no distinction
Of waters between us, and let us both give up our names,
So that you may pay a dowry to your daughter, and I give gifts to
    the bride.
Let Garda be the heir of both your waters and mine.
And it seems good that the lake, which, created here   145
From our streams, will fill this valley like a mighty sea,
So that ages to come might speak of our marriage
And bear everlasting witness to our affection,
Be called by the glorious name of Garda,
So that through me Garda may be renowned in every age."   150
    When he had heard these things, her father drives all fear
And hatred from his mind; he thinks that it is a good plan
For his daughter and himself, for both the marriage and the gift
    are great.
Thereupon, holding out his hand to the youth, he added these
    words as well:
"This, Sarca, does not come without the divine power of the   155
    gods;
The father of the heaven-dwellers breathes this idea into you
From high Olympus, he who, deciding that with hatreds buried
The affairs of each of us should prosper more happily, orders that
    we rule
These kingdoms in common, with like auspices, and with shared
    power.

160 Nulla tuis per me fuerit contentio dictis.
     Cuncta probo, gener ipse places ante omnia; natam
     Unica quae nostrae spes est iucunda senectae,
     Quod tibi quodque illi sit faustum, spondeo; dextra haec
     Polliciti et veri posthac sit pignus amoris'.
165 Inde manum pallentis adhuc multumque timentis
     Attollit natae, generoque innectit et: 'Esto
     Hic', inquit, 'tuus auspicibus dis, Garda, maritus,
     Cum quo mox pulchra videam te prole parentem'.
     Illa verecundo niveum os perfusa rubore
170 Sidereos terrae vultus et lumina figit,
     Insperata premens occulta gaudia mente.
         Ergo diem placuit certam statuisse, iugales
     Qua thalamos ineant, qua sollemnes hymenaeos
     Concelebrent: it finitimas vaga fama per urbes,
175 Perque agros, montes, vicinaque flumina, perque
     Silvicolas Dryades et amantes rura Napaeas.
         Antrum ingens fuit excelsa sub rupe cavati
     Montis, ab ingressu patulo quod protinus ore
     Panditur introrsum, mox in spatia ampla recedens
180 Humida per varios partitur tecta recessus.
     Desuper irriguo dependent pumice saxa,
     et circum viridi stant picta sedilia musco.
     Vestibuli ad dextram ramis florentibus hortos
     Aprici claudunt scopuli, quibus aspera nulla

On my part there will be no opposition to your words.   160
I approve of everything, above all, you yourself please me as son-
    in-law;
I promise, my daughter, who is the special sweet hope of my old
    age,
And may it turn out well both for you and for her; let this right
    hand
Be the pledge of my true and promised love from now on."
Then he raised up the hand of his daughter, still pale   165
And fearful, and joined it to his son-in-law, and said,
"Be this man your husband, Garda, under auspicious gods;
With him may I see you soon as the parent of beautiful
    offspring."
She, her snow-white face suffused with modest red,
Kept her face and starry eyes fixed on the ground,   170
Hiding the unhoped-for joys deep within her mind.
    Thus he was happy to appoint a certain day on which they
        might enter
Their nuptial chamber and celebrate their solemn marriage rites.
The story, spread abroad, reaches the neighboring cities,
It reaches the fields, mountains, and neighboring rivers,   175
The forest-dwelling dryads and the dell-nymphs, lovers of the
    countryside.
    There was a huge cave under the lofty cliff
Of a hollow mountain, which extends from its entrance at the
    wide mouth
Continuously inward, soon receding into wide spaces,
And dividing its watery dwelling into various chambers.   180
Rocks hang down from above, the soft stone dripping,
And all around stand seats colored with green moss.
On the right the sun-drenched rockwalls of the antechamber
    enclose
Gardens with flowering branches from which no rough storm

185   Tempestas viridem foliorum excussit honorem.
      Non annus variare vices, non tempora norunt.
      Semper odoratis pendet vindemia citris
      Aurea, surgenti semper subit altera foetu;
      Quaeque super gravibus pomis nova poma recumbunt,
190   Prospectu vario tabulata per alta renident.
          His quae Massylio quondam servata draconi
      Herculeae carpsere manus, his naufragus heros
      Dulichius quae Corcyreis miratus in hortis,
      Invidisse queant. Haec magni regia Sarcae
195   Tunc fuit; huc fessum se se referebat ab undis
      Cum libuit longo vires reparare labori.
      Hic ergo in mediis thalamus penetralibus ingens
      Erigitur pedibus pariter sublimis eburnis
      Et gradibus variis; tum sponda illusa figuris
200   Utraque, nunc auro nunc dente intexitur Indo.
      Hic natis coniuncta suis depicta Cytheris,
      Ut quondam levi devecta per aequora concha
      Rorantesque comas per colla effusa madebat,
      Cetera nuda, nisi ambrosiis quod tecta capillis.
205   Incensam manus una facem, manus altera ceston,
      Quo praecincta, tenet. Discordes iungit amantes
      Hoc illa et dulci unanimes enutrit amore.
      Illi Nereidum viridis chorus annatat exstans
      Pectoribus totis ab aqua roseisque papillis,
210   Quas super aligerum ludens volat agmen Amorum.
      Spicula torquentur vario distincta metallo.
      Ipsa etiam genitrix puerorum visere lusus

Ever struck off the green adornment of leaves.   185
Neither the year nor the season know any turn or variation.
Always a golden vintage hangs down from the aromatic citrus-
      trees,
Always a second crop climbs up the springing shoots.
And the new fruits that lie atop their ripened fellows,
Gleam high embowered with varied view.   190
   The fruit guarded by the Afric dragon which the hands of
      Hercules[2]
Once plucked or that which the shipwrecked hero
Ulysses marveled at in the gardens of Corcyra
Could have envied these. This then was the palace
Of great Sarca; hither he used to betake himself from his waters   195
When, tired from long toil, it pleased him to restore his strength.
Here, therefore, amid the inner rooms a huge marriage bed
Is erected, raised up on either side by ivory feet
And varied steps; the bed-frame, intricately worked on either side
With figures, was interwoven now with gold and now with   200
      Indian ivory.
Here was embroidered Venus with her offspring,[3]
As once when carried on a shell along the tops of the waves
She moistened the dewy hair spread out along her neck,
The rest of her naked, except where clothed by her ambrosial
      hair.
One hand holds a burning torch, the other the girdle   205
With which she herself is bound. With it she joins discordant
      lovers
And nurtures with sweet love those of one mind.
A band of Nereids swims up to her, rising from the water
To show their sea-green breasts and rosy nipples,
Over whom a wingèd band of cupids flies in play.   210
They hurl darts set off by parti-colored metal.
Even while the mother of the boys herself exults to see

Dum gestit, dulces dum admovit ad oscula natos,
Saucia non viso interdum praecordia telo
215   Sentit et occulto suspirat pectoris igne.
Conclavi torus in medio velatur amictu
Purpureo, spinis horrens quem carduus ambit
Aureus, et foliis et lento vimine limbum
Saepius intexens et eodem margine currens.
220   Parte alia priscis pendent variata figuris
Aulaea, intextis quae non Atrabata Gallis
Misere aut Morinum extremae gens ultima terrae,
Sed quae Parmensi doctae de vellere nymphae
Texuerant vario pariter distincta colore
225   Et facie. Satyros alibi colludere nymphis
Inspiceres, alibi insidias praetendere et illas
Frigus ad umbrosum furtim captare iacentes.
At procul hinc agmen ramosis comibus errat
Cervorum, incessu gestans capita alta superbo.
230   Illic auriti lepores, capreaeque fugaces,
Demissis aliae longis cervicibus herbas
Attondent, aliae per mollia prata recurnbunt,
Nonnullae arrectis pavitantes auribus adstant.
     Ergo dies optata aderat; montana relinquit
235   Proxima quisque; ruunt Baldi de vertice nymphae
Grandia vimineis portantes dona canistris,
Quaeque Nagum educto positum sub vertice, quaeque
Torbilis ima colunt oleis bene consita saxa.
Tum Melsemninae vallis quae rura frequentant,
240   Quaeque tuis, Lenaee pater, clarissima donis

Their play, while she urges her sweet offspring to kisses,
Her heart, wounded by an unseen weapon, feels its force
And she sighs for the fire hidden in her breast.   215
The bed in the middle of the chamber is covered with a robe
Of purple, around which winds a golden thistle bristling
With spines, its borders thickly interwoven with leaves
And pliant osier, running along the same edge.
On the other side hangs elaborate tapestries decorated   220
With ancient signs, which the Atrabatae, famed for
Gallic weavings, had not sent, nor the Morini, the last people
At the edge of the earth, but which expert nymphs had woven
From wool of Parma, variegated equally with different hues
And shapes. Here you can see satyrs playing together   225
With nymphs; there they hold out snares and stealthily
Seize the nymphs as they lie in the cool shade.
For on this side in the distance a herd of deer with branching
    antlers
Wander, bearing their heads high with a proud gait.
And on that side are long-eared hares and swift roes;   230
Some crop the grass with their long necks bent down,
Others lie about on the soft sward,
Some stand still, trembling with ears pricked.
    Thus, the longed-for day was at hand; each guest leaves
The nearby mountains; nymphs hurry from the peak of Baldus[4]   235
Carrying great gifts in osier baskets,
And those who dwell beneath the high summit of Nagus, and
    those
Who live on its lowest reaches well-planted with Torbilian olive-
    trees,
Then those who frequent the country areas of the valley of
    Melsemnina,
And those, father Lenaeus, who frequent estates, not far from   240
    here,

Praedia non procul hinc, mensas quis nulla secundas
Uberius decorant pomis aut dulcibus uvis.
  Quatuor ante alias forma venere sorores
Egregia, fidibus doctae et cantare peritae,
245 Nobilis antiquo Nogarolum a sanguine proles.
Harum si ingenii cultum respexeris, ipsae
Pierides poterunt cunctas genuisse videri.
Si libuit spectare manus, didicisse putabis
Pingere acu et tractare colos monstrante Minerva.
250 Vigilius pater ipse suo nam rure docendas
A teneris patrias annis curaverat artes;
Vigilius, quo non Musis dilectior alter,
Sive modis libet imparibus connectere carmen,
Sive libet fortes armare ad proelia reges.
255 Hae passim alternis inter se vocibus aptant
Quod canere ad thalamum carmen geniale parabant.
Aemula quis totidem mittebat clara puellas
Sirmio, quae docti numeros cantare Catulli
Assuetae, Aeoliis poterant contendere plectris.
260 Te quoque, coniugii licet averseris honores,
Virgineum statuens nunquam violare pudorem,
Huc misisse nurus perhibent, Tritonia virgo,
Illa ex arce tuo nomen quae a nomine sumpsit.
Ipsa etiam antiquum dederat quis Tuscia nomen
265 Moenia, turmatim laetos misere colonos.
Hos Hammone satus rex idem idemque sacerdos
Salodius pulcher ducebat, tempora sacris

Famous for your gifts and with whose fruit or sweet grapes
None decorate their second courses more luxuriously.
   Before the others come four sisters
Of glorious beauty, learnèd with the lyre and skillful at singing,
Noble offspring from the ancient bloodline of the Nogarola.[5]   245
If you had considered the cultivation of their minds,
The Muses themselves could seem to have begotten all of them.
If it pleased you to look at their handiwork, you would think that
    they
Had learned embroidery and wool-working under the tutelage of
    Minerva.
Vigilius himself, their father, on his own estate had taken pains   250
To have them taught their ancestral skills from a tender age;
Vigilius, than whom no other is more beloved by the Muses,
Whether it pleases him to weave together a poem of unequal
    beat
Or whether he enjoys equipping brave kings for battle.
These nymphs, everywhere in antiphonal interchange, are   255
    practicing
The marriage-song which they were preparing to sing beside the
    marriage bed.
Noble Sirmio in rivalry sent an equal number of maidens
Who, used to singing in the meters of learnèd Catullus,
Could contend against the lyres of Aeolia.
They say that you also, Minerva, though you shun all marriage   260
    rites,
Having decided never to violate your maiden chastity,
Sent hither young married women
From the stronghold which takes its name from yours.
Also the walls, to which Tuscia had given its ancient name,
Sent happy farmers in throngs.   265
Their king, the noble Salodius, son of Hammon,
Who was also their priest, led them, his temples bound

Incinctus vittis, qui post haud tempore longo
Fundavit dixitque suo de nomine pulchrum
270 Salodium, antiquam migrans quo transtulit urbem.
Adde Garignani cymbis quicumque frequentant
Littora piscosi; ponuntur retia, cessant
Cuspide depositi nodosae ab harundinis hami;
Qua libuit tuto lascivit piscis in unda
275 Nec timet insidias, impuneque seligit aurum
Carpius, in sicca naxae feriantur harena.
Ipse etiam horrisonis descendens montibus Oenus
Vicino cupiens Athesi placuisse roganti
Nympharum commissa viris longa agmina mittit.
280 Nymphis compressae corpusque et bracchia vestes
Substringunt, gremium crispo sinuatur amictu,
Colla humerosque breves claudunt velaminis orbes
Pectora nectentes et candida guttura nexu
Aurato, tum serta premunt his florea crines,
285 His flava incingunt gemmantes tempora cycli.
Intactis facies nivibus certare, capilli
Flaventi possunt auro, tum lumine partim
Caeruleo, partim glaucis variantur ocellis.
At iuvenes tunicas pertusi in mille fenestras,
290 Et patrio pictas gestantes more lacernas
Virgatosque sagos, incedunt ordine longo.
Tympana rauca animos et acuto tibia cantu
Exhilarant, gressumque sono moderantur eodem.
Arma illis humero ferratae cuspidis hasta
295 Et lateri fidus, qui numquam ponitur, ensis.

With holy fillets, he who not long after founded a city
And called it lovely Salodium⁶ from his own name,
To which he migrated, transferring his ancient city.   270
Add to these the people who with their boats filled the shores
Of Garignanum,⁷ abounding in fish; nets are put aside, and
    hooks
Cease their work, detached from the tips of the knotty rod.
Pleased thereby, the fish sports safely in the waves,
And fears no plot, and the carp picks up gold without peril,   275
While the fish-traps rest on the dry shore.
Even Oenus himself, coming down from the dreadful sounding
    mountains
And wishing to please Athesis, his neighbor, since he had asked,
Sends a big bevy of nymphs pledged to husbands.
Tight robes press on the bodies and arms of the nymphs,   280
Their bosoms are wound round by a fluttering garment,
Brief circlets of veiling, bound at their breasts
And gleaming throats with a knot of gold, cover their necks
And shoulders while flowery garlands press their hair,
And circles adorned with gems bind their gleaming temples.   285
Their faces could vie with virgin snow, their hair
With yellow gold, while some are graced
With deep-blue eyes and some with grey.
Moreover, young men, their tunics pierced with a thousand holes
And, according to the custom of their country, wearing variegated   290
    mantles
And striped cloaks, come forward in long ranks.
Hoarse drumbeats and the sharp sound of the flute
Make their spirits joyful, and by the same sound they govern
    their steps.
For arms they have on their shoulders a spear with an iron-clad
    point
And at their side a trusty sword which is never put down.   295

Ast Athesis magno Sarcae devinctus amore
Nec minus antiqua consanguinitate propinquus
Eligit ex omni numero turbaque clientum
Bis denos, quibus assueto compescere in alveo
300   Mandat aquas se absente, aliis hunc praeficit undis,
Hunc aliis, varient solitos ne flumina cursus.
Praecipit his curare sinus tortosque reflexus
Undarum, ast illis rectos intendere cursus
Per valles, campi spatiosa per aequora molles.
305   Ipse his compositis centum praemittit ab omni
Lectas natarum numero, totidemque ministris
Stipatus veteris petit alta palatia Baldi;
Atque ad neptis avum thalamos comitatur euntem,
Grandaevumque senem multo veneratur honore.
310   Illum mille viri laetantes, mille sequuntur
Matres atque nurus, pueri intactaeque puellae.
Illa patrem blando compellat Hamadryas ore,
Illa salutat avum, tendentes bracchia parvos
Protendunt aliae poscentis ad oscula natos,
315   Omnibus his tenues capitum velamina vittae
Exertis immissae humeris, virgataque multis
Palla modis late niveos circumtegit artus.
Tu quoque barbarico nimium Verona furori
Obvia et Alpinae infelix male proxima genti,
320   Posterior nulli officiis donisque fuisses,

Moreover Athesis,[8] bound to Sarca with great devotion,
No less than by his ancient blood-relationship as a kinsman,
Selects from the whole throng of his clientage twice ten
Followers, whom he orders to contain his waters in their usual
    channel
While he is away: this one to oversee some parts of the stream,   300
That one others, lest the river try to vary its accustomed course.
He orders these to see to the windings and the deep-curving
    bends
Of the stream, and those to direct a straight flow
Through the gentle valleys and the broad surfaces of the fields.
With these matters set right, he himself sends ahead one   305
    hundred daughters,
Chosen from his whole number, and he, with an equal number
Of manservants as attendants, seeks out the lofty palaces of old
    Baldus;
And he accompanies the grandfather as he goes
To his granddaughter's wedding, and attends that elderly man
    with full honors.
A thousand rejoicing husbands follow him and a thousand   310
    matrons,
As well as young married women, boys, and virgin girls.
The hamadryad addresses her father with gentle speech;
She greets her grandfather, and the others, extending their arms,
Stretch out their little children to ask for kisses.
All had, as a covering for their heads, gossamer fillets, dropping   315
Onto their naked shoulders, and a mantle, striped in a variety of
    ways,
Offers an ample cover for their snowy limbs.
You also, ill-starred Verona, too exposed to the madness of
    barbarians,
And, unluckily, too near the Alpine peoples,
Would have been second to none in courtesies and gifts.   320

Ni tua cinxissent fulgentes aere cohortes
Moenia, et horrisonis quateret tunc ictibus urbem
Plurima contorquens ferri grave machina pondus,
    His super advenit Phoebi Thebana sacerdos
325 Interpres Manto, quae post tibi, Mantua, nomen
Indidit, auspiciis postquam felicibus urbem
Filius et Musis dilectas condidit arces.
    Venerat Hesperiam paucis haec ante diebus
Crudeles fugiens Dircaea ex urbe tyrannos,
330 Cui pater ipse suas primis monstrarat ab annis
Solamen rapti quondam sibi luminis artes
Fatidicas dederatque ignaram haud esse futuri.
    Haec ut coniugium dis hoc auctoribus esse
Decretum atque huius venturum a stirpe nepotem,
335 Inferat ingenio qui se sublatus Olympo,
Praescia fatorum cernebat, laeta penates
Confertos hominum turba matrumque subibat,
Gratatura novis, quibus haec ignota, propinquis.
    Decedunt omnes vati, mirantur et omnes
340 Illam incedentem et longa se veste ferentem;
Tum lauro et niveis redimitam tempora vittis
Insigni ante alias venerati sede locarunt.
        Interea positis omnes longo ordine mensis
Discumbunt, epulas cumulatis lancibus alte
345 Praecincti apponunt famuli; tum pocula cuique
Stant sua Creteo primum spumantia Baccho;
Inde mero nigrum simulanti plena Falernum;

If troops gleaming with bronze had not girded your walls;
Were not numerous catapults, hurling a great mass of iron,
At that moment shaking the city with dreadful-sounding blows.
    Besides these, the Theban priestess, Manto, approaches,
Prophetess of Apollo, who later bestowed a name on you,   325
    Mantua,
After her son, under happy auspices, had founded
A city and citadels beloved of the Muses.
A few days earlier she had come to Italy,
Fleeing the cruel despots of the city of Thebes,
She to whom from her earliest years Jupiter himself had offered   330
Prophetic skills as comfort for her ravaged sight,
And had granted that she be fully aware of the future.
When she announces that this marriage is decreed on the
    authority
Of the gods, and that a grandchild would come from this stock,
    and when
Foreknowing the fates, she perceived that by his genius   335
He would be raised to Olympus, happily she approaches
The household gods, thronged with a crowd of men and
    mothers,
About to bring joy to her new neighbors to whom these things
    were unknown.
Everyone gives way to the seeress, and all marvel at her
As she approaches, clothed in a long robe;   340
Then, her temples crowned with laurel and white fillets,
They reverently place her forthwith on a seat before the others.
    Meanwhile all recline at the tables placed in a long row,
And servants, their garments gathered up, place before them
A banquet with platters heaped high; then, first, goblets are put   345
    down
For each one, foaming to the brim with Cretan wine;
Then goblets full with wine like dark Falernian;

Mox Tridentinae servant quae frigida cellae
Pressaque nobilibus ponuntur Rhaetica prelis,
350   Quaeque dedit fervens ardenti sole Maranum,
Quaeque incincta iugis Annonia vallis apertis.
Tum variare dapes pergunt semesaque tollunt
Fercula, substituunt alio condita sapore.
Integer has onerat mensas aper, has simul implent
355   Cervorum et verubus caprearum tosta colurnis
Viscera, non desunt lepores variaeque volucres,
Et pavo et perdix et habens a Phaside nomen,
Quem genitrix quondam crudeli caede peremptum
Apposuit patriis epulandum perfida mensis.
360   Postquam epulis fine imposito, sublatus edendi
Est amor, assurgunt choreis iuvenesque nurusque,
In numerumque pedes concordi lege moventes
Alternis agitant deductum cantibus orbem,
Aut bini inter se manibus per mutua nexis
365   Saltantes incompositos dant corpore motus.
Interea occiduo surgens optatus Olympo
Vesperus exacta referebat luce tenebras.
Ecce autem abductis sese penetralibus effert
Tecta verecundos croceo velamine vultus
370   Garda micans, roseo qualis cum Lucifer ortu
Oceanum linquens radianti luce tenebras
Excutit atque alios praecellens occulit ignes;

Soon the chill wine which the cellars of Trento preserve,
And Rhaetic, squeezed from noble presses, are placed before
    them,
And those vintages which Maranum produced, fiery from the   350
    glowing sun,
And those from the valley of Annonia, girt about with open
    ridges.
Then they proceed to vary the feast, and they carry off
The half-eaten dishes and put in their place savory food of a
    different flavor.
A whole boar weighs down these tables, and at the same time
They fill up the board with entrails of stags and roes, roasted   355
On spits of hazelwood, and there are hares, as well, and a variety
    of birds,
Both peacock and partridge, and the bird that takes its name
    from Phasis,
Which, done away with in cruel slaughter, a treacherous mother
Placed to be eaten upon his father's table.
    After they had made an end to feasting, and the desire   360
For food was sated, young men and women rise up in dance,
And moving their feet in rhythm according to harmonious
    agreement,
Make a drawn-out circle to alternating melodies,
Or in pairs, their hands intertwined with each other in mutual
    exchange,
Leaping, they make irregular movements with their bodies.   365
Meanwhile the longed-for Evening Star, rising in the western sky,
Brings on the shadows, even as the light is driven away.
See how Garda glitters as she removes herself
To her inner chamber, her bashful face covered
With a yellow veil, just as when the day star, leaving the ocean   370
In its rosy rising, drives away the shadows
With its gleaming light, and by excelling hides all other fires;

Haud secus illa alias forma supereminet omnes
Incedens: lecti neutro caruere parente
375 Qui pueri accenso praegestant lumine taedas.
Hanc cum egregio florentes corpore nymphae
Innumerae glomerantur concertantque iocosis
Proelia nocturnae dictis ridere palaestrae.
Quae dum sollicito meditans it pectore virgo,
380 Nunc metus ancipitem, nunc pulsant gaudia mentem.
 Tandem ubi marmoreo thalamo stratisque locata est
Purpureis, iuvenum coetu comitante procerus
Ipse vir ingreditur glauco velatus amictu
Et viridem quassans frondentis harundinis hastam.
385 Lascivire foris dictisque lacessere nuptam
Demissam vultus gaudent ipsasque puellas
Alterno invitant iuvenes contendere cantu.
Nec mora, prorumpunt Hymenaeum accire canentes,
Hi primum, argutis respondent vocibus illae;
390 Exultant iuvenes laeti, exultantque puellae,
'Teque, Hymenaee', vocant iuvenes, 'te, Hymenaee', puellae.
Et iam nox caeli medium perstrinxerat orbem
Indicens miseris curarum oblivia terris,
Cum turba et choreis et cantu fessa quievit,
395 Nec strepitu resonant ullo nec murmure tecta.
 Ecce autem varios vultu mutata colores
Assurgensque alta paulatim a sede sacerdos
Admovit thalamo se se Dircaea iugali;
Atque immota manens tacitis utriusque pererrat
400 Coniugis ora oculis, donec decreta deorum
Mente haurire queat venturaque discere fata.

In like manner does her beauty overtop that of all the other
    nymphs
As she enters; boys, chosen because they still have both parents,
Light the way with pine-torches.   375
Numberless glowing nymphs with lovely bodies
Gather round her and vie with happy words
To laugh at the battles of the night's contest.
While the maiden moves on, pondering with anxious heart,
Now fear, now joy beating in her uncertain mind.   380
    At last, when she had been placed in the marble chamber
On the purple coverlet, her tall husband, himself accompanied
By a crowd of youths, enters, covered in a grey-green cloak
And brandishing a spear made green with leafy reeds.
The young men delight to sport just outside the door and to   385
    tease
The bride, her face downcast, and they challenge
The maidens to contend with them in song for song.
Without delay, the boys break forth first in song
To summon Hymen, and then the girls answer with melodious
    voices;
The joyful youths leap up and then the maidens,   390
"You, O Hymen," call the boys, "You, O Hymen," call the girls.
And only when night had bound up the mid-circle of the
    heavens,
Declaring to the wretched earth forgetfulness of care,
Does the throng then quiet down, tired of dance and song,
Nor did the palace resound with any uproar or hubbub.   395
    Lo, now the Theban priestess, her face changed
From one color to another, rising slowly from her lofty seat,
Betakes herself to the wedding chamber;
And, standing still, she moves her silent eyes over the faces
Of the bridal pair, until she can draw into her mind   400
The decrees of the gods and learn their coming destiny.

Verum ubi caelestis visa est arcana senatus
Concepisse satis, tunc longa silentia rumpens
Expectata diu tandem haec in verba resolvit:
405   'Quis circum thalamos fulgor radiare decoros,
Quem video? Non hic facibus diffunditur alte
Demissis, nitor est humana lampade maior
Vividiorque, deos nobis denuntiat hic, qui
Ambrosius sentitur odor, venisse vocatos.
410   Ecce Hymenaeus adest auspex et regia Iuno
Pronuba, pulvinar thalami complexus uterque
Assidet, auratoque super Concordia lecto
Laeta volat. Citharam plectra Grynaeus eburno
Percutit auratam, viridis cui laurus obumbrat
415   Tempora, Cirrhaeo modo quam de vertice Musae
Decerptam molli contexuerant hyacintho.
Lanificas etiam tres hic adstare sorores
Cernimus intortis ducentes stamina fusis,
Immoto decreta Iovis quae condita fato
420   Distribuunt miseris mortalibus; aurea magnis
Fila trahunt heroibus, et qui fortibus ausis,
Et qui praeclaris potuerunt scandere caelum
Ingeniis, numeroque addi meruere deorum.
Talia sunt saeclis, ni fallor, Garda, futuris
425   Aurea, quae nostro debentur pensa nepoti.
Nam ne te fugiat, quibus ingrediare iugales
Auspiciis thalamos, quibus aut connubia fatis
Haec fieri voluit magni dominator Olympi,
Accipe, fatidicus quae dat mihi noscere Phoebus:

When she seems to have fully absorbed the secrets
Of the heavenly senate, breaking her long silence
She finally reveals these things in long-awaited words:
   "What is the brightness that I see radiating around the lovely   405
      chamber?
Whom do I see? The light spreading here does not fall from
Wedding-torches; its brilliance is greater than human lights
And more vibrant, it announces to us that the gods
Whom we called have come here; it is perceived as the odor of
      ambrosia.
Behold! Hymen is here as witness and royal Juno as the goddess   410
Of marriage; each having embraced the cushion of the marriage-
      bed,
Sits down, and over the gilded bedstead Harmony flies
In joy. Grynaeus strikes his golden lute
With an ivory pick, his temples dark with green laurel,
Which, plucked just now from the top of Parnassus, the Muses   415
Have interwoven with tender hyacinth.
We behold the three wool-working sisters present here,
Spinning the threads from their whirling distaffs,
They who mete out to poor mortals the decrees
Of Jove founded on immutable fate; they draw out   420
Golden threads for the great heroes, both those who from deeds
Of bravery, and those who from brilliance of their genius were
      able
To mount to heaven and deserve to be added to the number of
      the gods.
Such are the golden weights of wool, unless I am deceived, Garda,
Which in future generations are due our offspring.   425
For lest it escape you under what auspices you enter
Into marriage or by what divine laws
The ruler of great Olympus wished this union to be made,
Accept what prophetic Apollo gives me to know.

430 'Principio, Benace, tua, et tua flumina, Sarca,
Miscere inter vos et perdere nomen utrumque
Vallis ab ingressu primisque a faucibus huius
Inspicio; tum cuncta undis obducitur altis
Quam longe lateque patent quae cuncta videtis
435 Aggere seu longo lapidosis montibus arva.
Finitimi te, Garda, colent dominamque vocabunt
Reginamque lacus, quem mox velut aequoris undas
Ionii ventis et vastis fluctibus actum
Plurimus audaci sulcabit nauta carina.
440 Huius ad extremi lateris gens accola ripam
Moenia clara tuum nomen testantia ponet.
Haec tua regia erit, cedent hic sceptra volentes
Virque paterque tibi et totis dominaberis undis.
Hic quoque concipies plenaque gravaberis alvo.
445 Sed dum piscandi studio mollire tumentis
Langores uteri cupies, loca proxima adibis
Quae mox dicta tuo piscatu nomina sument.
Illic te decimus mensis gratique labores
Lucinae invadent inopinaque tempora partus
450 Corripient. Illic maturi pignora ventris
In lucem exsolves et magna vocabere mater
Ingentis nati. Hic materni limite regni
Nescius arctari collectis viribus alia
Franget claustra, minax Italas perrumpet in oras.

"To begin with, Benacus, I see that your stream and yours,   430
    too, Sarca,
Mix with each other and lose the name of each
At the entrance to this valley, indeed from its very mouth;
Then the whole valley, as far and wide as it extends,
Is covered with deep water, all the lands which you see,
As if in a long dam from the rocky mountains.   435
The neighboring people will worship you, Garda, and will call
        you
Mistress and queen of the lake, through which, just like the waters
Of the Ionian Sea, driven by the winds into huge waves,
Many a sailor will soon plow in his bold boat.
The people dwelling near the bank on the far side   440
Will build bright cities bearing witness to your name.
This will be your kingdom, your husband and your father will
Willingly yield power to you here, and you will govern all the
        waters.
Here also you will conceive and grow heavy with a full womb.
And when you will wish to soothe the swelling weariness of your   445
        womb
Through your fondness for fishing, the nearby places you go to
Will hereafter take their names from your having fished there.[9]
Thereafter the tenth month and the happy sufferings of the
        goddess
Of childbirth will fall to you, and at an unlooked-for moment
Birth-pangs will seize you. Then you will bring forth to the light   450
The love-pledge of your ripe womb and you will be called
The great mother of a mighty son. He will not know how to be
        contained
By the bounds of his mother's kingdom, but having gathered his
        forces,
He will break the high enclosure, and threateningly burst forth
        onto the lands of Italy.

455 Omnia vi patria primum loca proteret, agros
Agrorumque premet pelago mapalia vasto,
Ipsaque cum miseris rapiens armenta colonis
Regis ad Eridani fluviorum deferet undas.
Sed postquam Hesperiae caelum clementius ille
460 Hauriet et terras lustrare assuescet amoenas,
Paulatim Alpestres fremitus cursusque furentes
Exuet et patrios dediscet tempore mores,
Donec perspicuis labens et mollibus undis
Assuetas leni gaudebit flumine ripas
465 Lambere et innocuo per campos serpere lapsu
Mitius, unde agris, qua sese infundet, ab ipso
Mintius eventu dicetur nomine ducto.
Hic dum olim noster condet quas filius arces
Obductis incinget aquis stagnoque patentes
470 Piscoso campos et claram muniet urbem,
Gramineam ad ripam vitreis egressus ab undis
Comprimet Andinam nostro de sanguine nympham,
Quae non inferior forma nec nomine discors
Nec minor insigni partu te Atlante creata,
475 Qua divum interpres et culti maximus auctor
Editus eloquii, magni qui iussa parentis
Fertque refertque secans liquidas talaribus auras.
Dii magni, qualem nobis quantumque nepotem
Nostra haec Maia dabit! Felicior altera prole

First he will overrun every place with a force like his father's,   455
He will cover over fields and their habitations with a huge mass
    of water,
And snatching away the herds along with the wretched farmers
He will carry them forward to the waters of the Po, king of rivers.
But after he takes into himself the western skies in milder fashion
And becomes accustomed to survey the charming landscape,   460
By degrees he will cast off his alpine roaring and raging courses,
And will unlearn in time his ancestors' ways,
Until, gliding with clear and gentle waters, he will delight in
Lapping his wonted banks with tranquil stream
And in winding through the fields more gently with a harmless   465
Flow—whence, from the manner he pours himself over the
    fields,
He will be called Mincio, taking his name from that gentle
    movement.
Here our son will gird with spread-out waters the citadel
Which he will found, and with his covering waters and the broad
    reaches
Of the fish-filled lake he will fortify a famous city,   470
And going out from his green waves onto the grassy bank
He will mate with a Mantuan nymph of our blood,
Who is his equal in beauty and not inharmonious in name,[10]
Nor less than you, outstanding offspring of the daughter of
    Atlas,
From whom is sprung the seer of the gods, and the very great   475
Originator of the cult of eloquence, who brings and brings again
    the orders
Of our great Parent, cleaving the flowing breezes with his winged
    sandals.
Great gods! how extraordinary and how wonderful is the child
That our Maia will give us! There will not be on earth another
    more fortunate

480   Non erit in terris nec toto clarior orbe.
           Ecce novem iam nunc Aganippes fonte relicto
           Haud procul hinc tacito qua flumine Mincius errat,
           Aonias video parienti adstare sorores.
           Lucina exceptum puerum tibi tradit alendum,
485   Calliope, atque aliis curam partita Camoenis.
           Hae primum ex ipsa cui innixa puerpera lauro
           Infantem ediderat, decerptis frondibus illum
           Involvunt; hinc mollis amaracus atque rubentes
           Suave rosae et violae super insternuntur odorae.
490   Mox ubi ambrosium infundunt pro lacte liquorem
           Certatim Charites, Veneris quod munus ab alto
           Demissum attulerant haec ipsa ad munia caelo.
           Divinae huic inerat doctas vis mentis ad artes,
           Magnanimum heroum quis decantentur honores.
495   Quippe sui Venus Aeneae indignata iacere
           Nomen adhuc, scriptisque virum clarescere nullis,
           Cum Thetidis nati praeconia clara ferantur
           Docta per ora virum nullis non cognita terris,
           Constituit vatem primis effingere ab annis,
500   Qui Latios inter princeps Graiosque poetas
           Praecipuam sacro mereatur carmine laudem,
           Buccina Dardanium cuius per saecula regem
           Laudibus illustret toto resonantius orbe,
           Quam Larissaeum quae quondam ornarat Achillem.

In her offspring than she, nor one more renowned in the whole   480
     globe.
Behold now, even now, I see the nine Muses, their fountain
     abandoned,
Not far from the spot where the Mincio meanders
With silent stream, the Aonian sisters, standing near her in
     childbirth.
Lucina is handing your new-born son to you to nurse,
Calliope is there and she shares the task with the other   485
     goddesses.
These are the first to wrap him in the leaves which they had
     plucked
From the very laurel tree near which the woman in labor
Had given birth to her child; here soft marjoram and roses
Blushing with sweetness and odorous violets are being strewn.
Soon the Graces vie to pour out ambrosial liquid   490
For his mother's milk, which gift they had brought from high
     heaven,
Sent down of Venus for this very purpose.
The force of the divine mind was present that he might learn the
     arts
By which the glories of high-souled heroes might be sung.
Indeed Venus, offended that the name of Aeneas is still neglected   495
And that the hero does not shine in any writings—
While reports of the son of Thetis are famous, borne
By the mouths of men, known in every land—
Decided to fashion him as her poet from his very first years,
That he, prince among Latin and Greek poets,   500
Might earn extraordinary praise through his blest poem,
Whose trumpet will forever ennoble
The Dardan king with its praises more resoundingly
Throughout the whole world than that which
Once adorned Achilles of Larissa.

505 'Hic ergo ut florens annis adoleverit aetas
Musarum in gremio qua cura eductus, eadem
Pierias Phoebo sacer informabitur artes;
Et quia virgineum assuescet servare pudorem,
Virgineum insigni nomen cum laude merebit.

510 'Hinc patris ad ripas patulae sub tegmine fagi
Inter oves, inter bene olentia gramina, carmen
Trinacrium Latia primum cantabit avena.
Carmine quo taurus dulces oblitus amores
Deseret in silvis dilectam saepe iuvencam;

515 Ipsa quoque et vituli mater lactantis et herbae
Immemor ante pedes cantu stupefacta iacebit.
'Mox pastorales saltus et roscida linquens
Pascua per domitos cultu spatiabitur agros;
Quid faciat laetas segetes, quo sidere terram

520 Vertere conveniat, quis cultus apesque pecusque
Augeat, et viti quae cura adhibenda, docebit;
Ascraeumque canens Romana per oppida carmen
Primus Idumaeam referet tibi, Mantua, palmam.
'Hinc Phrygiam Hesperias classem deducet in oras,

525 Quam dux Dindymeae molitus monte sub Idea
Post varios casus, post mille pericula rerum
Dardanus ad Tuscas appellet Tibridis undas.
'Ante tamen Libycam vento Didonis ad urbem
Delatus magno reginam accendet amore;

530 Cui postquam occasum Troiae fraudesque Pelasgas
Erroresque suos narraverit, illa medullis
Concepti impatiens ignis submittet amori
Iampridem resides animos desuetaque corda.

"Therefore, when his flowering youth matures,   505
With the same care which reared him in the Muses' lap,
Will he, sacred to Phoebus, be shaped by the arts of Pieria;
And because he will be accustomed to guard his virgin modesty,
He will deserve the name Virgineus with special praise.[11]

"Then on the banks of his ancestral stream under the shelter   510
Of a spreading beech among the sheep, amid the sweet-smelling
      grasses,
He will be the first to sing Sicilian song on a Latin pipe.
Because of that song the bull, forgetful of delightful love
Will often abandon his beloved heifer in the forest;
The mother, forgetful of her nursling calf and of the grass,   515
Will also of her own accord lie before his feet, transfixed by his
      song.

"Soon, leaving the pastoral glades and dewy pastures,
He will make his way through fields tamed by cultivation;
He will teach what makes crops rich, under what star
It is fitting to turn the earth, what tending enriches   520
Bees and herds, and what care one should give to vines;
Reciting his Hesiodic poem through the towns of Rome,
He first will bring back the Idumaean palm to you, Mantua.

"After this he will lead to western shores the Trojan fleet,
Which the Dardan commander had built under the mount of   525
      Cybele's Ida,
And after many different disasters, after a thousand dangers
Will conduct it to the Etruscan waters of the Tiber.

"Before that, however, borne away by the wind to the Libyan
      city
Of Dido, he will enflame the queen with a great love;
After he has described to her the fall of Troy   530
The perfidy of the Greeks and his own wanderings, she, unable
To endure the fire conceived in her inmost being, will give over
To love a soul long quiet and an unaccustomed heart.

Sed postquam Iliacas monitu Iovis aequora puppes
535   E specula aequatis velis sulcare videbit,
Pertundet Phrygio flammantia pectora ferro.
    'Ille iterum Siculas vento compulsus ad oras
Persolvet patrio ludos et clara sepulcro
Funera. Chalcidicas post haec adnabit ad arces
540   Ingressusque lacus Stygios penetrabit ad umbras
Pallentes Erebi, obductis loca caeca tenebris
Elysiasque domos viset sedesque piorum.
Tantum amor et cari poterit suadere parentis
Magnanimo pietas nato laudumque cupido!
545   'Mox Superum reginae odiis, ubi semina belli
Clam sata Dardanios inter Latiosque vigebunt,
Coniuge promissa Phrygius fraudabitur heros,
Ipsaque causa novi rursus nova femina belli
Accendet formosa procos ad proelia reges.
550   Tum claros ad bella duces populosque ruentes
Urbibus ex variis vates varia induet arma,
Inque aciem turmas equitum peditumque catervas
Committens campos miseranda strage replebit
Arvaque purpureis obducet sanguinis undis
555   Ausoniae, donec decusso flore virorum
Et multis hominum demissis millibus Orco
Coniuge et aetherea Turnus spoliabitur aura.
    'Tunc vero invidia superum, ne munera tanta
Si possessa diu miseris mortalibus essent,
560   Clara potensque hominum nimio plus gloria surgat,

But after she spies from her watchtower the Trojan ships
Cleaving the sea with well-matched sails, because of Jove's   535
     warning,
She will transfix her burning breast with the Phrygian's sword.
     "He, again driven by wind toward the shores of Sicily,
Will pay his debt of games and a noble funeral at his father's
Tomb. Afterwards he will sail to the city of Cumae,
And, having entered upon the Stygian waters, will pass down   540
To the pale shades of Erebus, and will see the blind places
     covered in shadow
And the abodes of Elysium, and the seats of the blessed.
So much can love and piety towards a dear sire
Urge a high-souled son yearning for praise!
     "Soon, through the hatred of the queen of the gods, when the   545
     seeds of war
Sown secretly between the Trojan and Latin peoples begin to
     ripen,
The Trojan hero will be defrauded of his promised bride,
And a new and beautiful woman, the cause herself of a new war,
Will inflame the suitor-kings to battle.
Then the poet will clothe the famous kings and the peoples   550
Rushing to war from the various cities with many kinds of arms,
And forming into battle-lines the squadrons of horsemen and
Crowds of foot-soldiers, he will fill the fields with a pitiable
     slaughter,
And cover the land of Ausonia with red waves of blood.
Until with the flower of manhood cut down,   555
And many thousands of men sent down to the lower world,
Turnus will be robbed of both a spouse and the breath of life.
     "But then, lest so many gifts be possessed for a long time
By wretched mortals, lest the evident and powerful glory
Of men rise up too much, the ill-will of the gods   560

Eripieris humo mediisque locaberis astris
Aeternum caelo et terris victure poeta.
Victure aeternum, nam docta Neapolis ossa
Montibus in Calabris primum defleta, sacrato
565 Antinianeis tumulo tua condet in hortis,
Posteritas ubi te venerabitur omnis et aetas
Successura tuos imitabitur aemula cantus
Intendetque suos tua per vestigia gressus.
Tunc tibi vicinis lectos Sebetides agris
570 Et quae Pausilippi et quae Nesidos alumnae,
Certatim flores gremio calathisque ferentes
Ad tua odoratos effundent busta maniplos.
Immo etiam erectis aris tibi sacra quotannis
Thura dabit studiosa cohors, numenque vocabit
575 Ad sua quisque tuum conceptis carmina votis.
    'Te duce fraternas acies Thebanaque septem
Castra ducum dulci cantabit STATIUS ore
Carmineque Haemonium Latio illustrabit Achillem.
    'Te duce divinus longo post tempore vates
580 Proximus ingenio accedens IOVIANUS et arte
Prisca poetarurn studia intermissa novabit,
Advertens modulosque tuos numerosque decoros.
Nec temere hinc animos sumens sese efferet extra
Terrarum tractus, perque ardua nubila tranans,
585 Unde nives terris, unde imber et horrida grando
Dicet, et unde altos ferientia fulmina montes,
Donec olorinis sublatus ad aethera pennis

Will snatch you from the earth and will place you amid the stars,
A poet who lives forever in heaven and on earth.
O you will be forever living, for learnèd Naples will bury
Your bones, first mourned in the Calabrian hills,
In a blessed tomb in the gardens of Antinianeus,   565
Where all who come after will venerate you, and the age to come
Will imitate your poems in jealous rivalry,
And direct their feet in the path you have trtodden.
Then for you nymphs of Sebestos and those who are nurslings
Of Posillipo and of Nesis, bringing in the folds of their garments   570
And in baskets flowers that they have vied to pick in the
     neighboring fields,
Will pour out their sweet-smelling armfuls at your tomb.
Indeed at altars built for you a devoted band will offer
Holy incense every year, and each will summon your spirit
To his poems with carefully devised prayers.   575
     "Following your example Statius[12] with melodious speech will
          sing
About battle-lines of brothers and the seven camps of Theban
          leaders,
And will do honor in Latin poetry to Thessalian Achilles.
     "Following your example after a long time the divine Pontano,[13]
Approaching nearest in intellect and in art,   580
Will renew the venerable study of poesy which had been broken
          off,
Turning again towards your measures and stately meters.
Putting on your spirit, not rashly, he will take himself
Beyond the lands of earth, and moving through the lofty clouds
Will describe whence snow comes to earth, whence rainstorms   585
          come
And rough hail, and whence thunderbolts strike the high
          mountains.
Until, lifted to the upper air on swan's wings,

Perque domos caeli perque alta vagabitur astra,
Describens quae signa cadant, quaeque orta resurgant.
590 'Te quoque sollerti doctus suspendere carmen
Iudicio teneris imitari assuescet ab annis
ACTIUS, Arcadicis quem grex eductus ab agris
Et Glauci a liquidis chorus admirabitur undis,
Ad Mergellinas dum nectet carmina turres.
595 Hunc tu virgineos partus prolemque Tonantis
Ad nostras hominum delendas sanguine culpas
Demissam et poenas pro nobis morte luendas
Concinere et tecum numeris certare docebis,
Idque adeo in templo quod sumptu atque arte superbum
600 Egregia, divo gentili ponet ad ima
Collis tristitias animo curasque fugantis.
ACTIUS ille sua ornabit qui saecula cultu
Ingenii, clarisque viris tenerisque puellis
Deliciae, toto vivens cantabitur orbe.
605 'His ergo atque aliis post saecula mille futuris
Sidus ut Arctoum sulcantibus aequora nautis
Dux eris, aeternosque inter numerabere divos.
Salve, magne parens vatum antistesque verende
Musarum, ingenio quo non divinior alter
610 Ortus adhuc neque venturis orietur in annis.
Salve, magne nepos; tibi nunc orditur avorum

He will wander through the dwelling-places of heaven and the
      lofty stars,
Portraying which stars are falling and which in their rising are
      appearing again.
  "Having been taught how to craft a poem by skillful   590
      discernment,
From his tender years Actius[14] also will grow accustomed to
      imitate you
He whom the flock led out from the fields of Arcady
And Glaucus' band will admire from their flowing waves,
While he fashions poems by the towers of Mergellina.
You will teach him to sing of the virgin birth and the offspring   595
Of the Thunderer sent down to wipe out the faults of mankind
With his blood, and the punishments atoned for on our behalf,
And to vie with you in poetic measure,
And even more in the temple,[15] proud with costly
And glorious art, which he will erect to the patron saint of his   600
      family
At the foot of the hill which puts to flight the sorrows and cares
      of the spirit.
That Actius will adorn his age by the cultivation of his spirit
And, the delight of famous men and young maidens,
He will be celebrated throughout the world even while he still
      lives.
  "To these, therefore, and to another thousand poets in after   605
      generations
You will be guide, just as the North Star is to sailors
Cleaving the waves, and will be numbered among the everliving
      gods.
Hail, great parent of poets and revered priest
Of the Muses, up to now no one with a more divine talent
Has been born nor will be born in times to come.   610
Hail, great offspring; this marriage chamber now marks the rising

Hic thalamus seriem; hinc ortus primordia sumes;
Hinc tibi clara fluet clari natalis origo.
   'Sed vos interea, dextro quos sidere iunctos
615   Fausta maritali nunc arripit hora cubili:
Eia, agite, unanimes concordi ludite lecto
Legitimoque animos Veneris connectite nodo
Vernantesque iocis gratisque amplexibus annos
Transigite et laetam laeti exercete iuventam!'

Of the long line of your descendants; your birth marks the
     beginning;
From your glorious well-spring will flow a glorious race.
  "But meanwhile you, who have been joined under a propitious
     star,
The lucky hour of your marriage-bed now enfolds you.   615
Come now, come, sport with one mind on this harmonious couch
And knit tight your souls with the knot of lawful love
And spend your verdant years in playful and pleasing embraces
And joyfully indulge your happy youth!"

APPENDIX B

: I :

Echo

Quae celebrat thermas Echo et stagna alta Neronis,
    Deludit voces concava saepe meas.
Saepe hic Narcissum expecto, simul illa moratur;
    Si queror, haec queritur; si gemo, et illa gemit.
5   Quisnam clamor? Amor. Quisnam furor? uror. An Echo?
    Echo. Quae maior poena in amore? morae.
Expectas Narcissum? issum. Quae causa morandi?
    Orandi. Num haec dicta notabit? abit.
Affuerat? fuerat. Num isthic? hic. Quem fugit iste?
10   Is te, etiam me. Quam malum amare? mare.
Num veniet? veniet. Quae spes? aes. Vincitur auro?
    Auro. Victor ero prodigus aeris? eris.
Sunt pueri fragiles? agiles. Vi muneris? aeris.
    Quis docet haec? Echo. Cur bene clamat? amat.

: II :

Petri Bembi carmen

Fessus Amor ubi Mors se pallida forte tenebat
    Hospitium ignarus sole cadente subit.

POEMS VARIOUSLY ATTRIBUTED
TO BEMBO

: I :
Echo

Echo, who frequents the warm springs and deep pools of Nero,
    Hollow Echo often mocks my words.
Often I await Narcissus here, likewise she lingers near.
    If I moan, she moans; if I sigh, she sighs.
What is this shouting? Desire. What is this uproar? I'm on fire.   5
    Is it Echo? Echo. In love what pain is worse? Delay's a curse.
Is it Narcissus you await? He's late. Why is he delaying?
    He's praying. Will he heed what you say? He goes away.
He was here? Here. Near you? Near. Whom does he flee?
    Both you and me. To love, how evil a notion? Like the ocean.   10
Will he come? He will come. What hope that we join? Coin.
    Won by gold? By gold. Will I win if I spend extravagantly? I
        grant thee.
Are young men touched? Much. By the power of gifts, you say?
    Of pay.
    Who teaches such? Echo. Why does she cry out so? She
        loves, you know.

: II :
Pietro Bembo's Poem

At sunset Love, worn out, entered unaware the inn
    Where pale Death was by chance staying.

Post epulas ambo pariter dant membra quieti;
    Surgunt cum nondum fulgeret orta dies.
5   Sic imprudentes permutavere pharetras:
    Munus abit procul hic et procul illa suum.
Mors ut conspexit valido quos fixerat ictu
    In venerem curis incaluisse novis,
Mirata est; miratur Amor, quos blanda putabat
10   Oscula iuncturos succubuisse neci.
Iratus Mortem quaerit, Mors quaerit Amorem,
    Dum putat illusam se pueri esse dolis.
Concurrunt tandem et tumidi convitia primo,
    Mox arcu intento spicula uterque parat.
15   Quod ni se mediam Thaumantias ipsa dedisset,
    Mors sua sensisset et sua tela puer.
O Thaumantias, o <minime> mortalibus aequa,
    Quis furor has partes ut tuerere fuit?
Non ego acidalio gemerem nunc saucius ictu,
20   Tutus ab immiti condicione necis.

: III :

Lycda

Lycda, fugit tempus; lascivi, lude, iocare,
    Sunt dolor et lachrymae semper in insidiis.
Tantillum credas quod tantum dicimus; una est
    Quam trahimus vivi non mora, sed morula.
5   Lycda, manum da, Lycda, manum necte, imprime, stringe,
    O Veneris facies, tactilis o facula.

After dinner both laid their limbs to rest at the same time;
　　They got up when the rising sun was not yet shining.
And so, unaware, they took each other's quivers:　　　　　　　5
　　Duty took one far in this direction, the other far in that.
When Death saw that those whom he pierced with a powerful
　　　blow
　　Grew warm with the anxieties of new love,
He was amazed; Love marvels that those, whom he thought
　　Were about to join tender kisses, sank down in death.　　10
Angry, he seeks out Death, and Death seeks out Love,
　　Thinking the while that he is a victim of the boy's tricks.
At length they meet and at first each bursts with insults,
　　Soon each readies arrows with drawn bow.
If Iris had not placed herself between them,　　　　　　　15
　　Death and the boy would each have felt the other's weapon.
O Iris, O goddess least impartial to mortals,
　　What madness was it to separate the two sides?
I would not now groan, wounded by Love's blow,
　　And would be safe from the pitiless terms of death.　　20

: III :

Lycda

Lycda, time is flying; sport, play, make jokes,
　　Sorrow and tears are ever in ambush.
You would believe trifling what we call important; the life we lead
　　Is not a lingering, but a moment.
Lycda, give me your hand, Lycda, twine your hand in mine, press　5
　　it, bind it tight,
　　O shape of Venus, O little torch of touch.

Iunge labella; parum est, iunge altius, insere linguam,
    Sic ah sic facies oscula mollicula.
Lude intus, non ore exi, pro millibus unum
10   Basiolum da, quo se insinuent animae.
Sic ah sic animae miscentur, vertimur ambo,
    In te ego tuque in me, dulce tamen morimur.
Non morimur, vitam sed vivere discimus, in te
    Vivo ego, tuque in me mollius et melius.

: IV :

Ex Bembo

Uti nives post asperas, cum hiems vice
    Blandi Favoni pellitur
Nemore e virente, sole cum primo vagum
    Tenella cerva effert pedem,
5   Et nunc aprico in colle nunc ad limpidi
    Undas loquaces rivuli,
Ipsis procul pastoribus, villis procul
    Amata tondet gramina
Nullum sagittae ictum timens, nullum dolum
10   Cum latere vulnus accipit,
Sic ipse nullum suspicans miser malum
    Ibam die illo, Delia,
Tui quo ocelli fulgidis stellis pares
    Quas Vesper accendit Polo,
15   Tacente nocte, pectus hoc letalibus
    Tot sauciarunt spiculis.

Join your lips with mine; that's not enough, join them further,
  put in your tongue,
 Thus, ah, thus you will make tender kisses.
Play within, do not leave my mouth, instead of a thousand[1]
  Give me one special kiss, by which our souls will entwine. 10
Thus, ah thus, our souls are mixed, we both are altered,
 I in you and you in me, we die,[2] but how sweetly.
We do not die, but rather we learn to live life, I live
 In you, and you in me softer and better far.

: IV :

From Bembo

Just as after bitter snows, when winter in its turn
 Is driven away by the soft breeze of spring
From the greening grove, when at the first sun
 The tender doe lifts up her wandering foot,
And now on the warm hillside, now by the speaking waters 5
 Of the clear stream,
Far from the shepherds themselves, far from any houses
 She crops the grasses she loves,
Fearing no arrow's blow, no guile,
 She receives in her side a wound, 10
So poor me, suspecting no evil,
 When I was going along on that day, Delia,
Your eyes, like the glittering stars
 Which Vesper kindles in the vault of heaven,
In the silence of night, wounded this heart 15
 With their oh! so many deadly darts.

: V :

Ad Angelum Gabrielem gratulatio

Maxima facundae subiit certamina linguae
    Iam puer et, patriae caros amplexus honores,
    Rite salutavit venientia munera noster
    Angelus et primam gaudet decorare iuventam.
5   Nunc, o Phoebe pater, tuus est cantandus alumnus!
    Pande sacros latices inconcessumque profanis
    Limen, et, umbriferi grata inter frigora luci,
    Tende chelyn: doctae veniant ad plectra sorores
    Inque gyrum graciles, Clio ducente choreas,
10   Hanc pergant celebrare diem, Libethron et omnis
    Collis ovet, cupiantque ipsae descendere laurus.
    Tu modo iampridem, nostrae spes altera vitae,
    Et morum studiique comes, quem Tonis honestus
    Posceret, et caro laudaret Nisus amico,
15   Disce palatinos iuvenis perferre labores,
    Otiaque in magnas mutare Heliconia curas
    Et Musas vestire toga. Tibi protinus ipsa
    Monstrabit Fortuna viam, Virtusque magistra
    Ducet, ubi emeriti magna inter praemia ludi,
20   Candida perpetuae speres praeconia famae.
    Quis mihi, laudato (precor) et surgenti sodali,
    Laetitiae votique modus? Procul omnis abesto
    Livor edax tristesque metus curaeque malignae,
    Et properent hilares lusus et nuda voluptas,
25   Et favor, et laeta praestans victoria palma.

: V :

Song of Congratulation to Angelo Gabriel

Now the youth has taken upon himself great contests
   Of eloquent language and, embracing the precious honors
   Of his native land, our Angelo has duly recognized the duties
   That are coming and rejoices to win honor for his young
      manhood.
Now, O father Phoebus, we must sing of your foster-child!   5
   Reveal the sacred waters and the threshold not granted
   To the uninitiated, and within the grateful coolness of the
      shadowy grove
   Tune your lyre: let the learned sisters assemble at the sound,
   And with Clio leading their elegant dances in a circle,
   Let them hasten to celebrate this day, let Libethron and every   10
      hill
   Rejoice, and let the very laurels yearn to come down.
   For now you, the other hope of my life and long
   The companion of my ways and studies, whom upright Tonis
   Asked for and Nisus praised as its dear friend,
   Learn while a youth to undertake the tasks of government,   15
   To exchange the leisure of Helicon for greater responsibilities
   And to clothe your Muses with a toga. For you forthwith
   Fortune herself will show the way, and Virtue, ours teacher,
   Will lead you where, amid the great rewards of the completed
      contest,
   You may hope for the clear trumpets of undying fame.   20
   Shall I put a limit on joy and good wishes for my rising
   And (I pray) praiseworthy comrade? Let all gnawing envy
   Be far away, all sad fear and malicious anxieties,
   And let happy sports and naked pleasure hasten here
   And goodwill and victory sporting her joyous palm.   25

Spargite vos leves violas et olentia serta,
Naides, et virides huc huc afferte corymbos,
Fronde nihil tectae, quales cum caerula Tethis
Antra subit poscitque rosas; vos littora circum
30   Luditis, ac medio languescit ab aequore Triton.
Insanire lubet, neque non cum Troica castra
Fregerat et praeda spoliisque redibat opimis
Aeacides, fesso magis applaudebat amico
Patroclus, nec, post Cretei funera monstri,
35   Laetior Actaeo venientem in littore Theseum
Haemonius longis suscepit nexibus Heros.
O semper memorande dies semperque canende,
Felix, o niveo multum signande lapillo!
Sic primas spoliare genas, floresque iuventae
40   Carpere, ac audentes decet exordirier annos.
Aspicis ut lucis alius nitor, altera Caeli
Temperies? Nosterque suos ut torqueat ignes
Fortius, et tanto timeat iam Phoebus alumno?
Tales credibile est ipsum Pythone perempto
45   Adduxisse dies; sed quid nunc Aethere ab alto
Incendit nubes? heuque fragor? an ne Tonanti
Tristia suppositis mittuntur fulmina terris?
Ille quidem raro purus tonat, ite, profani.
En Deus (en, procul este, Deus), talaria cerno
50   Anguesque et subiti gestamina nota galeri.
Quisquis ades, precibus nunc nunc votisque favete,

You Naiads, sprinkle tender violets and fragrant garlands,
And bring hither, O hither, the green of ivy clusters,
Naiads, bare of even a leaf, such as when sea-blue Tethys
Enters her caves and asks for roses; you are playing
Along the shore and Triton tires of the deep sea.   30
It is delightful to play the madman as, when Achilles
Had shattered the Trojan camps and returned with booty
And rich spoils, Patroclus greatly cheered his exhausted friend,
Nor, after the death of the Cretan monster
Was the Thessalian hero any happier to receive   35
In a long embrace Theseus returning to the Athenian shore.
O day always to be remembered and always to be sung about,
   O happy day, much to be marked with a white stone!
   Thus it is fitting to shave his cheeks for the first time, to pluck
   The flowers of youth, and for the years of daring to begin.   40
   Do you see how there is the brightness of another light, a new
   Mildness to the sky? How our sun spins his fires more
      strongly
   And how Phoebus now fears for such a foster-child?
   It is believable that, with the Python killed, he himself has
   Brought days like these; but now what kindles the clouds   45
   From the high heaven? And O, is that a crashing? Are
      grievous
   Lightning bolts being sent to the low-lying earth by the
      Thunderer?
   Indeed, he is thundering, unwontedly, in the clear air; so
      depart, unclean ones.
   Lo, it is a god — lo, keep back! It is a god! — I see his winged
      sandals,
   His snakes, and the well-known ornaments of his priestly   50
      headdress.[1]
   Whoever you are, come near now, O now incline to our
      prayers and pleas,

Quidne ferat tacito, iubeatne attendite vultu.
Ipse Deum (si fas) paucis prius ore rogabo:
'Salve, magnorum scrutator fide Deorum,
55   Praevisum longe numero mihi, quae modo portas
Sint bona, sint multos multum iucunda per annos.
Sit laevum, sit triste nihil Te, grate, precamur.'
Vix bene finieram, cum protinus ille reductis
Sistit iter pennis, vacuumque per aera pendens
60   Sparsit odorato pandentes flore Penates,
Et timbrae foliis et amantis littora Myrti,
Atque ait: 'O nostra, iuvenis, dignissima virga,
Adriacos inter proles spectanda nepotes,
Non te fas sine me (redeant modo talia saepe)
65   Hanc, Gabriel, transire diem, mihi nec tua festa,
Nec chorus hic merito, nec tu fraudandus honore es,
Ipse huc ex alto mecum venisset Olympo
Iuppiter, ut stabat, non ullum versus in annum,
Sed labor e toto venientia numina caelo
70   Gratatum et laetos ista ob tua munera divos
Suscipere est illi; iam nec tam Dardana curae
Praeda, nec Iliacus tantum dilectus Iulus.
Is tibi (nec poterat maius dare munus) ab illa
Gente dedit patriam, quae cum bene plurima ponto
75   Imperet ut terris, ipsam illi subdere Cretem
Maluit, atque omnes iussit servire per annos.

Give ear to what he brings, attend to what he orders with
    silent aspect.
I myself (if it is right) will ask the god briefly with my own
    mouth:
"Hail, faithful watcher of the great gods,
We pray you, gracious one, that what you have just now   55
    brought
Be good, be filled with joy for many years,
Be in no way baleful, in no way sorrowful."
Scarce had I finished, when straightway with lowered wings
He checked his flight, and hovering in the empty air he
    sprinkled
My outstretched household gods with a sweet-smelling flower,   60
With leaves of thyme and the myrtle that loves the shore,
And said, "O youth, offspring most worthy of our wand,
One to be admired among the descendants of the Adriatic,
It is not right, Gabriel, that you pass this day without me,
(And may such days often return!); it is not right that your   65
    feast,
Nor this chorus nor you be cheated of the honor you deserve.
Jupiter himself would have come hither with me from high
    Olympus,
Where he was standing, turned toward no particular year,
But it is his work to felicitate the divinities coming
From all of heaven and to receive the gods   70
Happy because of your gifts; he showed less care for
Dardan booty; nor was Trojan Julus so beloved.
He has given to you (nor could he give a greater gift)
A fatherland from that race, which, since its excellent rule
    extends farther on sea
Than on land, has preferred to subdue Crete itself,[2]   75
And has ordered it to be subservient for all time.

Ille etiam, cum te nuper Lucina sub auras
Protulit, et teneros perfudit nectare vultus
Formavitque genas, ne non aequalis ab omni
80   Parte fores, grate concessit munera formae,
Binaque de nostro posuit tibi nomina caelo.
Tunc quoque cum primos coepisti fingere gressus,
Et pedibus te ferre tuis, meditataque verba
Promere, et ostensum blandus vocitare parentem,
85   "Huic steteris custos", dixit "mi nate, tuisque
Crescentem puerum comitatus gressibus, ore hoc
Primum iter, et facilis cursus moderate iuventae.
Discat opes animi, doctasque excalleat artes,
Et multum aequales, et multum disserat annos.
90   Post quoque cum veniet matura et serior aetas
Hunc doleant ipsi se non habuisse priores."
'Ex illo mihi tu cordi, ceu pulla columbae
Proles, aut Libycae modo nata leaenula matri,
Mox etiam, cum tu Adriacos transire per aestus
95   Hesperiosque sinus, mores cultusque locorum
Discere et insueto velles durare labori,
Assensi, iuvique vias, reditusque secundos
In patriam, tutaque dedi consistere terra.
Me duce, Caphareos scopulas, Syrtesque sonantes
100   Et Siculam rabiem posses atque ultima ponti
Littora et occiduam securus visere Thylem.
Sed iuvet hoc alios, et totum circuat orbem
Sisyphius sanguis: te magni grata senatus

He also, when the Goddess of childbirth lately brought you
    forth
To the air, and bathed your tender face with nectar
And shaped your cheeks, lest you be unequal
In any part, graciously granted you gifts of beauty,   80
And in our heaven he placed a twofold name for you.
Then also when you began to fashion your first steps,
And to stand on your own feet, and to produce thoughtful
    words,
And charmingly to call your parent by name when he appeared,
He said to me, 'Son, may you stand as guardian to this child,   85
And with your steps accompany the growing boy, by this word
Govern his first path and guide the easy journey of his youth.
Let him learn the riches of the mind, and let him master the
    learnèd arts,
And let him excel his peers, setting his years in good order.
Afterwards, too, when maturity and later age come   90
Let his elders themselves grieve that they did not have him for
    a peer'.
"From that time you have been dear to me, like the dark offspring
    Of a dove, or a little lioness born of a Libyan mother,
    Later, also, when you wished to cross the Adriatic Sea
    And the western bays, and learn the habits and customs   95
    Of other places and endure unaccustomed hardships,
    I agreed and I assisted your journey and favorable return
    To your native land, and I allowed you to come to rest on safe
        ground.
    With me as your guide, you can safely look upon the cliffs of
        Euboea
    And the roaring Syrtes, and the raging of Sicily and the farthest   100
    Shores of the Black Sea, and the Thule at the setting of the sun.
    But let the blood of Sisyphus[3] please others, and surround
    The whole world: it should be fitting that you hope for

Munera et egregias deceat sperare secures.
105 Hoc tibi, quid quoque nunc dubitas? defendere causas
Contigit, et patriae rectos perdiscere mores
Demissum a Superis. Macte, has, macte, accipe laetas
Primitias, et dona manu sunt haec tamen ipsa
Forte annis maiora tuis, sed parvulus angues
110 Vicerat in cunnis Tirynthius, et puer inter
Iam bellare viros mediis gaudebat Amyclis,
Cyllareas velox Castor perstringere habenas:
Est aliquid prima se se exercere iuventa,
Altius, et magnis praecingere pectora rebus.
115 'His alios, tibi, me functo, promittere honores
Iuppiter, atque alios iussit, <tu> cunctaque fata
Et Pylios, modo perge dies, atque Aesonis annos,
Digne puer, cui laeta suas ferat Africa messes,
Et Tagus et totis Aemus decurrat arenis.'

: VI :

Jacobi Synceri Sannazari epitaphium

Quid moror? aeterni te suspicit umbra Maronis,
Et tibi vicinum donat habere locum.

The pleasing gifts of the great senate and glorious supreme
    power.
Why now do you doubt this for yourself? It has come about   105
    that someone
Has been sent from the Powers above to defend our causes
    and learn
To the full the right customs of our native land. Well done,
    well done,
Take up these happy first fruits, gifts that are perchance greater
Than your years, but Hercules as a little child overcame the   110
    snakes
In his cradle, and swift Castor as a boy rejoiced to fight with
    men
In the midst of the Spartans and to pull tight on Cyllarus' reins.
It is important to train oneself more profoundly from early
    youth,
And gird one's breast for great things.
"When I am dead, Jupiter has given orders to promise you   115
    Other honors, and still others beyond these, and all the fates
    And days of Nestor and the years of Aeson;
    Only go forward, worthy boy, for whom joyful Africa will
        bring her harvests,
    And the Tagus and the Haemus flow over all their sands."

: VI :

Epitaph for Jacopo Syncerus Sannazaro

Why do I hold back? The shade of Virgil the Eternal watches
    over you
    And bestows on you a place near him.

: VII :

Raphaelis Sanctii Urbinatis pictoris epitaphium

Hic ille est Raphael, metuit quo sospite vinci
Rerum magna parens, et moriendo mori.

: VIII :

Nicolai Boni epitaphium

Ingentem patriae gemitum lacrimasque meorum,
    Flos iuvenum primo vere cadens, merui.
Nec fata arguerim: dulce est in limine vitae
    Evasisse brevi longa pericla via.

: IX :

Augustini Folietae epitaphium

Non secus ac gelidi summis in montibus Haemi,
    Aesculeam tetigit si Iovis ira trabem,
Prostratae immensam tellus stupet inscia molem,
    Et gemit infestis sylva agitata Notis,
5   Sic iacet ardentis deiectus fulmine plumbi

: VII :

Epitaph for Raphael Sanzio of Urbino, Painter

Here is that Raphael, by whom, when he lived,
   The great parent of all things feared to be surpassed
      And, at his death, feared to die.

: VIII :

Epitaph for Nicola Boni

Falling in my first spring as the flower of young men, I have
      earned
   The great grief of my country and the tears of those near and
      dear.
I would not argue with fate: it is sweet, while on the threshold of
      life,
   To have escaped a long road of dangers by taking the short way.

: IX :

Epitaph for Agostino Foglietta

Just as on the high peaks of icy Haemus,
   If Jove's anger has touched a huge oak,
The unknowing earth is stunned by the huge mass of the fallen
      tree,
   And the forest, disturbed by the dangerous South Wind,
      groans,
So Foglietta, light of Rome and of his fatherland,   5

Et Romae et patriae lux Folieta suae.
Effundunt questus septeni ad sydera colles,
    Et Tyberis solitam pernegat ire viam,
Lamentabilibus complet vada concava bombis,
10   Extremasque iterat flebilis Echo notas.
Phaebe pater, Phaebique Novem, pia turba sorores,
    Tuque Gigantae de capite orta Iovis:
Vos quoque quem viridi quondam cinxisse corona,
    Nec piguit vestris inseruisse choris,
15   Illius extincti lachrymis decorate sepulchrum,
    Nobilis et flentes sentiat umbra Deos.

Lies dead, struck down by a bolt of burning lead.
The seven hills pour out their laments to the stars,
    And the Tiber refuses to flow in its usual bed,
It fills the curved shallows with the noise of its mourning,
    And Echo, weeping, repeats its final notes.   10
Father Apollo, and his Nine, that dutiful throng of sisters,
    And you who are sprung from the head of Jove the Gigantic:
You also it did not shame to have crowned him with a green
        wreath,
    And to have made him a member of your dances,
Adorn the tomb of him now dead with your tears   15
    And let his noble shade sense that the gods are weeping.

DE AETNA LIBER

Ad Angelum Chabrielem

1 Factum a nobis pueris est et quidem sedulo, Angele, quod meminisse te certo scio, ut fructus studiorum nostrorum, quos ferebat illa aetas non tam maturos quam uberes, semper tibi aliquos promeremus. Nam sive dolebas aliquid, sive gaudebas, quae duo sunt tenerorum animorum maxime propriae affectiones, continuo habebas aliquid a me, quod legeres, vel gratulationis, vel consolationis, imbecillum tu quidem illud et tenue, sicuti nascentia omnia et incipientia, sed tamen quod esset satis amplum futurum argumentum amoris summi erga te mei. Verum postea quam annis crescentibus et studia et iudicium increvere, nosque totos tradidimus graecis magistris erudiendos, remissiores paulatim facti sumus ad scribendum ac iam etiam minus quotidie audentiores. Itaque, quas pueri miserimus ad te lucubrationes nostras numerare aliquas possumus, quas adolescentes non possumus.

2 Quo in consilio nobis diutius permanendum esse non puto: nam ut interdum non loqui moderati hominis est, sic semper silere cum eo, quem diligas, perignavi; neque Hercule, si in officio permansimus in prima aetate, debemus nunc, tanquam inexercitati histriones, in secundo aut tertio actu corruisse; praesertim cum aemulatio tuorum studiorum, Angele, nos non excitare modo languentes possit, sed etiam incendere, quippe qui multa et praeclara habuimus a te semper habemusque quotidie et consuetudinis nostrae testimonia et doctrinae tuae. Quare sicuti pueri scriptiunculas nostras, quasi lactentis ingenii acerbitatem, detulimus ad te, sic nunc deinceps etiam ad te adolescentiae nostrae primos foetus deferemus, non quo me ipse plus ames (nam iam id fieri posse vix

ETNA

For Angelo Gabriel

I am sure you remember, Angelo, how from boyhood I always   1
tried my very best to provide you with the fruits of my studies,
fruits which were plentiful enough for my age, though not yet ma-
ture. For whether you felt grief or joy, two of the sentiments most
natural to youthful spirits, you always had some written word   •
from me of comfort or of congratulation; you might have felt this
paltry and inadequate, like anything newborn at the start of life,
but even so it would have been proof enough of my unqualified
affection. Later on, however, as my studies and judgement alike
advanced with increasing years, and my education was wholly in
the hands of Greek teachers, I gradually came to lose interest in
writing and daily became less venturesome; so that I can count up
the childish compositions I sent you, though there is nothing from
my adolescence.

Now the time has come, I think, for me to change my ways, for   2
though silence may sometimes be the sign of moderation, failure
to communicate with one you love can only suggest indolence. If
indeed I could stick to my proper duty in early youth, I certainly
should not break down now like an unrehearsed actor in the sec-
ond or third act, especially when I have your own studies, Angelo,
to emulate. This should not only stir me out of my idle ways but
also fire me on, seeing that I have always had (and still have daily)
so many remarkable proofs both of the friendship between us and
of your own scholarship. So just as when as a boy I sent you my
humble efforts, the unripened fruit of my budding talent, now and
henceforward I shall send the fresh-gathered harvest of my ripen-
ing youth, not with the intent that you should love me more (for I
fancy that could hardly be possible) but because that is how it

puto), sed plane quia ita debemus inter nos: neque enim arbitror cariorem fuisse ulli quenquam quam to sis mihi.

3   Sed de his et diximus alias satis multa, et saepe dicemus. Nunc autem, quoniam iam quotidie fere accidit postea, quam e Sicilia ego, et tu reversi sumus, ut de Aetnae incendiis interrogaremus ab iis, quibus notum est illa nos satis diligenter perspexisse, ut ea tandem molestia careremus, placuit mihi eum sermonem conscriber, quem cum Bernardo parente habui paucis post diebus, quam rediissemus, ad quem reiiciendi essent ii, qui nos deinceps quippiam de Aetna postularent. Itaque confeci librum, quo uterque nostrum communiter uteretur.

4   Nam cum essemus in Noniano et pater se, ut solebat, ante atrium in ripa Pluvici contulisset, accessi ad eum progresso iam in meridianas horas die, ubi ea, quae locuti sumus inter nos, fere ista sunt. Tibi vero nunc orationem utriusque nostrum tanquam habeatur explicabo, non tanquam recenseatur. Igitur, cum illum multa in umbra sedentem comperissem, ita initium interpellandi eum feci:

5   PETRUS BEMBUS FILIUS. Diu quidem, pater, hic sedes, et certe ripa haec virens, quam populi tuae istae densissimae inumbrant et fluvius alit, aliquanto frigidior est fortasse quam sit satis.

BERNARDUS BEMBUS PATER. Ego vero, fili, nuspiam esse libentius soleo quam in hac cum ripae tum arborum tum etiam fluminis amoenitate: neque est quod vereare nequid nobis frigus hoc noceat, praesertim in tanto aestatis ardore. Sed fecisti tu quidem perbene, qui me ab iis cogitationibus revocasti, quas et libentissime semper abiicio, cum in Nonianum venitur, et nunc quidem nobis nescio quo pacto furtim irrepserant non modo non vocantibus sed etiam invitis.

BEMBUS FILIUS. De republica scilicet cogitabas aliquid aut certe de triumviratu tuo: saepe enim ex te audivi, si fieri possit, velle te, in agris cum esses, quoniam tibi id cum modice contingeret, tum

should be between us: no one, I think, has ever been dearer to any friend than you are to me.

On this subject I have often spoken elsewhere, and often shall; now I have something else in mind. For since you and I returned from Sicily, nearly every day has brought questions about the fires of Etna from people who knew we had investigated them personally with some care; I therefore decided to set down the conversation which I had with my father Bernardo a few days after our return, to which future questioners about Etna could be referred. And so I completed this script for both of us to use alike. 3

When my father and I were staying on his estate at Noniano and he had gone off, as he always did, to sit in front of his house on the banks of the river, I joined him round about noon; what we talked about then is pretty well what you have before you, for I intend to set down the words of the two of us just as they were spoken, unrevised. Accordingly, when I found him sitting in deep shade, I opened the conversation as follows: 4

PIETRO BEMBO. You have been sitting here a long time, father, and I am sure that this bank, kept green as it is by the river and the dense shade of your favorite poplars, is perhaps rather too cold for you. 5

BERNARDO BEMBO. But there is nowhere else, my son, where I can always be so happy as in these lovely surroundings of the trees, the river and its banks. I don't think you need worry about the cold hurting me, especially in such summer heat. But you have done me a good turn in recalling me from thoughts which I am always glad to put aside whenever I come to Noniano, and had now somehow stolen into my mind unbidden and indeed, unwanted.

PIETRO BEMBO. I suppose you were thinking about the state, or at all events about the responsiblities of your triumvirate in Venice,[1] for I have often heard you say that when you were in the country—since you rarely had that good fortune, or rather, all too sel-

etiam perraro, de iis, quae in urbe agantur, tanquam lethaeo aliquo sumpto poculo, nihil omnino recordari.

6 BEMBUS PATER. Est ita, ut dicis. Nam cum ab urbe propterea me frequentiaque hominum, tanquam a fluctibus, in hunc solitudinis portum recipiam, ut relaxem a curis remittamque paulisper animum meque ipsum restituam mihi atque ad reliquos confirmem labores, ut in ludis athletae solent, qui cum aliquo in cursu desudarint, considunt parumper revocantque sese, ut sint ad reliqua postea certamina valentiores, si tamen illae ipsae me rus etiam prosequuntur, quas fugio curas et sollicitudines, profecto nihil ago. Quod mihi quidem nunc ipsum evenit, qui cum solus in hac ripa consederim, ut dignum aliquid isto silentio meditarer, ecce nos ita etiam unda illa ipsa resorbuit urbanorum negotiorum paulatimque in triumviratus mei curas delapsus sum.

B.F. Ita sane coniectabar: visus es enim mihi iandudum nescio quid multa cogitatione commentari, neque eo vultu, quo esse hic soles, hilari et soluto sed, quo te in urbe conspicimus, contractiore interdum ac gravi.

B.P. Recte coniectabare. Sed ista tandem, quoniam nimis iam molesta sunt, obliviscamur.

7 B.F. Utinam ipse id possis, pater, tibique istud, quando ira te iuvat, tam facile factu esset quam mihi. Sed omnes curae, quae quidem sint maximae, ita se habent, ut, si insequaris, non fugiant, si fugias, etiam insequantur. Munus autem istud tuum cum est ipsum negotiosissimum per sese, quippe a quo fere omnes reipublicae nostrae partes pertractantur quodque universae civitatis caeterarumque urbium nostrarum advocationem agit et sustinet, tum vero illud etiam accedit, quod tu is es, qui maxime omnium tranquillitatem animi requietemque deames, quo fit ut magis etiam illa sentias, quae te premunt.

B.P. Est, fili, est sane causa illa quidem non levis, quae mihi labores adauget meos, sed tamen, ut verum fatear, aliud quiddam

dom—you would like, if it were possible, to drink a cup of the waters of forgetfulness and so remember nothing of the city's affairs.

BERNARDO BEMBO. Yes, you are right, for when I escape from 6 the city and its crowds of people, seeking solitude here like a haven from rough waters, I hope to find a brief respite from my cares and relaxation of the mind, so that I can feel myself restored and strengthened for the labors which still await me: just as the athletes in the Games sit down for a while to recover after sweating in some race, in order to return with added vigor for the remaining contests. But if the very responsibilities and anxieties from which I flee still pursue me to the country, I gain nothing, and this is what has happened to me just now. I sat down alone on this bank intending to concentrate on thoughts worthy of such silence, when lo and behold, I found myself swept up again by that wave of civic affairs and gradually drifted back into the sea of troubles which my duties bring.

P.B. I guessed as much, for you looked as if you had long been deep in thought, but you had lost the happy, carefree expression you usually wear here, and your face was serious, and sometimes drawn into a frown such we see in town.

B.B. You guessed rightly. But let us forget about all this, as it is so unpleasant.

P.B. I only wish you could, father, and that it was as easy for you 7 to do so whenever you wanted as it is for me. But it is the nature of all really serious cares not to flee if you pursue them, but to pursue you if you attempt flight. Besides, your office is so demanding in itself, as it handles almost every concern of the republic and gives judicial aid and support both to the state as a whole and to all the other cities under our jurisdiction; and in addition, peace and tranquillity of mind are what you value beyond all other things, so that you are the more conscious of what weighs on you.

B.B. That is certainly one cause, and no small one, of the growing burden of my cares, but, to tell the truth, there is a more pressing

maius me movet quod ipsum nuper me in urbem revocaverat, sic dum sederem; revocatque saepissime.

B.F. Quid illud tandem est?

B.P. Quod reipublicae causa non commoveri neque vellem, si possem, neque possem, si velim. Nam cum ab ineunte aetate ita vitam instituerim meam, ut patriae adessem semper, prodessem cum possem; potuerim autem nonnunquam vel iuvenis et domi et foris; illa vero me saepe muneribus reliquis, saepe legationibus honestarit; eam ipse si deseram nunc, cum et experientia et consilio et auctoritate plus valeo, quid sit aliud quam si tu me iuvenis senem destituas, filius patrem?

8 B.F. Duas igitur causas praedicas, pater, curarum tuarum, duras tu quidem illas et graves, verum, quia te sciente a te ipso proveniunt, perferendas. Nam qui te idem et actionibus tradidisti, quibus otio inimicius esse quid potest? et rus amas secessusque istos tuos, quae quidem, cum multo diutius ipsis careas quam fruaris, vitam tibi illam efficiunt molestiorem, dolendum tibi non puto, si te vel illis ipsis rebus condemnes, quas fugis, vel fugias omnino, quae te iuvant. Sed illud tamen quale est, quote dixeras reipublicae causa commoveri? an te fortasse, mi pater, motus ii Galliarum perturbant, qui feuntur?

B.P. Minime illi quidem, verum admodum gaudeo te e Sicilia rediisse. Nam si aliquid evenerit, malo te hic esse, ubi omnes sumus, quam illic, ubi neminem habes tuorum.

9 B.F. Equidem adsum ac libens, cum ea de causa tum quia vobis omnibus carebamus iam nimium diu. Cave tamen putes nobis hoc Siciliensi biennio quicquam in vita fuisse iucundius.

concern which had called me back to the city while I was sitting here just now, as indeed it often does.

p.b. What is that?

b.b. The fact that I would not wish not to be concerned for the state, were it possible, nor could I, even if I wished. From my early youth I ordered my life with a purpose, to be always at my country's call and to serve her when I could; and I was in fact able to do her service several times, even as a young man, both at home and abroad. She in her turn often honored me with the offices and embassies which still awaited me; so that if I desert her now that I have gained strength in experience, wisdom and authority, would it not be comparable to your abandoning me, your old father, when you are a son in the prime of life?

p.b. Then you can give two reasons for your anxieties, father; but 8 knowing as you do how they originate in yourself, though they are harsh and burdensome, you must endure them to the end. For you have dedicated yourself to public service, the arch-enemy of a quiet life, and at the same time you love the country and your retreat here; but as you have to do without these for far longer periods than you can enjoy them, they only make your life more irksome. I don't think then that you should complain if you have only yourself to blame for the matters you would leave behind you, or if you have to give up altogether what delights you when you are here. But what is it which you said was worrying you on our country's account? Are you disturbed perhaps by the reports of movements in France?

b.b. No, scarcely at all, but I am very glad you are back from Sicily. If something happens I would rather have you here with the rest of us than there, where there are none of your people.

p.b. I am happy too to be here for the same reason, and also be- 9 cause I felt I had been away from you all too long. All the same, you mustn't think that any time in my life has been more enjoyable than these two years in Sicily.

B.P. Gaudeo et id quidem, idque ipsum ex eo suspicabamur, quod nondum ad nos cogitabatis. Sed postea quam in eum sermonem incidimus, ut de Sicilia loqueremur, narra mihi quemadmodum ea se habent, quae de Aetnaeis ignibus et feruntur passim et perleguntur: te enim accessisse illuc cum Angelo tuo totumque montem perlustrasse audiebamus; et nobis quidem certe nunc vacat. Quid enim istoc aestu agamus meridiani? neque est, quod ego soleam libentius, quam de naturae miraculis audire.

B.F. Haec vero, ut libet, modo valeam recensere, et quidem eiusmodi sunt, ut tibi audienti afferre vel magnam possint, mihi certe narranti semper aliquam afferant voluptatem; quanquam quidem iam hoc ipsum facimus nimis saepe: quam enim multis nos eadem ipsa censes, postea quam e Sicilia reversi sumus, narravisse? Sed consurge, si placet, ab hac umbra: nam in ripis quidem omnis quae fit accubatio, ea si longior est, esse admodum gravior solet; atque ad illa buxeta nostra, si tibi videtur, sedesque pergamus.

10 B.P. Periniquum tu quidem facis, qui de ignibus loquuturus ab umbra et frigore decedendum putas, sed, quando ita vis, propter aquam potius in ripa deambulemus et cum fluvio sermoni reliquo demus operam loquentes: ita mihi videbor melius tuas illas flammas Aetnaeas, si me offenderint, Pluvici mei unda temperaturus.

B.F. Illae vero neque te offendent, cure absint longissime, neque hic si adessent, restinguere illas posse Pluvicus tuus, cure mare ipsum etiam cedat illis volentibus atque earum ardoribus contrahatur.

B.P. Magnum exordium inceptas, fili, ac iam plane vix credenda sunt ista quae dicis; verum, qui ita fiat, explana id etiam mihi.

B.F. Faciam, ut iubes; sed opus est, ante quam illo veniam, ut aliqua te praedoceam deque insulae deque montis natura, quibus cognitis ad ea, quae postulas, recta pergemus via.

B.P. Age, ut libet; modo ad illa etiam aliquando veniamus: quin etiam mihi feceris gratissimum, si ea lege inceperis, ut nequod pul-

B.B. I am glad of that, and I thought as much when up to now you hadn't spared a thought for us. But now that our conversation has turned to Sicily, tell me what truth there is in the widespread reports and written accounts of the flames of Etna, for I heard that you had been up to them with your friend Angelo and explored the whole mountain, and this is surely a moment when I am free to listen. Shall we spend our mid-day in the heat you felt? There is nothing I always enjoy so much as hearing about the marvels of nature.

P.B. So long as I can describe them as I should like, they should certainly be able to give you as great a pleasure while you listen, as they always give me when I talk about them, though I do so all too often. How many people, do you suppose, have heard the same account since our return from Sicily? Now, get up, please, and come out of this shade, for lying about on riverbanks is always rather risky, if it is prolonged. Let us go to our box wood where there is a seat, if you agree.

B.P. How contrary you are, to want us to leave the cool shade just 10 when you intend to talk about fire! But as that is what you wish, let us walk along the bank near the water, and continue our conversation with the river for company. Then if your flames of Etna reach me, I think I shall be better placed to quench them in the stream of my own river.

P.B. They certainly won't reach you, for they are too far away, nor could your river put them out if they did; the sea itself has to bow to their will and shrink before their heat.

B.B. That's a fine beginning, my son: what you say is already hardly believable. Now tell me how that happens.

P.B. I'll do as you ask, but first I must teach you something about the nature of the island and the mountain; after that we will go straight on to your question.

B.B. Just as you like, as long as we get there sometime. Indeed, you will please me best if you start with the principle that nothing

chrum praetereatur, sive vidisti aliquid, sive audivisti, sive quid es
ipse commentatus.

11 B.F. Ego vero, si placet, iter tibi nostrum omne ordine ipso, quo
factum est, recensebo, teque a Messanae menibus usque in Aetnae
cacumen perducam.

B.P. Placet et cupio: incipe igitur viamque ipsam omnem reminis-
cere et tanquam recurre, si potes.

B.F. Agam sedulo id quidem. Itaque, ne te teneam diutius, quar-
tusdecimus mensis agebatur, ex quo ego et Angelus meus apud
Constantinum praeceptorem graecarum litterarum studiis exerce-
bamur, neque sane adhuc vacuum ullum tempus dederamus nobis
laboris ac ne unum interea integrum remiseramus diem.

B.P. Nimium fuistis assidui vestris in studiis adolescentes vel
etiam superstitiosi. Annum et menses novae linguae rudimentis
incubuisse nullo intermisso die? mirum, si vos vel habitudo illa
prior destituit vel color! nos tamen e navigatione traxisse vos pallo-
rem istum et maciem putabamus.

12 B.F. Ita evenit; sed en tibi, iam tandem nos ipsos respeximus. Pla-
cuit enim ut Aetnam viseremus, atque interea, dum animi relaxa-
rentur, quod efficere vel occupatissimi debeamus, tantum naturae
miraculum etiam feriati nosceremus. Ita iocundis aliquot sumptis
comitibus, qui nos perducarent, consesso equo Messanam reliqui-
mus; sed iter facientibus nobis Taurominium usque memorabile
nihil conspectum est: summa enim littora eraduntur. A leva statim
Rhegium et Brutii agri parvo primum, mox latiori maris intervallo
aperientibus sese paulatim angustiis prospectantur; a dextra colles
continui imminent, Bacchi tota feracissima plaga et Mamertinis vi-
netis minus fortasse, quam olim fuit, tanquam ab ipsa vetustate
contritis iam laudibus, sed tamen satis nunc etiam percelebris. In
medio fere itineris vel paulo amplius castellum Nisus ex aeria
montis rupe viatoribus late prospicitur, unde illud devectum Ovi-
dianum

noteworthy shall be omitted, whether it is something you have
seen or heard, or some conclusion you have drawn yourself.

P.B. My idea, if you like it, is to recount the whole of our journey, 11
in the actual order of its events, and conduct you from the walls of
Messina right up to the peak of Mount Etna.

B.B. I should like that very much; so begin, recall every detail of
the road, tread it all again, if you can.

P.B. That is just what I shall do, with due care. And so, with no
further delay: it was the fourteenth month since my friend Angelo
and I had started our study of Greek literature under our teacher
Constantine,[2] and we had never allowed ourselves any free time
from work or a single whole day's holiday.

B.B. Then you were far too assiduous in your studies for young
men, or else too conscientious. Fancy spending more than a year
poring over the elements of a new language without a single day's
break! No wonder you looked different and lost your color! We
thought you had grown thin and pale on the sea voyage.

P.B. Well, that's what happened; but see how we took thought for 12
ourselves in the end. We decided to visit Etna and, while we were
giving our brains a rest, as we needed to do however busy we were,
to spend our holiday getting to know that marvel of nature. Ac-
cordingly, we chose some pleasant companions to be our guides,
took horse and left Messina. There was nothing special to see as
far as Taormina, for the coast-line is a good deal eroded. Reggio
and the Bruttian region[3] are immediately visible on the left, first
across a narrow stretch of sea and then a broader one as the straits
gradually open out. On the right rises a line of hills, and the whole
region bears a wealth of grapes, less perhaps in the Mamertine
vineyards than formerly, as if their fame had worn thin through
very age, but still enough to be renowned today. About half way,
or a little further, travellers can see from afar the fortress of Nisus
on its lofty mountain-crag, from which comes the line of Ovid

Nisiades matres sicelidesque nurus.

Incolae vallem etiam omnem, quae subest, Nisi regionem vocant.

13 B.P. Erit isto sane modo etiam aliquid infra Taurominium memorabile. Nam de hoc poetae versu, si recte memini, nobis pueris nondum inter grammaticos conveniebar: qua quidem in re adhuc illi arbitrum si quaerunt, plane video eam controversiam posse dirimi a Niso tuo, a quo nescio quam blande caeteri hospites suscipiantur. Te certe, ut illi dicerent, etiam elegantiorem remisit. Sed sequere.

B.F. Taurominii cure veterum monumentorum reliquiae plures visuntur, templa, sepulchra, aquaeductus, quin saepe temere graeca numismata passim effodiuntur, affabre facta illa quidem, neque in aes modo insculpta, sed in argentum, sed in aurum, quod etiam Syracusis plurimum et fere per totam insulam evenit; tum etiam coctile theatrum adhuc manet paulo, quam id quod Romae vidimus, minus, nisi quod illud amphitheatrum est. Quae quidem omnia eo inspexi diligentius, quod te recordabar plurimum semper veterum hominum imaginibus monumentisque, tanquam virtutum illorum et gestarum rerum testibus, oblectari. Urbs ipsa loco praecelso atque edito sita et montium angulo promissa in pelagus prospectum maris Ionii late hinc inde dominatur: theatrum ultimam anguli rupem insedit, qua collis conspicuus ante omnem urbem in circum planitiem ducens audentior procurrit in mare, atque hinc fluctibus, inde urbe medius ipse terminatur. E Taurominitano demissi iugo et littore paulatim relicto vallemque ingressi, quam a leva Aetnae radices, a dextra Taurominitani montes efficiunt, per eam Randatium usque pervenimus novum oppidum

Mothers of Nisus and daughters of Sicily.[4]

The local people also call the whole valley beneath it "the land of Nisus."

B.B. Then there is certainly something to remember below the heights of Taormina. If I remember rightly, there was still no agreement among grammarians about this line of the poet when I was a boy, and if they are still seeking judgement on the point, I see that their argument can be cut short by the Nisus you mention. I don't know how courteously he will receive other guests, but he certainly sent you home with a better choice of words, as they themselves would say. But continue.

P.B. At Taormina a good many ruins of the ancient monuments can be seen, temples, tombs and aqueducts, and Greek coins can be dug up quite casually anywhere, all skilfully made and stamped on silver and gold as well as on bronze; the same thing frequently happens in Syracuse and almost everywhere on the island. Parts of the brick-built theatre are still standing, rather less than we saw at Rome, though that is, of course, an amphitheatre. I looked at everything the more closely because I remembered what great pleasure you always take in the monuments and representations of antiquity, as bearing witness to the virtues and exploits of the past. The town itself is situated high up on a lofty site, built out on a spur of the mountains over the sea, so as to command a wide view on both sides of the Ionian Sea; the theatre is built on the furthest rock of the spur, from which a clearly-defined hill in front of the whole town encircles it with a plateau and runs boldly out to sea, bounded by the waves on one side and by the town on the other. We came down from the ridge of Taormina, and gradually left the coast to enter a valley formed by the foothills of Etna on the left and the mountains of Taormina on the right; through this we reached Randazzo, a modern town built at the base of Etna, on the side facing away from the sea. The whole of our journey from

et in Aetnae radicibus, qua parte mediterranea despectat, situm. Iter totum a Taurominio nobis quattuor er viginti milibus passuum confectum est. Vallis sonoro et perpetuo flumine scinditur et irrigatur. Platani numerosa sylva utrasque ripas inumbrantes maximam sibi vallis partem egregiae incolae vendicarunt.

14 B.P. Ain, tandem, platanos illae habent ripae?

B.F. Pulcherrimas illas quidem et multissimas, ut non Platonem modo aut Aristotelem, scholasque omnes mitiores suis umbris invitare possint ad philosophandum, sed etiam Gymnosophistas durissimos illos quidem homines et sole admodum delectatos.

B.P. Quam vellem, ut cum earum duabus possem ego vel tribus arboribus etiam omnes illas fructiferas arbores, quas in quinquuncem dispositas habemus, commutare.

B.F. Utinam illae tibi potius, pater, iis stantibus totum Pluvicum obduxissent. Poterant enim vel universum Nonianum; sed nescio an isto sub coelo provenirent.

15 B.P. Equidem arbitror: nam illis, posteaquam in Italiam travectae sunt et quidem ab ipsa Sicilia primum, multae urbes abundavere; quanquam posteriorum hominum negligentia deperierint. Nos enim, dum Romae essemus, unam, quae in ima ripa speculi est Dianae Aricinae, pro miraculo vidimus. Sed nihil est profecto, mihi crede, nihil est, fili, ut ego semper dicere soleo, quod effici ab homine cura diligentiaque non possit. Nos enim, ut de me ipso loquar, quibus tamen, ex quo hanc villam exaedificavimus, iam inde ante quam tu esses natus, consumere hic nondum etiam licuit triginta integros dies, neque quando licebit scio, cupiam certe semper et peroptabo, vides quam multos tibi possuerimus ordines pulcherrimarum arborum vel nostratium vel advenarum? Quod si etiam platanos habuissem, nunquam illae me vivo periissent, et haberes tu quidem nunc, quo melius invitare posses Faunum tuum, et ille quo libentius accedere.

Taormina covered twenty-four miles. The valley is watered by the resounding flow of the river which divides it throughout its length, arid thick woods of plane trees shade the banks on either side and are the most noteworthy occupants of the greater part of the valley.

B.B. Did I hear you say that there are plane trees on the banks? 14

P.B. Yes, and very beautiful and numerous they are; not only Plato and Aristotle and all the more civilized schools would accept their invitation to philosophize beneath their shade, but even those stubborn naked fanatics whose pleasure hitherto has been in the heat of the sun.

B.B. If I could have just two or three of them, how gladly would I exchange all my fruit trees in their formal rows!

P.B. I would rather have them overshadow all the river Pluvico, father, and leave your orchard standing. They could certainly do that to the whole of your property, but I doubt if they would flourish in the climate here.

B.B. I agree with you, for many cities used to have large numbers 15
which had been brought over to Italy, especially from Sicily, but they died out when later generations of citizens lost interest in them. I have seen myself a single remarkable specimen when I was in Rome, which was growing at the foot of the bank below the cave of Arician Diana. But believe me, my boy, there is absolutely nothing, as I am always saying, which man cannot achieve by care and perseverance. Take me as an example: ever since I built this house, before you were born, I have never yet been free to spend thirty days at a stretch here, and I don't know when I ever shall, though that is what I always long and pray for. Yet you can see how many rows of splendid trees I have planted, both native and foreign, with you in mind. If I had also had some plane trees, they would never have died in my lifetime, and you would now have something better worth inviting your Faunus to visit; he too would be more willing to come.

16 B.F. Vellem equidem, mi pater, sed, quando id effici non potest,
oblecta te populis tuis; tum etiam, si placet, sicuti matres filiorum
nomina, qui desiderantur, in eos saepe transferunt quos habent, ita
et nos platanos illas vocemus.

B.P. Mihi veto placet illas populos semper vocari; atque haud scio
an etiam cum eas tempestas vetustasve consumpserit, ut ait ille de
quercu Mariana, tamen erit in Noniano populus, quam Bembeam
populum vocent: ita mihi quidem videtur illas aeternitati com-
mendasse suis carminibus Aurelius noster. Quare

> Quae vitreas populus arduo
> > Bembeas ad aquas vertice tollitur
> > Vivum cespitem obumbrans
> > Intonsa bicolor coma

sit semper populus, crescat, surgat altius vel aquula ista, vel poetae
versu.

17 Sed, ut ad platanos redeam, non tam mea causa istud ipsum cu-
piebam, fili, quam tua. Ego enim me oblectavi satis; tum expe-
riendo illud didici, ut nequid admirarer; neque, si quid sero ali-
quando, quod facio semper, cum licet, sive aedifico aliquid aut
paro, propterea id facio, vel quia illis omnibus rebus putem me
esse usurum, cui me ipso uti iam meo ipsius iure non licet, vel
quia non facile illa possem contemnere, quibus carerem: quid enim
mihi potest iam ad eos dies, qui mihi reliqui sunt ad vivendum,
esse non satis? Vobis ista parantur, pueri, vobis ista, inquam, non
mihi. Scio enim quam a parentibus quaesita ista dulcius accipere
soleant filii, quam ipsi facile comparare, sive quod in quaerendis
rebus plerique laborem fugimus, in partis omnes voluptatem ama-
mus, sive quod in iis, quae nobis a maioribus nostris relinquuntur,
insit etiam memoria illorum, qui tradidere, quae illa nobis nescio
quo pacto, cure sanctiora efficiat, tum certe facit multo etiam iu-
cundiora.

P.B. I should have liked that myself, father; but as it isn't possible,   16
you must be content with your poplars. Of course if you wish, like
mothers who often transfer the names of children they have lost to
those they have later, we could call them plane trees.

B.B. No, I want them always to keep their name of poplar;
and when age or storms destroy them, I fancy there will still be
some tree growing here which, like Marius's oak, people will call
Bembo's poplar, for I think our poet Aurelio⁵ will have made them
immortal through his verses:

> Bembo's poplar, soaring high,
>   Reflected in the glassy stream,
>   Overshading living turf
>   With leaves unclipped, two-coloured.⁶

So may there always be a poplar to grow and soar higher than the
famous streamlet's source or the poet's verse!

But to return to the plane trees: it was not on my own account   17
that I had this wish but on yours. I have had pleasure enough, and
experience has taught me to desire no more; and if I build some-
thing or form some plan when I have the opportunity, as I always
do, though it may be rather late in life, it is not because I expect to
make use of all these things myself (since I am not free to dispose
of myself by my own right) or because I cannot easily dispense
with what I do not possess — for what could fail to suffice me for
the remaining days of my life? No, these preparations are for
you, my children, for you, not for myself. For I know how sons are
always happier to receive what their parents provide than to ac-
quire it easily for themselves, either because most of us shirk the
effort of making acquisitions while fully enjoying the pleasure they
bring, or because the memory of the givers remains in the posses-
sions handed down to us by our ancestors, and somehow makes us
value these with greater respect and certainly delight in them
much more.

18   B.F. Mihi quidem, pater, et nunc ista carissima sunt, quae, qua es in nos amoris exuberantia, a te video dici, et erunt semper, dum vivam, fixa animo et memoriae meae, cupioque, ut ex iis ipsis rebus, quae mihi a te quaeque fratri comparantur meo, longissimam ipse nobiscum percipias voluptatem. Sed si tibi nos unquam naturae lege supervivemus, habeo alia ego (ut de me tantum loquar: nam de fratre, quanquam multa possent dici, malo illi integram causam relinquere respondendi tibi), habeo alia, inquam, quae mihi sanctissimam tui memoriam semper efficient etiam absque Noniano tuo, quippe qui me puerum educaveris non diligenter modo, sed plane, quod vere mihi videor esse dicturus, etiam religiose; habueris tecum in legationibus tuis; imbueris optimis moribus omnibusque bonis artibus, quod in te esset, ita semper institueris, ut verear, ne sim prorsus ingratissimus, ultra haec mihi a te si quid unquam relictum optavero, tum si de iis ipsis tibi non ego semper maiores gratias habuero, quam si mihi magnificas villas construxisses. Quare ista quidem de causa nihil est sane quod labores.

19   B.P. Ego veto ac multum: nam qui tibi illa praeparaverim, quae sunt longe potiora meo quidem iudicio et, ut video, etiam tuo, curandum est etiam mihi, ista tibi ut ne desint, quae cum minora quidem sint, valde tamen sunt necessaria. Quemadmodum si te quis ad coenam vocet, ferculaque afferat cum varia tum sumptuosa, vina multifariam apponat, ministros adhibeat, calices quaerat et vasa vel aurea vel gemmata, nisi statuerit triclinium, aut mensas in hortulo disposuerit, ut tibi stanti coenandum sit, certe tu illum nihilo probes magis, quam si tam multa omnino non paravisset. Ita mihi eveniet patri: nam quod te recte instituerim a puero, mecum habuerim semper, utramque linguam te docendum curarim, id est ad coenam vocasse te satis dubiam et sumptuosam, in qua depasceres, animum tuum teque ipsum conviva elegans

P.B. What you have just said to me, father, in the fullness of the 18
love you bear us, is precious to me now and for as long as I live
will always be engraved on my mind and memory; and all you
have laid up for my brother and me will, I trust, continue to give
you pleasure, in our company, for a very long time. But if in the
natural course of events we outlive you, there are other reasons (to
speak only for myself: I could say much for my brother too, but
would rather leave him to make his own answer) — other reasons,
I say, why your memory will always be most sacred to me, quite
apart from what you leave us here. You saw to my education from
boyhood not only with care, but, if I am to speak truly, with devo-
tion; you took me with you on your embassies; you trained my
character in the best manner, instructed me in all the noble arts, to
the best of your ability, so that I fear I should show myself utterly
ungrateful if I expected anything at all from you beyond what you
have done for me, and certainly if I did not feel warmer gratitude
for this than for any splendid houses you might have built for me.
So there is no need for you to make any further effort on that ac-
count.

B.B. But I shall do so all the same, for though I may have pro- 19
vided you with what is far more important in my opinion, and, I
now see, in yours, I still have to make sure that you do not lack
what are possibly minor though very necessary essentials. Suppose
a man asks you to dinner, brings on a variety of rich courses, sets
out all kinds of wine, calls his servants, asks for drinking glasses
and gold and jewelled dishes: if he has provided no dining room,
or at least put out tables in the garden, and you have to dine
standing, you would certainly think no better of him than if he
had made none of all these preparations. That will be my lot as
your father: the fact that I gave you a proper training in boyhood,
always kept you with me, saw that you learned both Latin and
Greek, was your invitation to a rich and varied repast on which to
feast your soul and delight in being a discerning guest — for we are

oblectares convivae nanque sumus omnes, dum vivimus, neque
aliud est omnis vita nostra, qua sub ista mundi luce fruimur, quam
longa concoenatio, aut, ut iam verius dicam, convictio; quod si nec
sedem ullam tibi nec umbram aliquam praebuero coenanti, hoc est
nisi viventi diversorium secessumque gratum aliquem paravero
studiis et camenis tuis, profecto non tam in illis laudabis diligen-
tiam meam, quam in his etiam culpabis negligentiam, neque tam
pulchra ea tibi esse videbuntur, quibus abundaveris, quam fuisse
illa, quibus carebis, necessaria. Ita fiet ut, cum semel abiero, tu me
saepius accuses, quam probes.

20 B.F. O mi pater, mene tam impium unquam futurum, ut te au-
deam accusare? ego te unquam accusem, pater? quid si non tu me
saepe monuisses, et ego aliquando scriptum legissem a summis ac
sapientissimis viris, animi bona esse, quae beatos homines facerent
sola ipsa per sese quaeque opis externae non egerent? ea neque
eripi posse cuiquam nec aetate senescere nec morte interire? cae-
tera omnia manca esse, labilia, momentanea, quae quoniam for-
tuna et casu regerentur, tanto esse magis quenquam, quantum illa
contemneret, vel divitem vel etiam sapientem? animos nostros ex
aetherea sede in hanc corporis labem profectos ea lege, ut ad illam
ipsam purgati aliquando reverterentur, quae hic essent despicere,
ad illa se intendere quo properarent? me vero, quem ista quan-
doque docuisses, nisi mihi villam reliqueris sylvamque platano-
rum, putas tibi esse succensurum? Non est ita, mi pater, ne putes.

21 B.P. Non puto.

B.F. Neque me tam dementem existimes velim.

B.P. Non existimo.

B.F. Quid ita igitur loquebare?

B.P. Quia noveram mores hominum, tum etiam pertentare te
prorsus volui, quam recte ista sentires. Sed omittamus haec iam
tandem, fili, atque ad eam partem sermonis, ex qua egressi sumus,
revertamur.

all guests while we live, and all the life we enjoy in the light of this world is simply a long meal taken in company, or, more accurately perhaps, a sort of companionship at table; but if I provide neither seat nor shade for your meal, that is, no pleasant lodging for your lifetime and retreat for your studies and your Muse, you will certainly find less to praise in my care for the one than to blame for my indifference to the other, and what you possess in abundance will lose its charm in comparison with the necessities you lack. The result will be that once I am gone, you will blame me more often than you will recognise my worth.

P.B. Father, how could I ever be so unfilial as to dare to blame   20
you? Should I ever do such a thing? Have you not often told me yourself (as I have read in the writings of wise and noble men) that the true riches of the spirit are what make men happy alone and unaided and need no assistance from outside? And that they can neither be taken from us nor grow old with age nor perish with death? All other things are frail and fleeting, shortlived and governed by chance and fortune, so that anyone, be he rich or wise, gains in proportion to his contempt for them; and since our souls left their heavenly abode to endure the body's corruption on the understanding that cleansed of it they should one day return, they scorn what is here, looking only to what they hasten to re-gain.[7] If this is what you taught me, do you really suppose I should be angry with you for not leaving me a country house and a wood of plane trees? You must not think that, father.

B.B. I don't.   21

P.B. I would not have you think I have lost my senses.

B.B. But I don't.

P.B. Then why did you talk like that?

B.B. Because I knew what men can be like, and I wanted to test you and see if you had the right attitude. But let us leave this sub-ject now, and go back to the point in our conversation where we digressed.

B.F. Immo vero, pater, nec revertamur: quid enim amplius nobis cum platanis illis? de iis enim loquebamur. Sed, si placet, ad Aetnam potius, de qua sermo haberi coeptus est, properemus.

B.P. Mihi vero perplacet, ira tamen, ut ne festines: tibi enim ego omnes has pomeridianas horas dico. Sed quoniam me impellente nimium iam extra Aetnae terminos provecti sumus, non committam, ut te interpellem saepius, nisi quid erit, quod de ea ipsa te rogem.

22 B.F. Sane mons ipse situ, forma, magnitudine, fertilitate, incendiis mires, demum tota sui qualitate ac specie longe conspicuus et sibi uni par est. Ab aurora mare Ionium bibit et Catanam sustinet imo in pede; cum sole descendit in insulam, qua Tyrrenum pelagus est, et quae Aeoliae appellantur; laterorsus, in septentriones vergenti, Pelorus obiicitur et Italiae angustiae sunt; contra reliqua insula subiacet tractusque ii omnes, qui cum Lilyboeo in Africam protenduntur. Ipsa Aetna radices suas fere in orbem deducit, nisi sicubi orientem et meridiem versus promisso clivo paulisper extenditur: celebs degit et nullius montis dignata coniugium caste intra suos terminos continetur. Circumitur non minus quam centum milibus passuum ascenditur fere per viginti, qua brevior via. Imi colles ac omnis radicum ambitus per oppida, et per vicos frequens inhabitatur; Baccho, Pallade, Cerere feraces terrae, armentorum omnis generis supra quam credas feracissimae. Hic amoenissima loca circunquaque, hic fluvii personantes, hic obstrepentes rivi, hic gelidissimae fontium perennitates, hic parata in floribus semper et omni verna die, ut facile quilibet puellam Proserpinam hinc fuisse raptam putet.

23   Hic arborum multiiugae species et ad umbram valentium et ad foecunditatem, in qua etiam tantum excellunt caeteras omnes arbores, ut mihi quidem magis huic loco convenire videantur ea, quae de Alcinoi hortis finxit Homerus, quam ipsi Phaeaciae; in

P.B. No, father, not there: we were talking about plane trees, and there is no more we can say about them. If you don't mind I would rather we hurried on to Etna, where our conversation started.

B.B. I should like that very much, only please don't hurry, for I am giving up all these afternoon hours to you. And as it was I who led us on to go so far from the bounds of Etna, I will be careful not to interrupt too often, unless there is something relevant on which I want to ask a question.

P.B. The mountain itself is truly remarkable, in situation, shape,   22 size and fertility, as well as for its flames; in fact it stands out from afar and is unique in nature and form. On the east side it is watered by the Ionian Sea and has Catania resting on its foot, on the west it slopes down towards the islands (called Aeolian) of the Tyrrhenian sea; on the flank facing north it is confronted by the promontary of Pelorus and the straits of Italy, and at its foot on the other side lies the rest of the island, and all the regions which stretch from ancient Lilybaeum[8] towards Africa. Etna itself is almost circular at its base, except where a slope running out extends it slightly towards the east and south; it stands solitary and aloof from union with any other mountain, untouched within its own bounds. Its circumference is not less than a hundred miles, and its ascent, by the shorter route, is about twenty. The lowest slopes and the whole circuit of foothills are thickly populated with towns and villages; the soil is fertile for vines, olives and cereals, and unbelievably good for every kind of cattle. There are lovely scenes here on every side, resounding torrents and chattering streams, and the ice-cold waters of unfailing springs; here it is always spring-time, with flowers blooming every day, so that one could easily believe that this is the spot where Proserpine was snatched away.

Here too are many varieties of tree, both shade-giving and   23 fruit-bearing, so far surpassing all other trees that the lines which Homer wrote about the gardens of Alcinous seem to me to fit this

qua certe nos, cum e Sicilia rediremus, nihil eiusmodi vidimus, quod nos tantopere oblectaret; ut etiam non inurbane Angelus meus interroganti eum cuidam ex Phaeacibus, qui nobis urbem omnem ostentarant, quidnam illi videretur, ita responderit: 'Ego, Phaeaces, debere vos quidem—inquit—Homero permultum existimo, qui vobis plura etiam tribuit quam ipsa natura'. Referam, si potero, latine; vel certe ut potero: nam adverti propterea tum etiam diligentius illum ipsum Homeri locum.

> Hic nemora in coelum late crescentia surgunt
> Punicei pomum grani malumque pirumque
> Et dulces ficus et magnae Palladis arbor
> Non illis borealis hyems, non officit aestas
> Torrida, sed placidas zephyris spirantibus auras
> Arboribus totum superat foetura per annum
> Et pomo inseruere recentia poma priori
> Et nova iam miti superadvenit uva racemo.

24 Medius mons nunc variis arboribus late sylvescit, et praecipue pinis et fagis maximam in magnitudinem multitudinemque crescentibus, quarum illae inferius, hae sublimiores sunt; nunc nudo latere arabiles in plagas extenditur, et saepe usque ad imum descendit frumentis adeo foecundus, ut credita nonnunquam in centuplam segetem cultoribus ferat. Itaque prudenter, ut multa, illud etiam prisci viri, quod nobilissimum templum Cereris in Aetna constituere: ubi enim potius dea segetum coleretur, quam ubi fruges optimae provenirent? Atque id quidem tantum de segetibus, verum ab universa Aetnae fertilitate, ut opinor fabula etiam emanavit, Aristeum giganta eo in monte ita salvum esse atque vivere, ut neque ab Aetna prematur unquam, neque flammis coelestibus inuratur, quod optimi et uberrimi essent fructus, qui per Aetnae

place better than Phaeacia itself; we certainly saw nothing so de-
lightful when we visited Corfu on our way back from Sicily, and
when one of the inhabitants who were showing us all round the
city asked my friend Angelo what he thought of it, his reply was
rather witty: "I think you owe a great deal to Homer, who be-
stowed more on you than Nature herself." I will quote the lines in
Latin, if I can, or rather as well as I can, for I made a careful note
of the relevant passage in Homer at the time.

> Here far and wide the growing trees rise high,
> With swelling pomegranates, apples and pears,
> Sweet figs and mighty Pallas' olive-tree.
> Winter's north wind and summer's torrid heat
> Disturb them not; in zephyr's gentle breeze
> The trees abound in fruit throughout the year.
> Apples come fresh and age on earlier ones,
> New grapes are piled on clusters also ripe.[9]

The middle region of the mountain is partly extensively 24
wooded with trees of many kinds, especially pines and beeches
which grow in large numbers to an immense height, the pines be-
ing shorter with the beeches towering above them; but in the areas
free from woods it opens out into arable land, often right down to
its base, and is so rich in grain that it frequently multiplies a hun-
dredfold the seed the farmers have sown. And so the men of old
showed wisdom, as so often, in setting their noblest temple to
Ceres on Mount Etna; for where else could the goddess of corn
better be worshipped than on the spot which yields the best har-
vest? Here the reference is only to corn, but the general fertility of
Etna has given rise, I think, to the legend that the giant Aristaeus
is alive and unharmed inside the mountain,[10] where Etna's weight
never presses on him nor do the fires of heaven consume him; this
comes from the fact that the produce throughout the region of
Etna is so plentiful and of the best quality, attacked neither by de-

loca nascerentur, nullo telluris vitio, nulla aeris offensi malignitate. Nam et *aristeos* Graeci quidem illos vocabant, qui vicissent in certaminibus; quod verbum ab 'optimo' deductum esse credo, quia nisi optimi non vincerent; et gigantas scimus esse filios telluris appellatos. Ita, quonian fructus universos tellus quasi mater parit, cum fructus Aetnaeos esse optimos atque uberrimos vellent dicere, tanquam caeteros superarent, fabulae datus est locus non invenuste quidem, si tibi ira videtur. Expecto enim etiam, quid tu sentias, scire abs te.

25 B.P. Mihi sane videtur: itaque redde caetera.

B.F. Reddam, pater, atque illa ipsa quidem, quae a principio postularas er quorum causa ista omnia dicta sunt: ventum est enim ad id, ut iam de ignibus loqueremur.

B.P. Verebar sane tu ne me longius provectares; quanquam quid longum mihi esse hac in re, qua de nunc agimus, atque isto in otio potest?

B.F. Curabo id quidem, ne fiat, si potero, quam potero, diligenter.

B.P. Immo Hercle fiat potius, etiam id si facere ipse, ne fiat, potes: non enim impedio. Illud autem ideo dixeram, quia te putabam ante, quam istuc accessisses, aliquandiutius erraturum.

B.F. Ego vero existimabam, pater, erravisse me sic etiam nimis diu.

B.P. Non est ita, sed, ne nunc tandem erremus, perge de ignibus, ut proposuisti: verum autem, quid tu haeres?

B.F. Pergam equidem, ut iubes: sed scin, quam in salebram inciderim?

B.P. Nihil profecto minus.

26 B.F. Dum tibi ad ignes festino, eam Aetnae partem, quae nobis una restabat de tribus (sic enim partiri soleo), et qua sine ad ignes ipsos perveniri non potest, pene omiseram suboblitus: ita Aetnam,

fect of soil nor unkindness of climate. For the Greeks called their victors in athletics *aristei,* a word which I believe to be derived from their word for "best",[11] since they would not be victors unless they were the best; and we know that the giants were called the sons of earth. Consequently, as every kind of produce is born of Mother Earth, when they wanted to say that the produce of Etna was the richest and best and exceeded any other, they located the legend there, rather pleasantly, I believe, if you agree. I should like to hear what you think.

B.B. Yes, I agree; so tell me the rest.   25

P.B. Indeed I will, and that will include what you asked about at the start, which was the reason for all I have said; for we have now come to the point where I shall talk about the fires.

B.B. Well, I was beginning to fear you were taking me up by rather a long road; though nothing should really be long for me in the subject we are discussing, and with leisure to do so.

P.B. I will do my best, if I can, to see that doesn't happen.

B.B. No, no, let it happen, even if you can stop it; I'm not preventing you. I only spoke because I thought you were going to make a long digression before you actually reached your goal.

P.B. I had in fact been thinking that I'd already been digressing for too long.

B.B. That's not so, but let us not digress further now. Carry on about the fires, as you said you would; is there anything stopping you now?

P.B. I'll carry on, as you bid me; but I must tell you that I've come to a rough bit of the road.

B.B. No, surely not.

P.B. While hurrying on to the fires I had forgotten and nearly left   26 out the part of Etna which remained out of the three (as I usually divide them) and which has to be crossed before the flames can be reached; consequently I had killed Etna like the Chimaera, and

quasi Chimaeram, caecideramus et tanquam ream capite mulctave-
ramus imprudentes. Sed agam nunc tutius ac de utroque simul lo-
quar. Superior itaque montis pars (nam iam de iis, quae infra sunt,
diximus) usque ad summum cacumen nuda variam faciem praeos-
tendit. Nam alibi semiherbosi tractus sunt intersurgentibus to-
phis, qui etiam in pedemontana regione passim visuntur; alibi per
summa ora exundans incendium saxis fluentibus totas plagas inoc-
cupavit; alibi arenarum campi magnam in longitudinem et latitu-
dinem extenduntur. In supremo crateres duo sunt, quorum alte-
rum, qui minus altissimus est, ipsi vidimus in putei rotunditatem
angustum, emissis veluti gemina sponda hinc inde saxis sulfureo
virore fumigantibus. Hunc lapidea planities ambitu angusto cir-
cuntenet, quo ut primum inscendimus, sulfureis statim nebulis et
suburenti fumo, veluti e fornace percussi ora pene retulimus gra-
dum; mox increscente audacia, qua ventus perflabat, paulatim in-
gressi craterem ipsum tetigimus manu. Effundebatur inde, sicuti
ex camino, fumus non intermissa exhalatione. Is tamen etiam
scissa per longa incendia montis cute, ventis intus furentibus, qui
eo die imperiosius bacchabantur, multis in locis sibi faciebat
exeundi viam; interdum quoque de repente ipsis sub pedibus exi-
liens manere nos uno in loco non permittebat. Quin etiam illud
accidit, ut quem locum maxime contemplabamur, quod erat saxis
nuper effusis et adhuc ignem et sulfur retinentibus incrustatus, per
hunc, qua parte concesserat in rimam, interflueret igneus rivus ac
pedes ipsos inter emissa ex rivo saxa urentia prosilirent.

27   B.P. Quod ais, peream, ni me totum commoves, fili, atque etiam
perterrefacis tua ista oratione. Quid autem saxa illa? an etiam
quenquam vestrum interlaesere?

beheaded her like a criminal without realising it. Let me proceed more cautiously, and speak about the two subjects together. The upper part of the mountain, then (for I have already spoken about the lower parts) is bare right up to its summit, but presents a varied appearance. In some places there are areas partly covered in grass with lumps of tufa sticking out here and there, such as one also sees scattered about at the foot of the mountain; in others the flames streaming out of fissures on the surface have covered whole stretches with molten lava, and elsewhere large areas of sand extend far and wide. At the top there are two craters, and the lower one we saw for ourselves: it is quite small and round like a well, encircled by smoking stones of sulphurous green color which have been poured out on both sides as if from a double-lipped cup. A stony plateau, narrow in width, runs all round, and when we first set foot on this we stepped back at once, as the clouds of sulphurous vapor and scorching smoke like that from an oven almost hit us in the face; then becoming bolder we gradually advanced, on the side from which the wind was blowing, until we could touch the actual crater with our hands. Smoke was belching out continuously as if from a furnace and, where the surface of the mountain had been split by a long line of fires, under pressure from the winds inside (which on that day were raging quite violently), it also forced an exit for itself in many places; sometimes it even broke out beneath our very feet and would not let us stay still. It also happened that we might be watching some place particularly closely because it was encrusted with stones which had only just been poured out and were still smoking and sulphurous, when it would crack open somewhere, and a stream of fire would flood it, while the stones shot out with this would scorch our feet.

B.B. What! I declare you make me tremble all over and terrify me to death with your story. And what about these stones? Were any of you hurt?

27

B.F. Neminem profecto, pater: quin etiam eorum duo, cum re-
frixissent, quae manu capi poterant, Messanam deportavimus sul-
furis partem servantia, caetera subnigra.

B.P. Quid enim vos tam ultra temere procedebatis?

B.F. Quia cum licere illic nobis tuto consistere putabamus, tum
etiam perlustrandi studio vel potius aviditate ferebamur.

B.P. An nesciebatis Plinium illum maiorem ita occidisse, dum ni-
mium diligenter, ne dicam inconsulte, Veseviana incendia perten-
taret?

28 B.F. Quid ni sciremus, pater? verum tanta nos delectatio illius
spectaculi detinebat, tanta rei novitas, tantus invaserat stupor, ut
sui ipsius iam nemo satis nostrum recordaretur. Sed missa haec fa-
ciamus, atque ad illam planitiem, de qua modo dixeram, reverta-
mur, quae quidem ita tamen perurebat ipsa, ut manus, nisi exem-
plo retulisses, offenderentur: pedes duplici calciamento ita propter
ascensus difficultatem comparato tuebamur. Ab eo cratere, quem
dixi, mons per fundae iactum insurgit ascensu difficillimo partim
salebris impedientibus, partim tardantibus arenis, et clivus statim
etiam quoquoversus impendebat. Is universi corporis vertex sum-
mus est, et tanquam in urbem arx domina, sic ille in montem pro-
minatur. Ab eius inscensu detinuere nos potentissima vis vento-
rum et exhalantes fumi. Itaque tibi de illo referre quidem aliud
nihil possum, nisi tibi ea vis recenseri, quae ab Urbano monacho
accepimus postea, Messanae cum esset, homo ille quidem verissi-
mus atque harum rerum cupientissimus sciscitator: is enim paucos
ante nos dies per summam tranquillitatem totum verticem perlus-
traverat.

B.P. Immo vero cupio: novi enim ego illum atque amo, quod te
non latet; quo mihi futura sunt haec omnia illius etiam testimonio
gratiora.

P.B. No, none of us; in fact, when two of the stones had cooled enough for us to handle, we took them back to Messina; part of them was still sulphurous, and the rest burnt quite black.

B.B. How could you be rash enough to go so near?

P.B. We thought it would be possible to stand there in safety, and we were led on by our eagerness — or perhaps our greed — to see everything.

B.B. But didn't you know that Pliny the Elder died like that, when he was too thorough (I won't say too rash) in his investigation of the fires of Vesuvius?[12]

P.B. Of course we did, father, but we were so delighted with the spectacle, and filled with such amazement at the novelty of the phenomenon, that none of us gave a thought to himself. But no more of this; let us go back to the plateau I spoke of just now, which was actually burning so hot that it would damage your hands unless you took them away at once; our feet were protected by the double shoes we had provided for the difficulty of the ascent. From the crater I have described, the mountain rises for the distance of a sling's throw, and is very difficult to climb, partly on account of the rocky patches which bar the way, partly because of the sand which holds one back; moreover the slope was overhanging all the way. The peak is the highest point of the whole massif, and rears up above the mountain like a citadel dominating a city. We were prevented from climbing it by the smoke belching out and the extreme force of the wind, so I can tell you nothing about it unless you would like me to recount what we learned later from the monk Urbano[13] when he was at Messina, a most reliable man and the keenest of investigators into matters like this; for he had walked over the whole summit a few days before us when everything was perfectly quiet.

B.B. I should like that very much. I know the man and love him, as you are aware, so that any information will be the more welcome if it comes through him.

29   B.F. Aiebat ille igitur (quando ea tibi narrari postulas, quibus tamen ego tam accedo ut credam, quam omnino si perspexissem) verticem illum esse ab ingenti cratere occupatum ambitu circiter quatuor stadiorum, eumque non usque in imum descendere eodem hiatu, sed alvum sibi intus paulatim astringere eatenus, quoad in medio centro ad evomenda montis incrementa satis amplo ore foraminatur; tum esse in summa montis corona parvum tramitem, ubi pedes firmentur; ex eo si quis declinaverit, aut in craterem obrui, aut e monte deturbari; stetisse tamen se ibi tam diu, quo barathrum exploraret; eructasse tum montem magno strepore incendia caliginosa et perurentes petras supra os, quantum sagitta quis mitteret, vel eo amplius, insurgentes; atque eum, veluti corpus vivens, non perflasse semper, sed emissa semel anima cessasse diutule, dum respiraret; tum se copiam intuendi habuisse quae vellet; mox eiectasse iterum atque iterum pari intervallo usquequaque; interea ingemere intus cavernas auditas, intremere etiam tonitruis montem sub pedibus magno et formidoloso iis, qui aderant, horrore; ex quo illud mirum videtur, quod qui tum strepitus per tranquillitatem sentiebantur, eorum a nobis nihil auditum sit in tanta ferocia ventorum.

30   B.P. Illud vero nec videatur, fili, neque plane ipsum est mirum. Constat enim, quemadmodum scriptores tradidere, simul cum ventis Aetnae animam immutari; et quo flante fumos tantum et caligines exhalet, eo ponente modo puras modo crassiores flammas emittere pro surgentium ventorum qualitate; aliquando etiam effundi torrentes ignium varia exundatione, prout intra montis viscera pinguia vel exilia incrementa sunt. Qae cum ita se habeant, illud etiam posse fieri quis est qui neget, lenissima unius venti aura eos strepitus intra montem excitari, qui vel furente altero non

P.B. Well then, as you want me to tell you all this, let me say that I   29
am as sure of his accuracy as if I had seen everything myself. He
said that the entire summit was taken up by a vast crater about
half a mile in circumference, but the way down to its depths was
not always by the same aperture, since the bowels of the mountain
would remain closed for a while until they opened in mid-center
with a hole wide enough to discharge the accumulated matter
within. There was also a narrow path round the highest point of
the mountain which gave a firm foothold, but anyone leaving it
would fall straight into the crater or roll down the mountain side;
however, he stood there long enough to have a good look at the
chasm; then the mountain erupted with a loud explosion, shooting
out smoking flames and burning stones which rose above his head,
a bow-shot high or more. It did not do this continuously, but let
out a blast and then, like something alive, paused for a while to
take breath, which gave him a chance to see what he wanted. Then
it erupted again and again, always after the same pauses, while all
the time the abyss within could be heard groaning, and the moun-
tain quaked with thunder beneath their feet, with deep shudders
so as to strike terror into those who were present. It seems surpris-
ing that none of these sounds which were heard on a quiet day
was audible to us when it was blowing such a gale.

B.B. It should not surprise you, my son, for there is nothing re-   30
markable in this. It is generally agreed (in accordance with the
written tradition) that Etna's exhalations change along with the
winds. When one blows it may breathe out only smoke and
fumes, but as that dies down, it starts to emit flames which may
be clear or smoky, depending on the nature of the rising winds.
There are times too when streams of fire come pouring out, and
their floods vary with the material building up in the bowels of the
mountain which can be solid or light. Consequently no one can
deny that the uproar within can be set off by a gentle breeze from
a single wind, though another can blow hard and nothing hap-

queant? non enim quam perflet quis, sed quam intret in montem quamque se in cavernas illius inque viscera insinuet, est spectandum.

31 B.F. Intra montem igitur tu, tanquam intra pectus animam, sic accipi ab Aetna ventos putas, quibus illa modo spirat leniter, modo vehementius incitatur?

B.P. Sane quidem, nisi tamen veriora illa sunt, quae de Typhoeo, deque Encelado poetarum fabulositas concinnavit.

B.F. Verissima illa quidem fabella est; sed perge tu mihi atque etiam, pater huius incendii causas redde, si placet: nam ex incolis quidem inventus est nemo, qui ea nobis paulo verius explicaret.

B.P. Pergam, ut libet; sed non prius id faciam, quam mihi dixeris, quomodo illud sit, quod tu verissimam fabellam dixisti.

B.F. Quia sane ea demum verissima fabula est, quae nihil habet veritatis.

B.P. Pulchre nimirum; atque isto modo ego etiam dicere historiam falsissimam possum, ut ea sit demum falsissime historia, quae falsi habeat nihil.

32 B.F. Non sequitur istud, pater; sed nos dialecticen e captiosis sophistarum circulis coronisque ne avocemus: satis enim habet illic negotii. Quare age, mi pater; explana potius illa nobis, quae petimus: ea incendia unde oriantur et orta quomodo perdurent.

B.P. Tu vero postulas etiam sine dialecticis philosophari; quod quidem ipsum fieri quam possit, vel alio tempore ex te ipso cognosces vel cum voles audies de me. Nunc vero age, philosophemur. Interea tamen paulisper hoc in cespite considamus. Neque enim ullis adhuc Nonianis legibus cautum est, ne quis temere quoquo in cespite considat, quemadmodum olim urbanis ne quoquo in solio; et ego iam deambulando defessus sum.

B.F. Tu vero quiesce, ut libet et quandiu libet; ego autem et stare adhuc possum libentius et te ira melius auscultabo.

pens. It is not so much a question of which wind is blowing as how it enters the mountain and penetrates into its depths and innermost parts.

P.B. You think then that Mount Etna draws in the winds, as the 31 lungs draw breath, and these make it sometimes breathe gently and sometimes be more violently roused?

B.B. That is right, unless there is more truth in the legend the poets tell about Typhoeus and Enceladus.[14]

P.B. There is certainly a lot of truth in the fable; however, carry on, please, and tell me the cause of the fire, for I found none of the local people could give me an adequate explanation.

B.B. Certainly, as you want me to, but not before I hear from you why you said there was a lot of truth in the fable.

P.B. A fable is surely nearest the truth when there is no truth in its own account.

B.B. Well said; then according to your logic I can call history far from the truth, since it must be nearest falsehood when there is nothing false in its account.

P.B. That doesn't follow, father! But don't let us lure dialectic away 32 from the hair-splitting groups and gatherings of the sophists: she has plenty to keep her busy there. Come then, give me an answer to my question: how do these fires start, and once started, how have they gone on so long?

B.B. Then you are asking me to philosophize without employing dialectic? How that could be possible you'll have to find out for yourself one day, or else learn from me when you are willing to listen. However, for the moment let us be philosophers, and sit down on the grass for a while, for I don't think there is anything yet in the laws of this place against sitting where you like on the grass, as there once used to be a law for Roman citizens against choosing their own seats, and I am tired now of walking about.

P.B. You have a rest where you like and as long as you like, but I would rather stay on my feet: I can listen to you better that way.

33   B.P. Et quidem hoc etiam licet; sed quoniam ita vis ut, quibus de ignibus ego te antea interrogaram, de iis tu me nunc audias disserentem, brevi expediam quae sentio; neque enim nimis multa sunt. Tellus quidem omnis, Bembe fili, sicuti nostra corpora, foraminibus canalibusque distincta est et tanquam venis internotata; sive quod omnino coire non potest, quae specie quidem multum sibimet differat intra sese; sive quod aut gignit ipsa semper aliquid aut interimit et immutat, neque unum idem omnis atque eodem permanet; sive ut alii tradidere, et quidem principes in philosophia viri, quia plane vivit ipsa atque a mundi anima vitam trahens ab eadem mundi anima extra intraque perlustratur.

34   Sed in omni tellure nuspiam maiores fistulae aut meatus ampliores sunt, quam iis in locis, quae vel mari vicina sunt vel a mari protenus alluuntur. Nam cum exedit semper mare consumitque suopte contactu suaque natura omnia, tum autem, si partem est nactum aliquam debiliorem membraque non adeo robusta telluris, erodit illa multo facillime pergitque in viscera ipsa, quam potest. Itaque cum in aliena regna sibi viam faciat, ventis etiam facit: ex quo fit, ut loca quaeque maritima maxime terraemotibus subiecta sint, parum mediterranea. Quod si etiam in sulfuris venas venti furentes inciderint, tum incendia suscitantur sane non difficulter, quoniam et in sulfure concipiendi permagna ignis vis inest et venti etiam aliena succendunt vi sua. Haec autem tu ut in Aetna accidant omnia, vide, quippe, ut modo tute dixisti, quae mare in radicibus habeat, quae sulfurea sit, quae cavernosa, seu quod natura ita fuerit semper ipsa, seu quod salo aliquando subexesa ventos admiserit aestuantes, per quos idonea flammae materies incenderetur.

B.B. Well, that's also permitted. And now, as you want to hear me   33
discoursing about the fires about which I was previously question-
ing you, I can soon state my view, for I have not a great deal to
say.[15] The whole earth, Pietro, like our own bodies, is divided by
different orifices and channels and, as it were, marked out by
veins, either because nothing can be entirely combined into a
whole if its components differ widely from each other, or because
it is always spontaneously generating or destroying and changing
something, so that it never remains wholly one and the same; or,
as others have said, and among them leading philosophers, be-
cause it has its own independent existence, drawing its life from
the World Soul and pervaded by this same Soul within and with-
out.[16]

But throughout the earth there are nowhere broader channels   34
or freer passages than in places which are either near the sea or
continuously washed by it. For the sea is always eroding and con-
suming everything by its contact and its very nature, and, more-
over, if it has seized on some weaker place, some limb of earth
which lacks strength to resist, it eats its way through with the
greatest of ease, and is thus able to penetrate into the very vitals of
the earth. The path into alien territory which it thus makes for it-
self is also open to the winds; consequently, places near the sea are
particularly subject to earthquakes, though they seldom occur in-
land. Now, if strong winds come in contact with veins of sulphur,
fires break out quite easily, as sulphur has a great propensity to
catch fire and winds can set other elements alight by their own
force. You can see how all this happens in the case of Etna, for, as
you have just said, it has the sea at its foot, and it is sulphurous
and full of cavities, either because it has always naturally been like
that, or because at some time it has been eroded by salt water and
opened a way in for the pressure of winds which set fire to
inflammable material.

35   Habes, unde incendia oriantur Aetnae tuae; habe nunc quo-
modo etiam orta perdurent. In quo quidem nolo ego te illud admi-
rari, quod vulgus solet: magnum esse scilicet tantas flammas, tam
immensos ignes post hominum memoriam semper habuisse, quo
alerentur. Quid est enim magnum ipsi magistrae rerum omnium
et parenti naturae? quid arduum? quid illa tandem non potest?
Qui stellas, qui solem, qui coeli convexa, qui terras omnes ac ma-
ria, qui mundum denique ipsum, quo nihil est admirabilius, vel
potius extra quem nihil est quod admireris, saepe sine admiratione
intuemur, iisdem nobis esse Aetna miraculum potest? Cave sis
tam imprudens, fili, ut tu id putes. Nam si naturam respicimus,
nihil in Aetna est, quod mirum voces. Si rem consideramus ipsam,
nonne tibi etiam mira videantur cum alia loca permulta, tum vel
Aponi nostri fontes calidaeque illae purissimae, quibus natura non
tantum ut calefacerent dedit, quod erat tamen ab aquis alienum,
sed multum de iure quoque rerum omnium concessit, multum de
nostro, tum aliquid de deorum etiam et suo, ut morbis scilicet me-
derentur non modo sine ullo aegri dolore, qua de causa graeco
verbo Aponus nomen invenit, sed etiam cum voluptate? Itaque qui
curantur,

> Non venas reserant, (ut ait ille), nec vulnere vulnera sanant
> Pocula nec tristi gramine mista bibunt:
> Amissum lymphis reparant impune vigorem
> Pacaturque aegro luxuriante dolor.

36   Nam morbos quidem expellere hominum plane est rerum usum
multarum recte callentium; hoc autem, vel sine dolore id efficere
vel, quod multo est maximum, etiam cum voluptate, deorum mihi
quidem videtur esse proprium ipsiusque principis omnium et pa-
rentis naturae. Quod si cum uno Aponi fonticulo et canali pro-

That is how the fires of Etna start; now hear how, once started,   35
they continue. I don't think this should astonish you, as it does
most people; I know such vast flames, the greatest fires within liv-
ing memory, must always have had an immense source of nourish-
ment. But what is immense or difficult for Nature, the parent and
ruler of everything? What is there which she cannot do? When
we can look at the stars, the sun, the arch of heaven, all the lands
and seas, indeed, the entire universe which is more wonderful than
anything, or, rather, leaves nothing else to wonder at, and often
without any feeling of wonder, are we to see any special marvel in
Etna? Mind you are not so foolish, my son, as to think so. If we
reflect on Nature, there is nothing you can call remarkable in Etna.
If we consider Etna itself, you should find many other places just
as remarkable, and in particular, our own spring of Aponus with
its pure, warm waters, to which Nature granted not only the gift
of making us warm (which was not the usual property of water)
but also great influence over everything, including mankind, and
even to some extent over the gods and herself: I mean the power
to cure disease, and that not merely without pain for the sufferer
(the origin of the Greek word *aponus*, meaning "painless") but even
with positive pleasure. And so the poet says of those who are
treated there:

> They do not open veins, heal wound with wound,
> Nor swallow potions mixed with bitter herbs:
> Safely the waters bring them back lost health,
> And, as they revel there, all pain is soothed.

For men who are skilled in the proper use of many things may   36
certainly have the ability to banish disease, but to do so painlessly,
or, which is even more remarkable, with a feeling of pleasure, can
only (I think) be a gift of the gods and of Nature herself, the first
principle and parent of all. Still, if you compare the single tiny
spring and channel of Aponus with all the depths and outpourings

funda illa comparaveris inundationesque omnes Aetnae tuae, for-
tasse non verear, ne noster hic colliculus tuo illo monte sit minor.

37   Sed faciam, ut tibi pollicitus sum, et Aetnae incendia, quomodo
alantur, docebo. Quoniam igitur, ut scis, humore et calore omnia
concipiuntur, cum et semper ardeat mons et semper a mari perlus-
tretur, habes iam duobus istis verbis, quod petis. Ignis enim, qui
detrahit semper aliquid atque consumit, gignit etiam semper ali-
quid sibi, quod consumat, suo ipsius calore humectantibus undis
tellurem semperque igni materiam sufficientibus, quo alatur. Nam
et bitumen maxime, quod sulfuri simillimum est, fit ex terra et
limo exudante tellure: tum et eiusdem fere generis halumen, quod,
quia ex salo et terra conficitur, ita vocatur.

38   B.F. Unde autem saxa et pumices, pater, et eiectamenta illa, quae
vomit? Quid illa tandem sunt? an sulfur tantum, bitumen, halu-
men omnia?

B.P. Nequaquam, fili, sed tanta est vis ignium, praesertim incluso-
rum, et ventis intus furentibus, ut non viscera imbecilla modo, sed
plane nervi etiam fortiores corripiantur telluris et saxa ipsa duris-
sima liquefiant.

B.F. At ea ipsa saxa non aliquando defecisse, montemque sibi non
subsedisse, nonne illud est mirum, pater?

B.P. Neque id, fili, quidem mirum. Tellus enim semper foecunda
est sui ipsius semperque semet ipsa parturit; nisi tamen malis tu
cum Pythagora sentire, qui quidem apud Ovidium ita praecipiens
inducitur, ut audeat affirmare Aetnae incendia non esse usque-
quaque duratura.

B.F. Ego vero, quid sentiam, non sat scio; quanquam equidem
mallem Pythagoram quam Empedoclem imitari: ille enim quae na-
turae consentanea videbantur, credebat asserens mutari quidem
omnia, nihil tamen omnino interite; hic, dum curiosius naturae
causas perscrutatur, etiam se ipsum imperscrutabilem facit.

of Etna, perhaps I should not worry if our small hillock here is inferior to that great mountain of yours.

But now I must fulfil my promise and give you an explanation 37 of how the fires of Etna are fed. As you know, everything is compounded of water and fire, and since the mountain is forever burning and forever washed by the sea, you have the answer to your question in these two words. The fire which is always consuming and destroying is also always creating something for itself to consume out of its own heat and the waters which moisten the earth and always provide material to feed the flames. For bitumen, in particular, which is very like sulphur, is formed from earth and slime oozing out of the land, and alum, which is very similar in nature, is so called because it is a mixture of salt and earth.

P.B. But where, father, do the rocks and pumice stones come 38 from, and all the material the mountain spews out? What are they? Or is everything only sulphur, bitumen and alum?

B.B. Of course not, my dear son, but the fires are so powerful, especially in an enclosed space and when the winds are raging within, that not only the soft core of the earth but the stronger sinews too are weakened, and the hardest rocks are melted.

P.B. But surely, father, the fact that the rocks have never come to an end and the mountain has not subsided is something remarkable?

B.B. No, there is nothing remarkable in that. The earth is always spontaneously prolific and always renewing itself; unless you prefer to share the view of Pythagoras, who, according to Ovid, was moved to declare boldly in his teaching that the fires of Etna would not last forever.[17]

P.B. I really do not know what I think; though I would rather follow Pythagoras than Empedocles, for he believed and argued that everything which seemed to be in accordance with natural law was in a state of change but was never wholly destroyed; whereas Empedocles devoted himself to penetrating the causes of nature, but in so doing made his own words impenetrable.[18]

B.P. Sed valere nos illos sinamus, fili, et quoniam nos tibi Aetnae incendia unde fiant, diximus, id velim ego scire item ex te, ipsa ista quomodo fluant.

39 B.F. Iam istud quidem fieri sine ullo negotio potest vel una Hesiodi comparatione, qua ille in sua *Theogonia* fluxisse ait tellurem, ubi eam post fulminatum Typhoeum igne correptam describit isto, ni fallor modo. Ex quo sane libet mihi suspicari etiam pastorem illum Ascraeum aliquando Aetnam conscendisse atque inde sibi sumpsisse, quod de universa tellure scriptum reliquit:

> Uritur ipsa ingens tellus aestuque furente
> Liquitur, albentis quondam ceu lamina plumbi
> Arte virum, flammisque cava fornace liquescit,
> Seu ferrum, quanquam hoc maternae viscera rupis
> In duras aluere vires, cum ferbuit olim
> Vulcani domitum manibus, terraeque fatiscit.

40 Et quidem propterea illum ego plumbi et ferri exempla posuisse crediderim, ut alteri ea compararet, quae igne facilius corripiuntur et fluunt, ut sulfurea tellus omnis et eae telluris partes quae tenuiores sunt, alteri autem cum saxa omnia, tum ea quae flammae resistunt magis et sunt suapte natura duriora.

B.P. Mihi haec quidem certe non displicent ipsa per se, atque etiam delectavit me non nihil poetae ingenium, qui tam apte descripserit fluentem et ardentem tellurem; sed tamen tu, fili, nimium perparce respondes ad illa quae peto: non modo enim istud ita simpliciter cupio, ea incendia quomodo fluant, scire abs te, sed etiam, ubi descenderint, quam faciem capiant: tum si perdurant eadem semper an aliquando immutentur, audire.

41 B.F. Geram tibi morem, pater, et ea quae postulas, ut potero, explicabo. Pleno iam partu, ut maturior est omnis foetus, quicunque

B.B. Well, let us take our leave of them both; and now that we have discussed the origin of the fires of Etna, I should like to hear more from you about those floods you mentioned.

P.B. That can easily be done by means of a single simile from the   39
Theogony of Hesiod, where (if I am not mistaken) he describes in the way you mean how the earth was in a state of flood when it was set on fire after Typhoeus was struck by lightning. This makes me suspect that the Ascraean shepherd had climbed Etna at some time, and taken from it the description which he afterwards applied to the whole earth.

> Vast earth is burning, in the raging heat
> It melts: as once white lead in beaten strips
> Is liquified within the hollow furnace
> By fire and craftsman's art; and iron, so hard
> Built-up within the depths of native rock,
> Once it has glowed, now tamed by Vulcan's hand
> Cracks on the ground.[19]

I should imagine that he took his examples from lead and iron   40
so that he could compare with the one the elements which are more easily destroyed and melted by fire — all the sulphurous and weaker parts of the earth — and with the other the rocks and elements which are naturally harder and more resistant to flame.

B.B. I find these lines very pleasing in themselves, and I am also much taken by the poet's gift for giving such an apt description of earth which is melting and on fire. But you still haven't given me a full answer to my question: I want to know quite simply how these fires flow down, and also to hear what form they take when they have reached a low level, whether they remain always the same or eventually undergo a change.

P.B. I will comply with your wishes, father, and answer your ques-   41
tions as well as I can. Whatever takes form in the womb of Etna, once it has reached full term, like any other fully developed foetus,

in Aetnae matris utero coalescit, nisu parientis expellitur et eiecta-
tur quacunque prius rimam invenerit aut viam sibi paraverit vi sua:
saepe tamen exit ex cratere, quem ipsi vidimus; nunquam ex supe-
riore, quod vel eo inscendere gravis materia non queat, vel, quia in-
ferius alia spiramenta sunt, non sit opus. Despumant igitur flam-
mis urgentibus ignei rivi pigro fluxu totas delambentes plagas; ii
paulatim recedente calore priorem sibi naturam reposcentes, in la-
pidem indurescunt fragilem sane flammis enervantibus et, si com-
plectas, putrem. Stat ea confluvies veluti glacies concreta, usque ut
alteri descendant rivi. Ii nanque non suprafluunt, sed inter montis
arenosam cutem et priora concreta fluenta insinuantes sese cursum
sibi medium quaerunt.

42   Sic quae prius induruerant, quia friabilia sunt, ut dixi, novis in-
cendiis cedentia crepant et in partes disiecta prosiliunt quacunque
unda deurgens interfluit; deinde conglaciantem eam altera subiit
illuvies, atque ipsa tantundem facit, tum altera item et altera.
Non enim continuato fruore mons, sed per intermissos spiritus, ut
supra commemoravimus, eructatur; atque ita novissimis semper
vincentibus multiplicatoque in immensum incendio ex igneis flu-
minibus fracti lapides altissimo congestu magnam partem montis
inoccuparunt; atque ii, quo recentius fluxere, eo et nigriores sunt
et firmiores, aetate et pallescunt et resolvuntur. Inde ego esse are-
narum plagas omnis, quae circa cacumen visuntur, existimo. Mate-
ries omnis aridissima est, atque ideo minus multo, quam vivi lapi-
des, ponderosa: scabra adeo, ut brevi mora, tanquam a lima,
inscendentibus calcei exedantur.

B.P. Atqui ego sane in eo mallem Empedoclem imitari, qui ascen-
surus amyclis aereis utebatur; sed sequere.

is pushed and thrust out by the birth-pangs of its mother, at any point where it has previously found a fissure or has prepared a way out by its own effort. It often comes out of the crater which we looked at, but never from the upper one, either because the heavier material cannot rise so high, or because it does not need to when there are other, lower vents. Thus streams of fire come swirling down in a thick flood as the flames drive them on, and spread over all the surrounding country, but as the heat cools off they return to their former nature and harden into stone which is now brittle, since the flames have weakened it, and crumbles away if handled. The flood then stands hardened like a glacier, until a second lot of streams comes down, and these do not flow over it, but work their way through the sandy surface of the mountain and previous hardened floods and find themselves a course in between.

Thus what had hardened before, being friable, as I said, gives 42 way under the new fires with a loud crack, leaps into the air, and is scattered in all directions, wherever the stream exerts pressure and flows between. Then, as that one hardens, another inundation supervenes and does the same, and this happens again and again; for (as we said before) the mountain does not erupt in a continuous flood but in intermittent bursts. So as new downflows always overwhelm the old, and the flames break out repeatedly over a vast area, the stones broken by the streams of fire are piled high and have covered a large part of the mountain; those which have poured down more recently are blacker and harder, but in time their color fades and they begin to crumble. It is this, I think, which accounts for all the areas of sand to be seen around the summit. All the material is very dry, and consequently much less heavy than living stone, and so rough that climbers' shoes are soon worn away as if scratched by a file.

B.B. Then I would certainly choose to copy Empedocles, who wore shoes made of bronze for his ascent.[20]

43 B.F. Ea infra parvum craterem circumversus totum montem com-
plexa est, et cumulum eum, in quo maior crater est, sustinet; de-
mittitur inde alicubi per intervalla imum in montem obliquis fluxi-
bus, quaque Catana iacet, usque in mare, lata saepe qua visus
patet, horrendum sane spectaculum modo alveis hiantibus modo
impendentibus ripis. Inter maxima profluvia longe memorabile il-
lud est, quod paulo ante nostram aetatem usque intra Catanam
decurrens non parvam urbis partem incendio depopulavit: neque
sane descensus is minus quam per ducenta stadia conficitur. Quin
etiam portum eum de quo ait Virgilius:

> Portus ab accessu ventorum immotus et ingens
> Ipse, sed horrificis iuxta tonat Aetna ruinis,

ita implevere fluenta Aetnaea, ut iam errasse Virgilium putes,
quod portum ibi esse ingentem dixerit, qui pene nullus siet.
B.P. Istud nimirum est, quod a principio dixeras cedere illis volen-
tibus atque eorum contrahi ardoribus ipsum mare.

44 B.F. Est ita quidem, ut dicis; sed, ut ad propositum revertamur,
reptare per eas crepidines, quas dixi, duobus milibus passuum ne-
cesse est quemvis craterem visuros: reliquum iter in equis confici-
tur. Reptationis eius labor haud facile credas quam durus est
quamque indigens virentis genu; quippe quia degravante viatore
temere ingesti lapides concedunt et in ascensu raptissimo, ni probe
posueris pedem, dimoto uno tota congeries devolvitur et in te ip-
sum ruit. Adde quod etiam, si in plano cecideris, laedunt scabritie
sua, et manus crebro contactu, nisi contexeris, offenduntur. Magna
haec fortasse videbuntur, pater, audienti tibi; magna enim sunt, ut
mihi quidem videri solet, verum nusquam adeo ac nobis videnti-
bus fuere: nam Aetna quanta est, nemo quidem scit, qui non vi-

P.B. The sandy area beneath the small crater has spread all round   43
the mountain, and also supports the mound where the large crater
is; from there it descends at intervals everywhere in sloping
streams down to the base of the mountain, and in the region of
Catania, as far as the sea, often spreading out as widely as the eye
can see. It is indeed a fearful sight, its yawning chasms alternating
with towering banks. Amongst the greatest downpours, by far the
most memorable is the one a little before our time which ran down
as far as Catania and destroyed a considerable part of the town by
fire; the distance of the descent was certainly not less than twenty-
five miles. The harbor too, of which Virgil says

> The harbor there is vast, untouched by winds' approach,
> But Etna thunders near and fearsome showers fall[21]

must certainly have silted up with Etna's floods; you might imag-
ine that Virgil was mistaken in calling it vast, for it is scarcely any-
thing now.
B.B. That is not surprising, when you said at the beginning that
the sea itself had to bow to their will and contract in their heat.
P.B. It does indeed, as you say. But to return to the subject: if you   44
want to visit either crater, it is necessary to crawl over the stretches
I have described for two miles; the rest of the journey can be made
on horseback. It is difficult to believe how hard the effort of crawl-
ing is, and how strong you have to be in the knee, for the loosely
heaped stones give way beneath the weight of the traveller, and in
a hurried ascent you must place your feet carefully or a single stone
dislodged can bring the whole mass sliding down to bury you. In
addition, if you fall flat, the sharp stones hurt you, and your hands
are scratched by repeated contact unless you cover them. You may
find this remarkable only to hear about, as indeed it is; I have al-
ways thought so, but never so much as when I saw it for myself,
for no one can judge the size of Etna who has not seen it. From its
summit is a view of the whole island, the bounds of which appear

det. Ex summo vertice contemplari totam insulam licet: termini eius longe esse multo minus videntur quam sunt. Brutia ora ita tibi sub oculis iacet, ut eo posse traiicere pene quidem iactu lapidis putes; serena tempestate Neapolitani etiam tractus extimantur. Nivibus per hyemem fere totus mons canet: cacumen neque per aestatem viduatur.

B.P. Quid, quod hyemare tantum eas meminit Strabo?

45   B.F. At experientia ita te docet, ususque ipse auctor, quod quidem venia illius dixerim, non deterior. Quare illud, mi pater, etiam atque etiam vide, ne quid te moveat, si aliqua ex parte huius nostri de Aetna sermonis cum vetustis scriptoribus dissentimus. Nihil enim impedit fuisse tum ea omnia, quae ipsi olim tradire, quorum permanserint plurima in nostram diem, quaedam se immutaverint, aliqua etiam surrexerint nova. Nam, ut caetera omittam, quod cinerosa partim esse summa cacumina dictavere, eius rei nunc vestigium nullum apparet. Cinis enim, qui queat conspici, toto monte nullus est. Neque id tamen omnibus annis fuit: nam multorum testimonio accepimus, qui videre, annos ab hinc quadraginta tantos ex Aetna cineres evolasse, ut per totam eam insulae partem, quae versus Pelorum iacet, universam oleam abstulerint, eos etiam in Italiam ventis ferentibus latos.

46   Sed, ut ad nives illas redeamus, addebat idem Urbanus Kalendis iuniis ascendente se satis largiter abundeque ninxisse; tum iterum, qui septimus fuerit post eum diem, dum ipse Randatii moraretur, in universam montanam plagam nives fere in pedis altitudinem descendisse: in quo ipso licet et Pindarum suspicere, scite cognomento usum, qui Aetnam nivium nutricem appellarit.

47   Quo latere subest Catana, media fere inter ipsam et cacumen regione purissimus et perennis fons erumpit dorico vocabulo Crana ab incolis appellata. Caeterum toto monte supra radices

much smaller than they really are. The Bruttian coast lies under your eyes, so close that you think it is no more than a stone's throw across, and in fine weather even the area round Naples can be seen in the distance. In winter practically the whole mountain is white with snow, and the peak never loses this throughout the summer.

B.B. But didn't Strabo say snow was there only in winter?[22]

P.B. Well, one learns in practice, and experience is as good an authority as Strabo, if he will forgive me for saying so. And so you will frequently have to guard against being surprised if some part of my account of Etna disagrees with the ancient authors. It may well be that at the time they wrote, everything was as they described it, and a great deal has remained the same down to our own day, though there have been some changes and some new features. To give a single example, they have repeatedly said that the top of the mountain is partly covered in ashes, but there is no trace of this now—there are no ashes to be seen anywhere on the mountain. Yet this has not been so at all times, for we learned on the authority of many people who were eyewitnesses, that forty years ago so much ash was carried down from Etna that throughout the whole region of the island in the direction of Pelorus the entire olive-crop was destroyed, and the winds scattered it far and wide in Italy.

But to return to the snow: Urbano added that when he was making the ascent on the first of June it snowed quite heavily over a wide area, and again, while he was staying at Randazzo a week later, snow fell over the whole mountain to the depth of about a foot. On this point you can also refer to Pindar and his apt choice of epithet when he calls Etna "nurse of snows."[23]

On the side above Catania, about halfway between the town and the mountain peak, gushes out a perpetual spring of purest water which the local people call by its Doric name, Crana; otherwise throughout the mountain above the foothills, there is no wa-

nullae aquae sunt, nisi quae vel ex nivibus emanant, cuius quidem
rei etiam Theocritum testem habemus, in quo dum Galateae Cy-
clops enumerat divitias suas haec etiam interserit:

> Est glacialis aquae rivus mihi quem sylvosa
> Nectareum in potum nivibus fluit Aetna solutis

aut si quae intra fagorum truncos pluviis descendentibus relin-
quuntur.

48   Atqui res et locus me monuere ut quod ibi vidimus pulcherri-
mum natura opus et mirati fuimus maxime, non praeterirem.
Altissima in specula, qua sylva deficiente liberior prospectus in in-
sulam et Tyrrhena fluenta dominatur, herbidus campus leni de-
cumbit clivo: hunc pini procerae pari distantes intervallo ducta co-
rona circunsepiunt. In medio fagus densissima quadrifido robore
se subiiciens celsior quam caeterae veluti regina ipsa consurgit. Ea
non statim ex imo discriminatur, sed a tellure per spatium cubita-
lem uno trunco contenta est: inde se in ramos consimiles aequali-
bus intervallis dispartitur. Interne usque ad imas radices arbor
deficiens undis pluvialibus urnam ex sese facit: illae montano pur-
gante aere ac umbris solem arcentibus et fontanis gelidiores sunt et
putealibus puriores. Ambigeres ibi tu quidem, pater, si quid eo-
rum tibi laudandum esset, quidnam potissimum laudares, an pros-
pectum eius loci an locum, tum an arborem an undas: ita scite in
alteris decorandis, quasi quidem id agerent, ut quid magis pul-
chrum esset ambigeretur; et Hamadryas et Nais convenere. In ho-
nestandis vero alteris admirabile quidem est, quantum gratiae ve-
nustatisque sibi invicem afferant Iupiter Genio et Genius Iovi: quo
fit ut in utrisque multum Venus etiam permista sentiatur.

49   B.P. O pulchras naturae delicias vel etiam Deorum, ut poetis pla-
cet, si qui sunt qui eum montem colant.

ter except what comes from melted snow, and for this we have confirmation from Theocritus; the passage where the Cyclops enumerates his riches to Galatea contains these lines:

> I have a stream of icy water which wooded Etna
> Pours down from her melted snows for a nectar-sweet drink.[24]

There may also be some left among the boles of the beech trees after rain has fallen.

But now this topic and site have reminded me not to leave out a particularly beautiful work of nature which we saw there and especially admired. On a high promontary where the woods have thinned and the view opens out over the island and the Tyrrhenian sea, there is a grassy meadow spread over a gentle slope and enclosed by a ring of tall, evenly spaced pine trees. In the center a beech with dense foliage towers above all the other trees like their queen; it grows from a trunk split in four, but is not divided at the root, for a single bole can support it for a height of nearly two feet, and then it branches out into boughs of similar shape and size at regular intervals. Inside the tree, right down to the roots the trunk is hollow and makes a vessel for rain water out of itself; and because of the clear mountain air and the shade which keeps off the sun, this is colder than spring water and clearer than what is drawn from a well. You would find it difficult to decide, father, which to praise most if you had to choose between the view from the site or the place itself, the trees or the water: so skilfully have the nymphs of woods and streams combined to beautify both, as if their object was to create doubt about which is the more lovely. But if we pay tribute to both, we can only marvel at the charm and beauty which Jupiter of the heavens and the spirit of the place have brought each other, and in so doing enabled Venus to feel that her beauty permeates them both.

B.B. O lovely delights of Nature! Or indeed of the gods, as the poets say, if there are any who have the mountain in their care.

B.F. Sunt, pater, ut aiunt, atque incolunt illo ipso quidem in loco.

B.P. Mirabar, si haec temere dicerentur provenire, praesertim a Siculis, quos quidem constat propter sermonis impunitatem et licentiam etiam trilingues vocatos. Sed quis inhabitat Deus?

B.F. Fauni esse fontem illum dicunt.

B.P. Fabellam te video inchoare; sed quoniam in Faunum incidimus, sequere: detineri enim me ab illo facile patior, cum quo te scio libenter etiam carminibus ludere interdum solere. Istud autem qui sciunt? an ita fortasse coniectantur.

50 B.F. Videre se aiunt pastores ipsum Deum passim errantem per sylvas et pascua; tum etiam sedentem sub illis arboribus coronatum pinu et tacentem saepius, interdum tamen etiam fistula solantem amores. Sed continebo potius me hic, pater: levia enim ista sunt, et mihi loqui tecum, nisi reverenter, non licet. Quanquam quidem, si pergerem, faceremus ipsi hac in re, quod facere etiam reges in coenis solent, qui quidem inter apros et pavones, quibus abundant quotidie, interdum tamen et allium poscunt et betas. Neque sane animus noster vacare semper rebus severioribus potest, neque si vacet, tamen ex illis tam plenam capit iucunditatem, quam si ea ipsa remitteret interdum et mox non longo intervallo intermissa revocaret. Ita nos quidem nunc gravia illa philosophiae studia, quibus quidem certe id omne tempus soles, quod tibi per rempublicam licet, impertire, melius etiam fabellis istis levioribus condiremus, et quidem licet maxime vel in Noniano fabulari.

51 B.P. Sane quidem licet, dum illud tamen semper teneatur, ut cerato remige Sirenas, quod aiunt. Et profecto poeta ille sapientissimus nunquam Ulissi concessisset, quem prudentissimum semper facit, ut Sirenarum cantus audiret, nisi liceret etiam gravibus et sapientibus viris, quorum tamen in numero me non pono, minus se-

p.b. There are, so people say, and they dwell in this very place.

b.b. I should be surprised if this were lightly said to be so, especially among the Sicilians, for they are known to be so free and unbridled of speech that they are generally called triple-tongued.[25] But what god lives here?

p.b. They call it the spring of Faunus.

b.b. I see you're off on a legend, but as we have started on Faunus, carry on; I can willingly put up with being detained by him, for I know how you sometimes amuse yourself with him in verse.[26] But who knows this? Or are they perhaps only guessing?

p.b. Shepherds say they have seen the god himself moving about   50 through the woods and pastures, and also sitting under those very trees, wreathed in pine-branches, generally silent, but sometimes solacing his loves on a pipe. But I would rather stop at this point, father, for these are trivial matters, and when I talk to you I should be serious. However, if I were to go on, we should only be like kings at their banquets, who sometimes ask for beet and garlic amongst the wild boar and pheasant which are served in plenty every day. Our minds cannot always be given to serious subjects, and if they were, we should not find such full enjoyment as when we give such things a rest sometimes and then resume them after a brief interval. So we might do better to season that profound study of philosophy, on which I know you spend all the time you are allowed from state affairs, with those lighter subjects of legend; and we should feel especially free to tell out tales when we are here in the country.

b.b. Certainly we should, as long as we always keep to the rule   51 that we hear the Sirens, as they say, while the oarsmen have their ears stopped. The greatest and wisest of poets would surely never have allowed Ulysses (whom he always makes so far-sighted) to listen to the Sirens' song unless thoughtful and serious men — though I don't count myself one of them — were not sometimes permitted to take part in less serious matters and seize the oppor-

riis adesse interdum rebus et lusus captare non adeo severos; modo
ne remiges audiant, hoc est ne sensus pateant voluptatibus, quibus
et demulcentur ipsi semper et, nisi ratione occlusi sint, saepe etiam
facillime capiuntur. Quod tibi esse faciundum in vita maxime sem-
per censeo, Bembe fili: nam nisi te ita informaris, ut voluptatum
illecebris animum impervium geras, non possum dicere quam
multae tibi occurrent species earum, quae te non adolescentem
modo, ut es nunc, demulcere possint et delinire ac iam etiam de-
bellare et devincere, sed plane etiam virum.

52   Itaque illis aut magnanimiter imperandum est, quod fecerunt
viri omnes magni et boni et ii, quos propterea deos etiam appella-
vere, vel omnino turpiter deserviendum; in quo quidem tu, si me
audies, non committes ut reiecta continentia atque ipso amore vir-
tutis ex illorum sis grege, de quibus praeclare Horatius

> Nos numerus sumus et fruges consumere nati,
> Sponsi Penelopes, nebulones, Alcinoique
> In cute curanda plus aequo operata iuventus,
> Quis pulchrum fuit in medios dormire dies et
> Ad strepitum citharae cessantum ducere curam.

Sed quoniam iam advesperascit, procedamus in atrium: nugae au-
tem pastorales istae tuae sub umbris sunt potius et inter arbores,
quam intra penates recensendae. Quae cum dixisset et iam in
atrium pervenissemus, ego finem loquendi feci, ille cogitabundus
in bibliothecam perrexit.

tunity for lighter-hearted amusement; provided that the oarsmen do not hear, that is, the senses are not exposed to pleasures which will always allure them, and, unless reason restrains them, all too easily often take them prisoner. This is always my chief advice to you throughout your life, Pietro; for unless you train yourself to make your mind impervious to the allurements of pleasures, they will assail you in countless forms, entice and ensnare you, even defeat and overpower you, not only when you are young, as you are now, but also when you are a grown man.

And so we have to choose between highmindedness, thereby 52 imposing our will on them, as all great and good men have done, as well as those whom they deemed gods for that very reason, and complete submission in the shame of slavery. If you listen to me on this subject you will not make the mistake of abandoning self-control and love of virtue to join the herd of those of whom Horace says so well:

> We are mere ciphers, born to devour earth's fruits,
> Penelope's idle suitors, Alcinous' young men,
> Who spend their time unduly on their looks,
> Thinking it fine to slumber until noon,
> To rest their cares with music and the lyre.[27]

But now evening draws on, so let us go home; those pastoral fancies of yours are better suited to the shade beneath the trees than to conversation indoors.

After he had spoken thus and we had entered the house, I said no more; and he went off to the library to his meditations.

Note on the Text

The *editio princeps* of Bembo's *Carminum Libellus* was printed posthumously in 1552–53 as *Petri Bembi carminum libellus* (Venetiis, 1552; colophon: Venetiis, Apud Gualterum Scottum, 1553). The text used in this translation, that of Rosanna Sodano (Turin: Edizioni Res, 1990), follows the *editio princeps* with only minor corrections of orthography and punctuation, respecting, as Sodano says, "as much as possible humanist spelling, but with the elimination of typographical errors." The Sodano text was recollated with the *editio princeps* for this publication. Readers interested in the textual evolution should consult Sodano for the readings of earlier redactions.

Bembo's Latin poetry was printed in full a century and a half later in *Opere del cardinale Pietro Bembo ora per la prima volta tutte in un corpo unite*, 4 vols. (Venice, 1729). That edition, under the supervision of Anton Federico Seghezzi, added to the corpus four poems, including "Echo" and "Nicolai Boni Epitaphium", whose authorship was uncertain. There were two other eighteenth-century editions of Bembo's poetry, containing the Italian *Rime* and the Latin *Carmina* together in one volume, both by Pier Antonio Serassi, but there were no printings of his poetry in the nineteenth century. In 1959 Marco Pecoraro challenged the authenticity of the *editio princeps*, arguing that MS 635 of the Biblioteca Antoniana of Padua was the only assured manuscript source (Pecoraro, *Per la storia*, cited fully in the Bibliography.) His assertions, in particular that Scotto, under Gualteruzzi's direction, adjusted the contents to suit the reform atmosphere generated by the Council of Trent, were rebutted by the great Bembo scholar, Carlo Dionisotti, in his important review of Pecoraro's book in *Giornale storico della letteratura italiana*, 138 (1961): 573–592.

The text of the seven poems which Bembo excluded from the *Carmina* he had prepared for printing is based on Pecoraro's edition of MS 635 (known as the Antonianus). The nine poems which follow them in the present edition (as in Sodano's) have various manuscript sources. "Petri Bembi Carmen" and "Lycda," the first from a codex in the Marciana, the second from a codex in the Biblioteca Estense of Modena, were brought to light by Guido Pesenti in 1915 and 1917 respectively. "Ad Angelum Gabrielem Gratulatio," which is in codex 52.II.1 of the Biblioteca Universitaria of Bologna, was first printed by Pecoraro in an appendix to his book. The Sodano edition also contains an expurgated version of "Sarca" as found in *Spicilegium Romanum*, vol. 8 (Rome, 1842), pp. 488–504. The complete text used here is found in Codex Vindobonensis 9977, ff. 143r–156v, of the Österreichisches Nationalbibliothek in Vienna as edited, with an accompanying German translation, by Otto Schönberger in *Sarca: Petrus Bembus: Einleitung, vollständiger Text, erste Übersetzung und Anmerkungen* (Würzburg, 1994). I am much indebted to his painstaking work, both for the full text of this gem of a poem and for the careful scholarship of his notes and commentary.

The text and translation of the *Etna* are reprinted, with permission, from a rare bibliophilic edition of 125 copies published in 1969 by Hans Mardersteig and the Officina Bodoni of Verona. The Latin text was taken from the *editio princeps* of 1496, as revised for that edition by Carlo Dionisotti. The English translation is by the English classicist Betty Radice, former editor of Penguin Classics. The notes have been added by the General Editor of this series, James Hankins.

NOTE TO THE REPRINT EDITION

We have taken the opportunity of the second printing (2012) to correct a number of errors in the first printing (2005). Most of these corrections were noted in a review by John N. Grant in *Mouseion: Journal of the Classical Association of Canada* 7, no. 1 (2007): 93–97. Some additional corrections, not found in the review, were kindly supplied for this second printing by Professor Grant.

J.H.

Notes

꙳꙳꙳

LITTLE BOOK OF POEMS

I. Choral Prayer of the Shepherds
Source: Sodano, pp. 5–8   Meter: hendecasyllabic

Theocritus wrote a number of pastoral poems with verse and refrain. Eclogue 8 of Virgil is the most famous Latin example. Spenser's "Prothalamium" and "Epithalamium" offer parallels in English Renaissance poetry.

II. Faunus Speaks to the River Nympeus
Source: Sodano, pp. 9–10   Meter: elegiac distich

The figure of Faunus is roughly equivalent to the Pan of Greek myth, though Bembo makes them separate entities in the eighth poem, *Galatea*.

III. Faunus Speaks to the Nymphs
Source: Sodano, pp. 10–11   Meter: elegiac distich

On this poem, an elaboration of the speech of Polyphemus in Ovid's *Metamorphoses* 13, see the article of John N. Grant cited in the Bibliography.

IV. Iolas Speaks to Faunus
Source: Sodano, pp. 11–12   Meter: elegiac distich

V. Thestylis Prays to Faunus
Source: Sodano: p. 12   Meter: elegiac distich

For the convention of making an inscription and offerings to a deity in nature see Theocritus, *Inscriptions, passim,* and Horace, *Odes* 3.22.

VI. Daphnis Prays to Faunus
Source: Sodano: p. 12   Meter: elegiac distich

VII. GALATEA

Source: Sodano, pp. 13–15   Meter: elegiac distich

The story of Acis and Galatea, a favorite with writers of pastoral, can be found in Ovid, *Metamorphoses* 13.732–894. There Acis is described as Faunus' son. This invention of Bembo's seems based on the convention that Faunus spent much of his time fruitlessly chasing nymphs. Cf. Horace, *Odes* 3.18.

VIII. PRIAPUS

Source: Sodano, pp. 16–19   Meter: elegiac distich

In this poem Bembo has softened and civilized the character of Priapus as found in classical literature. Except for Tibullus' treatment of him (1.4), the Priapus of antiquity is coarse and crude, his phallus used to frighten thieves from the garden. Bembo's Priapus is genially seductive and quite attuned to the uses of sexuality for pleasure and comfort.

1. The two flowers in this stanza are the sunflower and the hyacinth. For the story of Hyacinth see Ovid, *Metamorphoses* 10.162 ff.

IX. THE TOMB OF LEUCIPPUS AND ALCON

Source: Sodano: pp. 19–20   Meter: elegiac distich

In the codex Antonianus the title reads: *Alcippi et Alconis Tumulus ad Faunus*

X. TO MELINUS

Source: Sodano, p. 21   Meter: elegiac distich

The model for this poem is Propertius 2.18.1–4; see the article of John N. Grant cited in the Bibliography.

XI. TO TELESILLA

Source: Sodano: pp. 21–22   Meter: elegiac distich

XII. TO LUCREZIA BORGIA

Source: Sodano, pp. 22–24   Meter: elegiac distich

Bembo's love affair with Lucrezia Borgia is beautifully documented in *The Prettiest Love Letters in the World* by Hugh Shankland. The affair was warmest in the years between 1502 and 1504, but Bembo always remained devoted to the much-maligned and unfortunate duchess.

1. For the notion of love as shipwreck see Horace, *Odes* 1.5.

XIII. A Lady-Friend Speaks to Gallus
Source: Sodano, pp. 24–28   Meter: elegiac distich

Whoever this contemporary Gallus was, the Gallus of classical times was Gaius Cornelius Gallus, an Augustan poet and creator of a new form of love-elegy in which the mistress was the dominating figure.

1. This and the following fifteen lines are a reprise of *Aeneid* 4.

XIV. To Lygdamus
Source: Sodano, p. 29   Meter: elegiac distich

XV. Concerning a Lady-Friend Guarded Most Carefully by Her Husband
Source: Sodano, pp. 30–35   Meter: elegiac distich

1. Podalirios, son of Aesculapius, was skilled in medical art. Chiron, wisest of the Centaurs, was renowned for his skill in music and hunting, as well as in medicine.

XVI. About Galesus and Maximus
Source: Sodano, pp. 36–37   Meter: elegiac distich

XVII. To Sempronius
Source: Sodano, pp. 38–39   Meter: hendecasyllabics

In the codex Antonianus the title reads: *Ad Sempronium maternum sermonem non esse fugiendum* ("To Sempronius: that one should not abandon the mother tongue").

XVIII. Benacus
Source: Sodano, pp. 39–47   Meter: dactylic hexameter

Giovan Matteo Giberti (1495–1543) was in the service of Giulio de' Medici, who became Pope Clement VII in 1521. He handled all Clement's diplomatic correspondence and undertook a number of embassies to Spain, France, England, and Germany. He was named bishop of Verona in 1524 and became, in that post, a great pre-Tridentine Italian reformer. This poem was first printed in 1524, but then appeared again together with the "Hymn to St. Stephen" in an Aldine edition in 1527. For the arrival of the rivers, see Ovid, *Metamorphoses* 1.565 ff.

1. The classical Latin name for the Lago di Garda.

2. As papal ambassador Giberti had attempted to forge a Franco-papal-imperial alliance against the Turks who were beginning to invade southeastern Europe.

3. The area around Verona had been devastated by the French armies prior to Giberti's appointment.

4. "The Tuscan Father" is the Florentine pope, Clement VII.

5. As an assiduous papal ambassador Giberti had more than his share of difficult journeys.

6. The Pyrenees mountains which stretch across the Iberian peninsula from the Atlantic to the Mediterranean.

XIX. Prayer on Behalf of Gorytius to the Gods
Source: Sodano, pp. 47–8   Meter: dactylic hexameter

The Gorytius of the title was Johann Goritz of Luxemburg, a curial prelate and one of Rome's leading humanists, who always entertained literary and artistic friends on the feast of St. Anne. The sculpture which he commissioned is *The Virgin and Child with St. Anne* by Andrea Sansovino found in the church of San Agostino in Rome. This poem first appeared in print in 1524 in a collection of poems dedicated to Goritz titled *Coryciana*.

1. This and the following line are missing from the poem as it was printed in the *Coryciana*.

XX. Hymn to Saint Stephen

Source: Sodano, pp. 48–50   Meter: dactylic hexameter

Because of the references to gathering armies and magistrates unable to provide calm this poem can be dated as having been written for the feast of St. Stephen on December 26, 1526. The poem was published in 1527, (see note to "Benacus"), but before the Sack of Rome, which began on May 6 and continued for well over a month. The story of the martyrdom of St. Stephen is found in *The Acts of the Apostles* 7.54–60, 8.1.

1. Bembo had every right to fear for Rome. On September 23, 1526, the Colonna family under the leadership of Cardinal Pompeo Colonna had attacked the Vatican and carried off a great deal of treasure. As the year ended, the imperial armies were bearing down on the city. When the sack occurred, no one and nothing was spared, and by mid-June over 45,000 people had either been killed or had fled the city.

XXI. The Golden Bracelet of Lucrezia Borgia, Duchess of Ferrara

Source: Sodano, p. 51   Meter: dactylic hexameters

XXII. Concerning the Boy Julius

Source: Sodano, p. 51   Meter: elegiac distich

XXIII. The Horse Pegasus, My Father's Insignia

Source: Sodano, p. 51   Meter: elegiac distich

Pietro's father, Bernardo Bembo (1433–1519), was a Venetian diplomat and bibliophile, whose collection of manuscripts, both classical and medieval, was one of the most important in Italy.

XXIV. Accompanying a Gift of White Tapers Sent to the Monk Bernardo

Source: Sodano: p. 52   Meter: elegiac distich

XXV. Inscription for a Forge

Source: Sodano, p. 52   Meter: elegiac distich

XXVI. The Tomb of Poliziano

Source: Sodano, p. 52–3   Meter: elegiac distich

Angelo Ambrogini of Montepulciano, known as Poliziano (1454–1494), was a renowned poet and humanist, a professor of Greek and Latin, a protégé of Lorenzo de'Medici and tutor in the Medici household. His *Orfeo* was one of the earliest plays in Italian.

1. When Lorenzo de' Medici, his patron, died in 1492, Poliziano wrote an elegy, "Quis dabit capiti meo aquam", which was composed in a free metrical style. (See l. 8.)

XXVII. Epitaph for Gallus

Source: Sodano, p. 53–4   Meter: elegiac distich

XXVIII. The Supreme Pontificate of Julius the Second

Source: Sodano, p. 54–5   Meter: elegiac distich

The oak tree, oak leaf, and acorn were symbols of the Della Rovere family, of which Pope Julius II was a formidable member. They are to be found on various monuments which Julius caused to be built in Rome. The acorn can be seen as the finials on the papal chair in Raphael's portrait of the aging pope. In the codex Antonianus the title reads: *De Julii pontificatu*.

XXIX. Epitaph for My Brother Carlo Bembo

Source: Sodano, p. 55   Meter: elegiac distich

Carlo Bembo (1472–1503), Pietro's younger brother, died in Rome while Pietro was on a mission for the pope. In a letter to Lucrezia Borgia he describes Carlo as "my dear and only brother, my life's sole support and delight." (Shankland, Letter XIX).

XXX. Epitaph for Ercole Strozzi

Source: Sodano, p. 55–6   Meter: elegiac distich

Ercole Strozzi (1469–1505) was a trusted member of Lucrezia Borgia's court and a close friend of Bembo. A gifted classicist and poet, he did much to foster Bembo's affair with the Duchess.

XXXI. Epitaph for Marco Antonio Gabriel of Venice
Source: Sodano, p. 56   Meter: dactylic hexameters

Marco Antonio Gabriel was the grandson of Bembo's dear friend and contemporary, Trifone Gabriel.

XXXII. Epitaph for Filippo Beroaldo the Younger
Source: Sodano, p. 56   Meter: elegiac distich

Filippo Beroaldo, junior (1472–1518), nephew of the great humanist teacher Filippo Beroaldo, senior, wrote three books of poems and one of epigrams, all published posthumously. Bembo composed this epitaph for Beroaldo's tomb.

1. Giovanni de' Medici, Pope Leo X.

XXXIII. Epitaph for Scytha, Poet of Feltre
Source: Sodano, p. 57   Meter: elegiac distich

Giovanni Baptista Scytha, rhetor and poet, was a friend and correspondent of Aldus Manutius.

XXXIV. Epitaph for the Philosopher Certaldo
Source: Sodano, p. 57   Meter: elegiac distich

XXXV. Epitaph for Longolius
Source: Sodano, p. 57   Meter: dactylic hexameters

Christophe de Longueil or Longolius (1491–1522) was a French humanist and champion of the Ciceronian style. He was attached for a while to the court of Leo X, but followed Bembo to Padua where, before his early death, he became a Franciscan friar.

XXXVI. Epitaph for Leonico
Source: Sodano, p. 57   Meter: elegiac distich

Niccolò Leonico Tomeo (1456–1531), a native of Venice, was professor of philosophy at the University of Padua and Bembo's teacher during the time he lived in Ferrara.

XXXVII. Epitaph for Telesilla
Source: Sodano, p. 58   Meter: elegiac distich

It is interesting to speculate about the identity of Telesilla. She is addressed as a daunting lady-love in Poem XI, and since that poem stands just before the poem to Lucrezia Borgia, she could be Maria Savorgnan, Bembo's previous *inamorata*. But the placement of her epitaph here, only four poems before the end of the *Carminum Libellus* as Bembo arranged it, suggests that she might be Faustina Morosina, his devoted mistress of many years and the mother of his children.

XXXVIII. Epitaph for My Puppy
Source: Sodano, p. 58   Meter: elegiac distich

XXXIX. A Fiction in the Ancient Manner
Source: Sodano, p. 58–9   Meter: elegiac distich

XL. Epitaph for Jacopo Syncerus Sannazaro
Source: Sodano, p. 59   Meter: elegiac distich

Jacopo Sannazaro (1458–1530), known to his academic intimates as Actius Syncerus, was one of the most important humanists of his day. Among his works is a series of Latin eclogues titled *Piscatoriae Eclogae*. Modelled after those of Virgil, they have for characters fishermen and sea deities instead of shepherds and wood-nymphs; they were much praised and imitated by his contemporaries. The work for which Bembo likens him to Virgil is the *De partu virginis*, a long hexameter poem about the birth of Christ. He was buried very near Virgil's traditional tomb at Posilippo.

XLI. Epitaph for Lucilio Bembo, My Son
Source: Sodano, p. 59   Meter: elegiac distich

Lucilio Bembo was the eldest of the three children whom Faustina Morosina bore to Bembo during their fourteen years of shared domesticity. Ben Jonson's "Epitaph For My Son" contains a similar sentiment.

APPENDIX A

I. About Faunus and Galatea
Source: Sodano, p. 69   Meter: elegiac distich

II. On the Marble Christ of Pyrgoteles
Source: Sodano, p. 70   Meter: Phalaecian hendecasyllabics and elegiac distich

Pyrgoteles was the academic name of the Paduan sculptor Giorgio Lascaris (d. 1531), who was probably of Greek descent. Only two of his works have been securely identified, a Madonna in the lunette over the portal of Santa Maria dei Miracoli in Venice, and a small statue of S. Giustina in the basilica of Sant'Antonio in Padua. This poem documents the existence of a third statue.

III. A Fig for the Poets
Source: Sodano, p. 70   Meter: elegiac distich

The humor of these lines is more apparent in Latin because of the similarity between 'poma' and 'poema'.

IV. The Same Subject
Source: Sodano, p. 70   Meter: dactylic hexameters

V. On the Po in Flood
Source: Sodano, p. 71   Meter: elegiac distich

VI. On the Marble Statue of Arion
Source: Sodano, p. 71   Meter: elegiac distich

For the story of Arion see Ovid, *Fasti*, 2.79 ff.

VII. To Lycoris
Source: Sodano, pp. 72–78   Meter: elegiac distich

This poem was printed for the first time by the librarian of the Biblioteca Antoniana for the Carreri-Spilimbergo wedding as *Epitalamio latino del cardinale Pietro Bembo* (Padua, 1887).

1. This vignette of Penelope and her father, Icarius, is not in Homer's *Odyssey*. In book 2.96 ff. the suitors say that Penelope told them she was weaving a shroud for her father-in-law, Laërtes.

VIII. SARCA

Source: Schönberger, *Sarca*, pp. 28–56   Meter: dactylic hexameter

'Balbide' in line 44 has been changed to 'Baldide' (see lines 235 and 307).

Bembo's myth about the creation of the Lago di Garda and about the derivation of place-names associated with the lake and its surrounding country-side was not unusual. But the affection he evinces both for this area of the Veneto and for his classical models make his epyllion particularly endearing.

1. The river Sarca rises at the top of the Val di Genova near Monte Adamello.

2. The Golden Apples of the Hesperides.

3. The description which follows bears a remarkable likeness to Raphael's fresco of the nymph Galatea in the Villa Farnesina in Rome.

4. Monte Baldo, Torbole, Nago, Malcesina (modern spellings) are all situated along the eastern shore of Lago di Garda.

5. The Nogarola family from San Vigilio (the Vigilius of line 250) produced four accomplished daughters, the most famous of whom were Ginevra (1417–1461/8) and Isotta (1418–1466). The latter was considered one of the most learned women of her day and was an ardent feminist, engaging the Venetian Francesco Foscarini in a long epistolary debate on the relative guilt of Adam and Eve.

6. Modern Salò lies on the southwestern shore of Lago di Garda.

7. Modern Gargnano is half-way up the western shore of the lake.

8. The river Adda (ancient Athesis) rises in the Alps near the Stelvio pass to the west of Sarca's source.

· NOTES ·

9. The local place name is Peschiera del Garda.

10. The Maia of line 479.

11. The following brief descriptions of Virgil's works are a pastiche of quotations from the texts being described: the *Eclogues*, *Georgics* and *Aeneid*.

12. Publius Papinius Statius (45–96) was one of the greatest of the Silver Age poets. His most famous work was the *Thebais*, an heroic poem in twelve books, about the expedition of the Seven against Thebes.

13. Giovanni Gioviano Pontano (1426–1503) was a humanist and poet. His *Urania sive De stellis libri quinque*, a long hexameter work embodying the astronomical science of the age, won him the admiration of Italy. It was published in 1533 by Aldus Manutius

14. For Actius or Jacopo Sannazaro see note to Poem XL.

15. The church of Santa Maria del Parte built by Sannazaro on his estate at Mergellina. It is the hill of Posilippo that puts to flight sadness and care—this from the etymology of the word in Greek, "putting a stop to care and sorrow."

APPENDIX B

I. ECHO

Source: Sodano, p. 91   Meter: elegiac distich

The story of Echo and Narcissus is found in Ovid, *Metamorphoses* 3.358 f.

II. PIETRO BEMBO'S POEM

Source: Sodano, p. 92   Meter: elegiac distich

Sodano's 'conditione' in line 20 has been changed to 'condicione.'

III. LYCDA

Source: Sodano, p. 93   Meter: elegiac distich

1. Here Bembo is referring to Catullus 5.

2. In both classical and Renaissance literature "to die" can mean to achieve sexual release.

263

IV. From Bembo
Source: Sodano, p. 94   Meter: Iambic

V. Song of Congratulation to Angelo Gabriel
Source: Sodano, pp. 95–99   Meter: dactylic hexameter

Angelo Gabriel (1470–1533) served Venice in various posts, both political and military. He accompanied Bembo to Messina to study Greek in 1491, and their friendship lasted a lifetime. After Gabriel's death Bembo's devotion continued for Gabriel's children and grandchildren. These verses read like a graduation poem.

1. These are the attributes of Mercury, messenger of the gods.

2. Shortly after the end of the Fourth Crusade (1202–1204), Venice bought Crete from the marquis of Montferrat. She retained control of the island until 1669.

3. Sisyphus, son of Aeolus, was king of Corinth. Although famed in myth for his punishment of always having to roll a huge stone uphill, he was considered a type of Christ in the Renaissance because he bound the god of death, stopped his power, and was for a long time able to escape Hades. The blood of Sisyphus is equivalent to the blood of Christ, and by these words Bembo seems, therefore, to be directing his friend away from the life of a cleric and towards a career in politics.

VI. Epitaph for Jacopo Syncerus Sannazaro
Source: Sodano, p. 120   Meter: elegiac distich

For Sannazaro see Poem XL.

VII. Epitaph for Raphael Sanzio of Urbino, Painter
Source: Sodano, p. 120   Meter: elegiac distich

This epitaph was published as Bembo's for the first time in 1576 by Matteo Toscano in *Carmina illustrium poetarum italorum*. It can be read on the side of Raphael's tomb in the Pantheon in Rome.

VIII. Epitaph for Nicola Boni
Source: Sodano, p. 120   Meter: elegiac distich

IX. Epitaph for Agostino Foglietta

Source: Sodano, p. 120   Meter: elegiac distich

Agostino Foglietta (1450–60–1527) of Genoa was attached to the papal court and served as secretary to three popes, Julius II, Leo X, and Clement VII.

ETNA

1. Bernardo Bembo's "triumvirate" must refer to his service on the Venetian Consiglio di Dieci, or Council of Ten, the most important civic council; Bembo held the office at various times, including 1496–97, as *On Etna* was being published. For Bembo's distinguished public career, library, and writings, see Nella Giannetto, *Bernardo Bembo, umanista e politico veneziano* (Florence, 1985), and Margaret L. King, *Venetian Humanism in an Age of Patrician Dominance* (Princeton, 1986), pp. 335–339.

2. Constantine Lascaris (1434–1501), a Greek scholar who emigrated to Italy from Constantinople after the fall of that city to the Turks in 1453. After working as a copyist of Greek manuscripts in Milan, he came to Messina in Sicily in 1466 and taught Greek there for many years. He was the author of the first book printed in Greek, the *Erotemata*, a guide to Greek grammar (Milan, 1476).

3. The Bruttian region: i.e. lower Calabria, the toe of the Italian peninsula, inhabited in pre-Roman times by the Bruttii, an autochthonous people.

4. Ovid, *Heroides* 15.54.

5. Giovanni Aurelio Augurelli of Rimini (c. 1456 – 1524?), a minor Neo-Latin poet, author of the *Chrysopoeia*, a didactic poem on alchemy in three books. Bernardo Bembo was Augurelli's patron, and he may have taught the young Pietro Bembo, whose poetry he influenced. One of Augurelli's *Carmina* (2.6) is a poem in praise of Pietro Bembo. On him see the article by Roberto Weiss in the *Dizionario biografico degli italiani* 4 (Rome, 1962), pp. 578–581.

6. From Book I, ode V of Augurelli's *Carmina*, a poem entitled "Optat Iulium Alexandrum Capellam sub populo in amoenissima villa Bernardi

Bembi Veneti Senatoris clarissimi sita amoris curas solari" ("He wishes to console Giulio Alessandro Capella for the cares of love beneath a poplar in the most pleasant villa of Bernardo Bembo, the distinguished Venetian Senator"). Text in Giovanni Aurelio Augurelli, [*Opera poetica*] (Venice: Aldus, 1505), sig. k8v. This text has a slightly different first line: "Quae, *Iuli*, vitreas populus ardua." Bembo probably dropped the vocative to make the poem fit more smoothly into his dialogue.

7. Bembo here seems to embrace a Neoplatonic view of the descent of the soul into the body, a view he might have imbibed from the Florentine Platonist, Marsilio Ficino, who was a close friend, client and correspondent of his father. The doctrine is difficult to reconcile with orthodox Christianity.

8. Modern Marsala.

9. Homer, *Odyssey* 7.114–121.

10. Presumably the giant Antaeus, son of Gaia and Poseidon, not the demigod Aristaeus, patron of beekeepers; the Latin text should perhaps be corrected to "Anteum."

11. *aristos*.

12. See Pliny the Younger, *Letters* 6.16.

13. Urbanus Valerianus (c. 1443–1524), known as Bolzanio, son of a blacksmith from Belluno, joined the Conventual Franciscans before studying classical languages in Treviso and Venice. (He was not a monk, as is stated here, unless Bembo was merely trying to avoid unclassical language.) Later he served as tutor to Giovanni de'Medici, son of Lorenzo, the future pope Leo X. He studied at Lascaris' academy in Messina where he, too, investigated the volcanic activity of Mount Etna. He wrote a Greek grammar, the *Institutiones graecae grammaticae* (Venice: Aldus, 1497) and later helped Erasmus prepare the Venetian edition of his *Adagia*.

14. See Hesiod, *Theogony* 820–868 (part of which Bembo quotes below); Callimachus, *Hymn IV to Delos*, 140; Horace, *Odes* 3.4.53–56; Virgil, *Aeneid* 4.174f.; Propertius 3.9; Statius, *Thebiad* 3.594. Typhoeus was a giant defeated by Zeus and imprisoned beneath Mount Etna. The giant

Enceladus was defeated by Athena, who buried him under Sicily, "which burns with the burning yet of that immortal giant" (Quintus Smyrnaeus 5.640).

15. The account that follows of the nature and source of volcanic fires is taken from the pseudo-Virgilian poem *Aetna*, ll. 445f., in the *Appendix Vergiliana*.

16. An allusion to the Platonic doctrine of the World-Soul (*Timaeus* 34a–36b), which Bembo could have known about from numerous Latin and Greek sources as well as through his association with Ficino. (Betty Radice's translation, "universal spirit," has been altered here.)

17. Ovid, *Metamorphoses* 15.340–341.

18. On Empedocles' obscurity see Aristotle, *On Generation and Corruption* 1.1.

19. Hesiod, *Theogony*, 862–868.

20. Diogenes Laertius 8.69, a text Bembo could have known in the Latin translation of Ambrogio Traversari (1429) as well as in the original Greek. Empedocles of Agrigento (c. 483–c. 423 BC), a natural philosopher and a follower of Pythagoras, was supposed to have committed suicide by jumping into Mount Etna.

21. Virgil, *Aeneid* 3.570–571.

22. Strabo 6.2.8.

23. Pindar, *Pythian Odes* 1.15.

24. Theocritus, *Idylls* 11.47–48.

25. Apuleius, *Metamorphoses*, 11.5.

26. See the Introduction, p. xiii.

27. Horace, *Epistulae* 1.2.27–31.

Bibliography

Castagno, Luigi. "Il *Politiani Tumulus* di Pietro Bembo." In *Aevum* 3 (1995), pp. 533–553.

Dionisotti, Carlo. "Pietro Bembo." In *Dizionario biografico degli italiani*. Rome: Istituto della Enciclopedia italiana, 1966, pp. 133–151.

Dionisotti, Carlo. [Review of Pecoraro as below]. In *Giornale storico della letteratura italiana*, 138 (1961), pp. 573–592.

———. "Per la storia del *Carminum libellus*." In *Italia medioevale e umanistica* 8 (1965), pp. 278–291.

Grant, John N. "Propertius, Ovid and Two Latin Poems of Pietro Bembo." In *International Journal of the Classical Tradition* 1.4 (1994–95), pp. 48–62.

Kidwell, Carol. *Pietro Bembo: lover, linguist, cardinal*. Montreal: McGill-Queen's University Press, [in press].

Pecoraro, Marco. *Per la storia dei carmi del Bembo. Una redazione non vulgata*. Venice and Rome: Istituto per la collaborazione culturale, 1959.

Reinecke, Ilse. "Der *Benacus* des Pietro Bembo." In *Res Publica Litterarum* 12 (1979), pp. 177–183.

Salemi, Joseph S. "*Priapus* by Pietro Bembo." In *Allegorica* 5 (1980), pp. 81–94.

———. "The Faunus Poems of Pietro Bembo." In *Allegorica* 7 (1982), pp. 31–57.

Schönberger, Otto, ed. *Sarca: Petrus Bembus: Einleitung, vollständiger Text, erste Übersetzung und Anmerkungen*. Würzburg: Königshausen und Neumann, 1994.

Shankland, Hugh. *The Prettiest Love Letters in the World*. Boston: David Godine, 1987.

Sodano, Rosanna, ed. *Pietro Bembo. Carmina*. Turin: Edizioni Res, 1990.

Index

❧

References are by poem number (where appropriate) and line number. References to the Introduction are by page number. A = Appendix A; B = Appendix B; E = *Etna*; L = *Carminum libellus*; hn = headnote; n = note.

Aurelio (Giovanni Aurelio
  Augurelli), E16
Ausonia, L20.43; A8.554

Bacchus, L3.3; E12, 22
Bactria, L18.78
Baiae, L2.5
Baldus, *mountain*, A8.44, 235, 307
Bembino, *puppy*, xv, L38.1
Bembo, Bernardo, vii, L23hn; E3,
  16, 16n5
Bembo, Carlo, xv; L29.3; L29hn
Bembo, Elena, xi
Bembo, Lucilius, xi, xv; L41;
  L41hn
Bembo, Torquato, xi
Benacus, xvii, L18.7, 62; A8.13,
  44, 48, 126, 133, 430
Bergamo, xii
Beroaldo, Filippo Minor, xv;
  L32.7
Black Sea, B5.101
Boccaccio, Giovanni, viii
Bologna, xvi
Bolzanio. *See* Urbano
Boni, Nicolai, B8
Borgia, Lucrezia, ix, x, xiv, xvii;
  L12.18, 42; L12hn; L21.3;
  L3ohn; L37hn; A5.2
Bruttian region, E12, 44
Burckhardt, Jacob, xviii

Calabria, E11n2
Callimachus, E31n14
Calliope, L27.7; A8.485
Calypso, A7.97
Canopus, A7.9

Castiglione, Baldassar, ix, x
Castor, B5.111
Catania, E22, 43, 47
Catullus, xiii, xvii, xviii; A8.258;
  B3n1
Caucasus, L18.146
Centaur, L15n1
Ceres, L8.11; L27.14; E24
Certaldus, L34.1
Chimera, E26
Chiron, L15.157; L15n1
Circe, L15.32
Clement VII (Giulio de' Medici),
  xi, xii; L18hn, n4; B9hn
Clio, B5.9
Clymene, L3.6
Cocytus, L15.82
Colonna, Cardinal Pompeo,
  L20n1
Concordia, A8.412
Contarini, Gasparo, xii
Corcyra, A8.193
Corfu, E23
Corinth, B5n2
Crana, E47
Cressa, L3.4
Crete, L15.79; L18.58; B5.75; B5n2
Cumae, A8.539
Cupid, L15.135; A8.65
Cybele, L2.35; A8.525
Cyclops, L7.6; A1.4, 6, 7; E47
Cyllarus, B5.112

Daphnis, L6.2
Day-Star, L29.1; A8.370
Death (Mors), L26.1, 13; B2.2, 7,
  11, 16

Publication of this volume has been made possible by

The Myron and Sheila Gilmore Publication Fund at I Tatti
The Robert Lehman Endowment Fund
The Jean-François Malle Scholarly Programs and Publications Fund
The Andrew W. Mellon Scholarly Publications Fund
The Craig and Barbara Smyth Fund
for Scholarly Programs and Publications
The Lila Wallace–Reader's Digest Endowment Fund
The Malcolm Wiener Fund for Scholarly Programs and Publications

Publication of this volume has been made possible by

The Myron and Sheila Gilmore Publication Fund at I Tatti
The Robert Lehman Endowment Fund
The Jean-François Malle Scholarly Programs and Publications Fund
The Andrew W. Mellon Scholarly Publications Fund
The Craig and Barbara Smyth Fund
for Scholarly Programs and Publications
The Lila Wallace–Reader's Digest Endowment Fund
The Malcolm Wiener Fund for Scholarly Programs and Publications